T0303985

ROUTLEDGE LIBRARY EDITIONS: THE ECONOMICS AND BUSINESS OF TECHNOLOGY

Volume 15

NEW TECHNOLOGIES AND WORK

NEW TECHNOLOGIES AND WORK

Capitalist and Socialist Perspectives

Edited by
ARTHUR FRANCIS AND PETER GROOTINGS

Routledge
Taylor & Francis Group

LONDON AND NEW YORK

First published in 1989 by Routledge

This edition first published in 2018
by Routledge
2 Park Square, Milton Park, Abingdon, Oxon OX14 4RN

and by Routledge
711 Third Avenue, New York, NY 10017

Routledge is an imprint of the Taylor & Francis Group, an informa business

© 1989 European Co-Ordination Centre for Research and Documentation in Social Sciences

British Library Cataloguing in Publication Data
A catalogue record for this book is available from the British Library

ISBN: 978-1-138-50336-6 (Set)
ISBN: 978-1-351-06690-7 (Set) (ebk)
ISBN: 978-0-8153-6832-8 (Volume 15) (hbk)
ISBN: 978-1-351-25492-2 (Volume 15) (ebk)

Publisher's Note
The publisher has gone to great lengths to ensure the quality of this reprint but points out that some imperfections in the original copies may be apparent.

Disclaimer
The publisher has made every effort to trace copyright holders and would welcome correspondence from those they have been unable to trace.

NEW TECHNOLOGIES AND WORK

Capitalist and Socialist Perspectives

edited by Arthur Francis and Peter Grootings

for the European Co-ordination Centre for
Research and Documentation in Social Sciences

Routledge
London and New York

First published 1989 by Routledge
11 New Fetter Lane, London EC4P 4EE
29 West 35th Street, New York, NY 10001

© 1989 European Co-ordination Centre for Research
and Documentation in Social Sciences

Printed in Great Britain by Billing & Sons Ltd, Worcester

British Library Cataloguing in Publication Data

New technologies and work: capitalist and socialist perspectives.
   1. Work. Effects of technology. Social aspects
   I. Francis, Arthur II. Grootings, Peter, *1951–* III. European
   Coordination Centre for Research and Documentation in Social
   Sciences
   306'.36

   ISBN 0-415-00399-7

Library of Congress Cataloging in Publication Data

New technologies and work.

   Includes index.
   1. Machinery in industry – Europe – Case studies.
2. Machinery in industry – Europe, Eastern – Case studies.
3. Technological innovations – Economic aspects – Europe – Case
studies. 4. Technological innovations – Economic aspects – Europe,
Eastern – Case studies. I. Francis, Arthur. II. Grootings, Peter,
1951– . III. European Coordination Centre for Research and
Documentation in Social Sciences.
HD6331.2.E85N48 1989   338'.06   88-32548
ISBN 0-415-00399-7

Contents

v

Contents

Figures

Figures

Tables

Contributors

Georg Assmann (b. 1933) is Professor of Sociology at the Institute for Marxist-Leninist Sociology at the Humboldt University, Berlin, German Democratic Republic.

Jan Berting (b. 1930) is Professor of Sociology at the Erasmus University Rotterdam, the Netherlands.

Hans van de Braak (b. 1943) is Senior Lecturer in Sociology at the Erasmus University Rotterdam, the Netherlands.

Arthur Francis (b. 1944) is Senior Lecturer in Sociology at Imperial College, London, Great Britain, and co-ordinator of the programme on Competitiveness of British Industry with the Economic and Social Research Council.

Peter Grootings (b. 1951) from 1981-87 was co-ordinator of the programme on Work and Technology at the European Co-ordination Centre for Research and Documentation in Social Sciences, Vienna, Austria.

Jaroslav Jirasek (b. 1926) is Senior Researcher at the Institute for Philosophy and Sociology at the Czechoslovak Academy of Sciences, Prague, Czechoslovakia. Former director of the Research Institute of the Engineering Industry.

Roger Kesteloot (b. 1957) until 1986 was researcher at the State University of Antwerp, Belgium. Presently works as a journalist.

Pertti Koistinen (b. 1948) is Senior Researcher at the Finnish Academy of Sciences, Lecturer in Sociology at the University of Joensuu and Assistant Professor at the University of Tampere, Finland.

Vitalina Koval (b. 1930) is Senior Researcher at the Institute for the International Labour Movement at the Soviet Academy of Sciences, Moscow, Soviet Union.

Jolanta Kulpinska (b. 1928) is Professor of Sociology at the Institute of Sociology, University of Lodz, Poland. Former President of the Research Committee Sociology of Work of the International Sociological Association.

Otfried Mickler (b. 1940) is Professor of Sociology at the University of Hannover and Director of the Sociological Research Institute (SOFI) in Göttingen, Federal Republic of Germany.

Detlev Nagel (b. 1950) is a member of the sociological research group with the State Committee for Broadcasting.

Katalin Nagy (b. 1954) is researcher at the Institute for Labour Research, Budapest, Hungary.

Michael Nochevnik (b. 1937) is Senior Researcher at the Institute for the International Labour Movement at the Soviet Academy of Sciences, Moscow, Soviet Union.

Slawomir Skalmierski (b. 1954) is Assistant at the Institute of Sociology, University of Lodz, Poland.

Rudhard Stollberg (b. 1931) is Professor of Sociology at the University of Halle, German Democratic Republic.

Preface

This is the second book resulting from a rather ambitious international comparative project in which we have tried to make a contribution to the development of a non-technological deterministic approach in the study of technology and work.[1] Our project has been ambitious not only in its aims, but also in the way it has been organised, that is as co-operative research by teams from different East and West European countries. Basically, what we have tried to do is to compare the introduction and implementation of new technology at work in similar enterprises in East and West European countries and to see to what extent characteristics of the country and the socioeconomic system create specific conditions for the introduction and use of technology. Changes in work would, in our view, be the result of the complex combinations and interactions of such conditions and technology, rather than of technology per se. As a consequence, we have not been so much interested in the 'impact' of new technology and whether this impact varies or not under different socioeconomic and political conditions, but rather in the mechanisms and processes that are at work when new technology is being introduced. This has been our argument for organising international comparative research.

The research has been undertaken within the framework of the European Co-ordination Centre for Research and Documentation in Social Sciences in Vienna (Vienna Centre), which has as its general goal the promotion of co-operation and comparative research between social scientists from Eastern and Western Europe. Preparations for the project started in 1981 and involved at that time researchers from 17 countries. By the end of 1986, for different reasons, ten research teams had remained, and it is the result of their work which is presented in this volume. In the introductory chapter a full analysis will be given of the conceptual, methodological and organisational assumptions of the research and of their development over time when our work proceeded. After reading about the history and the experiences one will understand that all of us are quite satisfied that it has been possible to conclude the work in a - for international projects of this kind - relatively short time with some material results. When reading the national chapters that follow, one should bear in mind that these are already the result of a certain comparative analysis. It is clear that in a project such as ours, based as it is on the working together of researchers from such different backgrounds, scientific arguments easily become intertwined with political and ideological ones. As a research group we have not been and cannot be isolated from the outside world. However, as much as possible research results of each team have been repeatedly subject to the critical questions and remarks of other colleagues (frequently also a mixture of scientific and ideological ones), which have not only forced everyone to defend and explain their interpretations but have also led to a clarification of what each of us tended to assume as self-evident. It is this process of mutual understanding that has led to the chapters of this book. We are aware that this is just a first step towards true international comparison and that it does have advantages and disadvantages. The major advantage of this way of organising international research is, as already mentioned, that it leads to a basic understanding of how things work under different conditions. It also leads to an understanding of what it is possible to do and what not. The major disadvantage is, obviously, the difficulty of arriving at a higher level of sophistication. This is much easier to realise if the research is done by one researcher or by a small homogeneous group of researchers, which in turn, however, has a number of other disadvantages and may not always be feasible.

We are, of course, aware of the many factors that have restricted our 'discourse' but for none of us has this taken away the enthusiasm to do international comparative research, nor our interest in East-West comparisons. On the contrary, many of us have been looking for ways to continue co-operation on a smaller basis and there is no doubt that the experience from our international co-operation will have an impact on our research work at home as well.

One sine qua non for research projects such as ours is that researchers can meet across the borders. There are still many obstacles for this but we are grateful to all those institutions and persons who have made it possible for our group to meet several times over the past five years in different places of Europe so that we could develop insights and understanding and - no less important - good 'human relations'. We would like to thank especially our colleague Joanna Ambrus, who has so skilfully taken care of the administrative and social aspects of our research and who has helped us with the preparation of this publication. Thanks also to Luise Zimmermann for her help in editing all those different versions of European English, to Ralph Kinnear for helping with the technical problems during the preparation of the camera-ready copy, and to Waltraud Salimi for typing the manuscript several times.

Oxford and Vienna

Arthur Francis, Peter Grootings

Note

1. Peter Grootings (ed.) (1986) *Technology and Work. East-West Comparison*, London, Croom Helm reports on the conceptual and methodological preparations.

The final comparative analyses will be published in Peter Grootings, Jolanta Kulpinska and Otfried Mickler (eds.) *Work, Society and Technology: Eastern Europe and Western Europe*. The results from our comparative research in offices will be published in Peter Grootings, Liisa Rantalaiho and Paul Willman (eds.) *New Technology and Women's Work in Banks and Offices* (provisional title).

1

Conditions and Consequences of the Introduction of New Technology at Work

Peter Grootings

Introduction

This book contains a number of studies that have been undertaken within the framework of an international comparative research about conditions and consequences of the introduction of new technology at work organised and co-ordinated by the European Co-ordination Centre for Research and Documentation in Social Sciences (Vienna Centre). Teams from seven West and five East European countries have taken part in this research.[1] Both the title of the research and its international comparative character need some clarification and this will be done in this introductory chapter. I shall subsequently present the history of the project, the main theoretical and methodological ideas, its design, the methodology that has been applied in the national and international analyses and the organisational structure that has evolved in the course of our work. In the last section I shall describe the research process and point at the number of problems that we encountered during the five years spent between our first meeting and the finishing of the contributions for this publication. Both the initial conception and the analysis of its realisation should give the reader the appropriate frame of reference for reading and evaluating the results of our work.

In search of new 'paradigms'

First preparations for the project started at the end of 1981 with a careful evaluation of the experience from a previous project co-ordinated by the Vienna Centre on Automation and Industrial Workers.[2] This and a review of the international literature gave strong evidence for a growing anti-deterministic climate among social scientists in Eastern and Western Europe (Grootings ed. 1986). No consensus seemed to exist yet for a well-developed alternative paradigm. Several - sometimes conflicting - theoretical approaches existed, each of them sharing, however, a basic interest in opening what so long had been treated as a black box: How is technological change really taking place inside enterprises? Theory and research have made great progress since then, but at the beginning of the 1980s the situation was still very vague, indeed.

Our review of the research in Europe also showed considerable unevenness and heterogeneity, not only concerning the spread and introduction of new technologies but - related to this - also in the state of research.[3] Moreover, it became clear that different research questions were posed in different countries, depending on research traditions but also on dominant ways of defining social problems and on the role of social research in solving them. Despite all these differences there seemed to exist, at least at the theoretical level, an increased interest to develop an alternative paradigm for technology and work instead of traditional technological determinism. It was clear, moreover, that this would imply also different ways of doing international comparative research.

Technological determinism and its 'strategic' and 'systemic' criticisms

The relationship between technology and work has been a central issue of research in Europe for the past three decades.[4] This has resulted in a great variety of conceptual, theoretical and methodological approaches, which makes it very difficult to come to a good comparative assessment of the findings of this research.

The technological determinist approach has been the paradigm dominating social science, though in different degrees, in all European countries up to the middle of the 1970s. Two assumptions formed its hard core. The first implied that technological change was the result of progress in science and as such had an intrinsic logic of development, was unavoidable, neutral and pervasive. Technological determinism, secondly, also assumed that techno-

2

logical development had necessary consequences, especially for employment (both quantitative and qualitative), which should be accepted. About the nature of these consequences, however, opinions differed. This approach was also connected with the view that societies were converging during the course of their technological or industrial development.

Most of the research in the past had been focused on the implications and consequences of technology and technological change questioning the forces behind it. Very often it had been guided by the assumption that a certain technical equipment was always connected with one specific form of work organisation. Given such a contingency ('the one best way'), it was thought to be sufficient to choose a number of typical cases of technological development and to extrapolate from them predictions for the future (Lutz 1984). However, exactly the growing evidence of diversified or even radically opposite implications that one and the same technology appeared to have in different cases led to the conclusion that a strict relationship between technology and work did not exist. As a matter of fact, the organisation of work and division of labour appeared to be the main reason for the flexibilities found, and a given technology apparently allowed for considerable variation in the organisation of work. Subsequently, the attention of research has shifted to the question as to which other factors, given a certain technology, influence the shape of work organisation.

International comparative research has greatly contributed to this line of argument. Various publications (Burawoy 1985, Dore 1973, Dubois and Makó 1980, Gallie 1978, Lutz 1976, Maurice *et al.* 1982, Sorge *et al.* 1981) have shown that enterprises using a similar technology, but located in different countries, have different organisational, manning and qualification structures. Also, these enterprises employ workers whose attitudes and behaviour differ considerably. From these studies we now know the relevance of specific societal characteristics for shaping work organisation. Such characteristics have been located mainly in structures and developments of educational and industrial relations systems and in industrial and market structures.

The relative autonomy of work organisation with respect to technology seems now to be accepted in principle, both among East and West European social scientists. This is consequently also the case of the 'social makeability' of work organisations. Connected with this we have seen a change of research interest from consequences of technology towards the study of the

3

conditions of its development and implementation.

While the search for a new theoretical paradigm goes on, there is no agreement about an alternative. As a matter of fact, different approaches raise different arguments against technological determinism and it is exactly because of this that it would be futile to expect a major consensus to be developed soon. However, since the sharing of a paradigm, even a negative one, is a condition for co-operation and comparison, it is necessary to look in more detail at the various perspectives and to analyse on which points they might be compatible.

Critics of technological determinism have above all developed the argument that technology is an instrument for social actors to reach certain objectives or to solve certain problems, rather than an autonomous source. Differences occur with respect to the definition of the nature of the social actors, the character of their objectives and their degrees of freedom for action. One can distinguish approaches that are action or strategy-oriented apart from those that focus on the constraints or context for action.[5] The debates have basically centred around how to combine strategic and systemic analyses, the point of agreement being that work and technology are shaped by strategies of social actors, but that the social actors themselves are guided by specific interests and have to act within definite social environments.[6]

Up to the end of the 1970s most of the discussion was more or less directly concerned with the argument of technological determinism. One can summarise the major criticisms in five points:

- first, technology itself is designed and introduced by people who, in so doing, try to realise their own interests;
- second, a given technology leaves room for different alternative organisational solutions;
- third, these solutions are the result of social relations between people that are, however, not always and everywhere based on domination;
- fourth, social actors are socialised by their environment, which also shapes the nature of their social relations;
- fifth, the impact of technological change depends on the aims and goals of its introduction, both under capitalist and under socialist conditions.

In a sense the criticisms were located at different levels of analysis (from the micro-level of individuals in the Sociotechnical System approach to the mega-level of socioeconomic systems in Marxist approaches), although attempts were also undertaken to relate the different levels. Being concerned with technological determinism as such, these points of criticism had little to do with the specific character of the new technologies, nor with the specific socio-economic situation of the end of the 1970s, characterised by fundamental restructuring of enterprises and national economies.

In this respect the 1980s marked a turning point for research on the relations between technology and work (Maurice *et al.* 1986). The new research did not look at the introduction of new technologies in terms of a continuation and intensification of old trends. It argued that not only had the paradigm of social science changed, but technological and organisational paradigms themselves were changing, with the traditional technology based on the mechanical model becoming replaced by one based on the cybernetic model (Hirschhorn 1984), and the classical Taylorist model of work organisation being replaced, at least in specific branches, by post-Taylorist forms of work organisation no longer based on hierarchical control and a strict division of labour. Changes in work organisation, despite their great variety, are generally aimed at a broader and more comprehensive utilisation of workers' qualifications and experience. They are above all connected with greater flexibility in deployment of workers (Grootings *et al.* 1987). However, although the fundamental principles of these new paradigms are clear to a certain extent, they have nowhere been fully developed yet.[7]

It is interesting to note that the new research tries to combine both strategic and systemic analyses, not only at the level of enterprises but also at the level of countries and systems. The research has also a strong international comparative character and is more future- than past-oriented. Changes in technology and work organisation are considered to be intimately connected with survival strategies of individual enterprises and national economies. In the West, the increased competition on the international markets has made criteria like quality, product variety and quick market responsiveness at least as important as costs of production. Neither the old 'rigid' technologies nor the traditional Taylorist forms of work organisation can compete with such new demands. The socialist countries of Eastern Europe are confronted with problems connected with the transition from extensive to more intensive production systems, internationalisation (COMECON) and competition on the world market, and are increasingly seeking solutions with the help of new technology and changes at the level of direct production. While the new technologies as such do not automatically lead to new forms of production, they do - as against the 'old' technologies - have a flexible potential.

New technologies differ from old technologies especially in that they offer better possibilities for non-Taylorist forms of work organisation.[8] Although offering flexibility, non- or post-Taylorist forms of work organisation do not automatically develop as a reaction to new technologies. Besides technology, as was shown by research from the previous period, other factors play a role as well. On the other hand, attempts to change traditional work organisation did not begin with the coming of new technologies but in most countries started already in the 1960s, carried by highly educated workers and strong trade unions (Grootings *et al.* 1987). One could argue that the new models of work organisation developed at that time on an experimental basis, together with the underlying developments in education and industrial relations, have to a certain extent paved the way for the implementation of new technologies. They have contributed to the development of new products, production methods and social relations in the enterprise. In this respect then, socioeconomic developments have contributed to the implementation of new technologies as much as the other way around (Maurice *et al.* 1986: 4).

Also this new wave of research, therefore, gives strong arguments against the traditional approach, according to which technological change is the result of developments in science and engineering of which merely the consequences and implications can and should be measured. In contrast, a conception of technology as a social phenomenon would argue that an appropriate assessment of the impact of technology is only possible when also the impact of the social and economic environment on the development and implementation of technology is investigated.

At this point, then, some writers see signs of fundamental changes. Piore and Sabel (1984), for example, claim that the present situation is above all characterised by a crisis of the traditional system of mass-production, and the way out of this crisis is the change towards another system of production, based on 'flexible specialisation'. Both systems are characterised by their own specific constellations of a certain technology and institutions (work organisation, qualification structure, reward system, social relations) macroeconomic policy, and some countries are better 'equipped' than others to make such a transition (Sabel 1982). A similar argument can be found with Hirschhorn (1984), who speaks of an 'industrial age' based on mechanical technology and Taylorist work organisation and the coming of a 'postindustrial age' based on cybernetic technology and socio-technical work organisation, depending above all on political action. Kern and Schumann (1984) see in key sectors of the German economy developments towards 'new production concepts' based on management strategies, and Maurice *et al.* (1986) observe similar trends towards 'a double change of paradigms' in France. While these publications are certainly not undisputed they do add another element to the discussion about technology and work by embedding new technology and work organisation in rationalisation strategies that differ fundamentally from the traditional ones.

Thus, instead of looking only at the impacts of technology it seems to be more important to investigate the interrelationships between technology and society (Von Thienen 1983). International comparative research has argued that such interrelationships at enterprise and national level are the outcome of nationally specific historical and institutional developments that show a certain 'systemic' coherence. In other words, one can find in various countries consistent patterns of relationships, in which relevant social actors have their own specific identity.[9] It is within such national patterns that new technologies are being implemented and which provide also the specific societal conditions for their use, both in terms of resources and barriers. It can be assumed that different national patterns exist not only within the capitalist countries of Western Europe, but also among the East European socialist countries. To what extent this is the case and in which way system-specific characteristics shape these patterns has not been dealt with satisfactorily until now.[10] But one general question has become dominant: How do individual countries, given their specific historical and institutional character, cope with the challenge offered by the new technologies?

It is with this question in mind that we have developed our research on conditions and consequences of the introduction of new technology. We have assumed that the relation between technology and work is dependent on given structures of organisation, qualification and regulation in the enterprise that are themselves strongly interrelated with national patterns of work organisation, education and industrial relations. Such patterns vary among countries and systems, but also change over time, depending on the socioeconomic situation. The wide-scale introduction of new 'flexible' technologies indicates the transition to new patterns, but is not solely responsible for this. Changes in the societal environment and on the markets have to be taken into account as well. Each enterprise in each country confronted with coping with these developments will look for its own solutions while making use of its own resources and trying to overcome its own barriers.

The introduction of new technology at the enterprise level, therefore, can be regarded as the outcome of a decision-making process in which social actors seek to introduce new technologies to solve certain problems. The implementation and use of these new technologies can be regarded as a learning process in which given divisions of tasks, qualifications and rewards are modified in order to make optimal use of the possibilities offered by the new technology. Technology is not only a social phenomenon in the sense that it has been designed by humans, but also in the sense of being a 'resource' that becomes socialised. This also implies that whenever similar trends with respect to technological change will be found in different countries and systems, such trends cannot be simply interpreted in terms of a convergence since they will be modified by the specific characteristics of individual systems and countries. As Maurice *et al.* (1986) put it, there are not only nation-specific patterns, but also nation- (and system-) specific ways of coping with new technology.

Connected with the change in theoretical approaches also the methodology of international comparative research has changed. I shall turn to this in the next section.

From cross-national to international comparative research

There are very different ways of doing international comparative research and - like every methodology - none of these ways is completely neutral in the sense that they imply certain theoretical assumptions. The traditional view underlying most of the comparative research from the 1950s and the 1960s sees it as a methodological approach which allows for the extension of the analysis of a certain social phenomenon to a larger number of geographical, national or cultural entities. Nowak, in summarising this position, writes that we simply do not know in advance whether phenomena of the sub-national level do not 'interact' with (or are conditional upon) the national level characteristics and

8

whether the range of variation of our variables in one nation necessarily covers all the values of the variables involved, necessary to reveal the nature of the relationships we are interested in.

'Therefore, in order to formulate and to test our theory in its general formulation, we usually need a cross-national study. In order to test how general and how unconditional this theory is, we try to obtain the *replications* of findings from one national sample in the sample drawn from other nations' (Nowak 1977: 15).

This type of 'cross-national' comparative research (CNR) poses problems which are actually not very different from national research, just a little more complicated from an organisational and technical point of view.[11]

In general, this approach is certainly relevant for the attempt to generalise the results of research undertaken in different countries. However, it also raises some questions especially concerning 'context-boundedness'. It is this problem that is largely neglected by traditional cross-national approaches, while a new approach to international comparative research might actually contribute to 'solving' this problem. What do we mean by 'context-boundedness'?

In every international analysis one can distinguish at least two levels: The particular phenomenon that is studied (micro-level) is related to certain characteristics of the society in which it is located (macro-level). The traditional cross-national comparisons deal with these levels in a very specific way. Although information is collected about both the country and the social phenomena, the former appear in the final analysis only as descriptive background information, their sole function seeming to lie in indicating that the countries are indeed different. There are no systematic attempts to analyse how country characteristics influence the particular social phenomena. The two levels remain separate from each other and the comparison is merely descriptive, i.e. the findings show in comparative perspective 'how things are' in the countries compared, 'where they stand' on specific dimensions of comparison, where one can find the 'similarities' or 'dissimilarities'. The alternative approach, which we shall call international comparative research (ICR), looks exactly at the relationships between the micro- and the macro-levels and

9

therefore poses a number of quite specific methodological problems.

The two ways of doing international comparative research are related to different theoretical assumptions. But the latter are not always made explicit. The basic assumption underlying CNR is that the national context (or the macro-level) does not exert any fundamental influence on the micro-level at all. Most researchers from the technological deterministic tradition who argue that the impact of technology on work is similar in different countries follow this methodology. The theoretical assumption is translated into a research design in which the social phenomena on both the micro- and the macro-level are defined in terms of universal dimensions. In many research projects, in fact, this assumption is taken for granted and covered by a technical procedure. The social phenomenon is operationalised in terms of one or more standardised variables and the countries are then given different values for the same variable(s).[12] Comparability is in this way secured by the research instruments but at the same time the very possibility to analyse the influence of the national context is excluded. For ICR, on the other hand, comparability is not so much a technical problem of designing research instruments, but a fundamental theoretical and methodological problem. Its basic assumption is that micro- and macro-level phenomena are very much interrelated (or 'context-bound') and that strictly speaking similar social phenomena in different countries are *a priori* not comparable. The role of international comparative research in this view is not so much studying the same phenomenon in different situations in order to test a general theory. Instead, it becomes a more heuristic activity through which the typicality (or 'context-boundedness') of social phenomena and also the processes that make them typical are analysed. Comparability is taken as a theoretical problem to the understanding of which ICR can contribute, rather than as a technical problem in CNR, and the comparison functions as a methodological help rather than as a goal in itself. In Figure 1.1 I have summarised the two ways of comparative analysis. There is no reason at all to maintain that ICR as described so far is of relevance to every study, nor can only this approach give the full and final depiction of a social phenomenon. ICR has the special focus on the relationships between social phenomena and their national or societal context and, therefore, seems to be especially useful in those cases where such relationships theoretically are expected to be relevant. This is the case for various anti-technological deterministic approaches that have been described in the previous section.[13]

Figure 1.1: Ways of Handling Micro- and Macro-Levels in CNR and ICR Projects

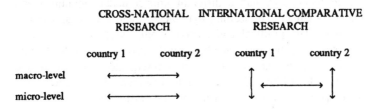

International research has greatly contributed to the development of an anti-technological deterministic climate in the social sciences. It has shown that organisations using the same technology, but located in different countries, organise their work in quite different ways; have diverging manning, qualification and reward structures and employ workers who think in different ways about their position and who also behave differently, both individually and collectively.

However, such contributions have not always been intended by the research hypotheses and the research design; much rather they have occurred despite their initial intentions generally aimed at establishing universally valid relationships. But even in cases where the guiding working hypothesis has stated a relationship between societal factors and technology, research findings have sometimes caused problems of interpretation, which has to do with what Mokrzycki (1982: 84) called the most fundamental methodological problem of comparative research: '... if the meaning of social phenomena is bound up with the social system, then how can this relation be transcended in the research process?'

I have argued so far that the main difference between CNR and ICR is that CNR treats micro- and macro-levels independently from each other (if it makes the distinction at all), while ICR explicitly looks at their interrelationships. Cross-national research is typical of technological deterministic approaches, while international comparative research better suits the approaches that look at technology as a social phenomenon. In order to illustrate my argument with concrete research experiences it may be useful to shortly describe some aspects of a previous Vienna Centre project on Automation and Industrial Workers.

It is interesting to read in Rantalaiho's (1986) account of the history of the Automation project how its main hypothesis was finally formulated as a compromise between two opposed theoretical approaches: one that was assuming that the impact of technology was universal and another which maintained that the use of technology had a different impact under capitalism and under socialism. The leading hypothesis, then, was formulated as follows: 'The political and socioeconomic system of a country exerts an essential influence both on the processes of introduction of automation and on its social consequences' (Ussenin and Nochevnik 1979: 23). Although research instruments were developed to collect information on different levels (socio-economic system of the country; management; trade unions; work process and workplace; individual workers), only the latter two have been systematically related to each other in each individual country. The core of the research design envisaged to compare in various countries in a similar type of industry (automobile) differences between individual workplaces and workers' attitudes in non-automated units (NAU), on the one hand, and automated units (AU), on the other (see Figure 1.2).

Figure 1.2: Comparative Design Automation and Industrial Workers' Study

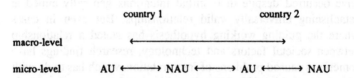

Also the design seems to have been the result of a compromise, since it gave to both theoretical approaches the possibility to pursue their research aims: those who assumed that system differences were present directly at the workplace level, and those who assumed that the differences were due to types of technology. Information, finally, was collected with the help of standardised research instruments (questionnaires and workplace observation schemes). Thus, though the main research hypothesis was formulated in terms of anti-technological determinism, the research design can be regarded as typical of CNR (see for more details Rantalaiho 1986, Koval and Nochevnik 1986, Forslin *et al.* 1979 and 1981). All in all the project appears to be a fine example of Kulpinska's (1986) argument concerning the gap between macro-level arguments and micro-level research in the research on technology and work in the socialist countries. With respect to the latter, as Rantalaiho noticed, the project firmly stands in the Anglo-Saxon research tradition of the 1960s.[14] Since any possible differences were made comparable in advance with the help of standardised research instruments, it is hardly surprising that the national studies did not show too many differences, at least not enough to allow acceptance of the working hypothesis. One can also understand that this situation, given the initial differences in theoretical approach, opened the way for a lot of ad hoc interpretation of the data during the comparative analysis.

The history of this study illustrates well the transition in theoretical and methodological paradigms that took place during the 1970s and would seem to support our argument that the present anti-technological deterministic climate is forcing us more or less towards the ICR type of research. It also makes clear, however, that ICR only becomes possible when technological determinism is not any more the dominating paradigm.

So far I have dealt with the theoretical and methodological discussion around international comparative research on Technology and Work. There is a third aspect that usually does not receive much attention but that is equally important for the practice of empirical research and that is its organisational dimension. This aspect will be dealt with in the following section.

Co-operative forms of international comparative research

Although is is not always recognised, organisational, conceptual and methodological dimensions in every research are very much interrelated. A choice for a specific organisational form basically determines what is feasible in terms of conceptual and methodological aims and vice versa: a certain conceptualisation implies specific methodological requirements and its own organisational structure. Vienna Centre research is characterised by a very specific organisational structure in that projects are undertaken in co-operation by national teams of researchers and co-ordinated by the Vienna Centre's staff. Also for our project this was something given and we had to look for the right 'balance' with our substantive aims.

In Figure 1.3 I have summarised the 'typical' type of co-opera-

Figure 1.3: Forms of Co-operation in Vienna Centre Research

Stages of research	Forms of co-operation		
	exchange of literature/ expert talks, conferences	workshops or joint research meetings	joint research
conceptual design	*	*	*
instruments	*	*	*
fieldwork			
analysis			*
interpretation		*	
comparison			*

tion in Vienna Centre projects. It appears that co-operation is actually of relatively low intensity and true for only very specific phases of the research. As a matter of fact, in crucial stages no co-operation can take place at all (fieldwork) and it practically does not go beyond the form of joint research meetings.

In view of the theoretical and methodological discussions that have been described so far, one could consider such a restricted co-operative structure as adequate for the typical cross-national research strategies. For research based on the theoretical and methodological assumptions of international comparative research, such organisational possibilities are far from ideal, and as I shall describe in the final part of this chapter, they have, indeed, limited the chances to realise our aspirations. While more intensive forms of co-operation, for instance in internationally composed research teams, were not (yet) possible within our organisational framework, we tried to find alternative ways of dealing with the heuristic role that comparative analysis in our conception should fulfil. The organisational structure of our project has developed in close connection with our initial research design, and it is to an analysis of this process that I shall turn next.

What I wanted to show in the foregoing was how our research has been conceived as a contribution (and not more than that) to the search for new paradigms: the theory of technology and work, the methodology of international comparative research, and that in the course of this it has been confronted with the problem to develop new forms of co-operative organisation.

Research design: aims, contents and methodology

Aims and contents

After the elaborate presentation of the main ideas on the basis of which we have developed our project on Conditions and Consequences of the Introduction of New Technology at Work, we can be relatively short about the principles of the initial research design.

The aim of the project was to contribute to a better understanding as to how societal conditions have an impact on consequences of the introduction of new technology at work. The project was to deal with conditions and consequences of the introduction of three specific types of new technology in production departments of enterprises:

- computer numerical control (CNC);
- process control (PC);
- office automation.

It was designed as an international comparative research making use of case study reports provided by national research teams, each of whom was responsible for the collection of national data. No standardised research instruments were to be developed. Societal conditions would be studied at the enterprise level by analysing the decision-making process in introducing new technologies and at the level of the broader national context in which the enterprise and its actors were located. On the level of the society the research was to focus primarily on the relations with:

- the educational system;
- the industrial relations system;
- the social and economic policy of the state;
- the structure of industry.

The relationships between these societal levels (enterprise and society) were to be the main focus of interest. Consequences of the new technologies would be studied in five areas that also form the conditions for their introduction at the enterprise level:

- changes in the overall organisation of work;
- changes in work content and load;

15

- changes in qualification structures;
- changes in workers' culture;
- changes in industrial relations at the enterprise level.

It is obviously the first one (changes in the division of work) which is the central research dimension. Indeed, the quality of individual workplaces (content and load), the resulting qualification structure (relationship between available and defined qualifications), the social relationships within the enterprise (social status of different groups, both formal and 'real'), and the structure and content of interest representation depend to a high degree on the way in which work has been divided and organised in tasks, jobs and departments, each with its own professional and social responsibilities.

In the first phase a national report was to be prepared by each research team. These reports should contain two parts: case descriptions and national background information.

The case descriptions should give a historical descriptive analysis of the social process of the introduction of new technology at the plant level. Every case should also include an analysis of changes in work organisation. Other research dimensions were to be covered by at least two participating teams to make an international comparison possible. We called this a module working procedure. The choice of research techniques and instruments was left to the participants according to their possibilities. As a guide for the description a topic list was jointly elaborated for every research dimension.

The national reports should include background data thought relevant by researchers for explaining national specificities. Additional background information was to be provided when asked for at later stages of analysis.

The national studies were to provide the basic empirical material for the second stage of the project: the international comparative analysis. This analysis should be undertaken by participants themselves through an intensive confrontation of their own case study results with those reached by other teams. The comparative analysis would thus start as early as possible, and be a co-operative endeavour with each team participating according to its possibilities and concrete interests. It should concentrate mainly on:

- the strategies of social actors applied in the process of

16

decision-making, introduction and implementation of new technology as well as solving of the problems that arise;
- the outcomes of the introduction of new technology in terms of changes in work organisation, job content, qualification structure, workers' culture and industrial relations;
- an analysis of the 'why' questions: the processes, causes, interrelations underlying and leading to the observed outcomes and strategies.

Methodology

Both our research hypothesis and the envisaged content of the study entail their specific methodological demands. The assumed national and system-specific effects of microelectronic technology call for an international analysis of countries that belong to different socioeconomic systems. The complex content of the study calls for detailed and in-depth analyses which are guaranteed the most by the case-study method. Case studies allow for a variety of research techniques such as expert interviews, observations and the study of written documents, and use can even be made of questionnaires. The case study makes it possible also to analyse a social phenomenon in a dynamic way in terms of the processes, mechanisms and social relations that have led to a certain situation. It makes, however, quite a difference whether the case-study method is used in national or in international research.

A major problem frequently discussed in connection with case studies is that of representativeness. Is it possible to generalise findings of case studies or not? Usually two different answers are given to this question. The first denies the possibility to generalise case-study findings and sees it basically as a heuristic method giving qualitatively rich insights that should be tested by some other, more rigorous method. In this view case studies as such cannot test or prove anything. The second answer is more optimistic and relates the degree of generalisation to specific criteria for the selection of cases.

Different as they are, still both answers share a basic concern with the problem of representativeness. But one could argue that this problem itself is rather an operational and technical one based on a specific way of thinking as well as on a specific definition of research aims. To start with the last point: the problem presents itself only if one would like to make statements of a general nature about a certain universe (for example about a country). Since it is impossible to investigate the whole universe, one has to restrict oneself to selected parts of it. How to select these parts of the whole and how to generalise the findings of such partial research into general statements then becomes indeed the problem. Our research aims have in fact been much more modest and in a way we have not been too much concerned with the generalisation issue. This was also implicit in our conceptual and theoretical assumptions. The principle of 'context-boundedness' of social phenomena has led us to distinguish in our study several interrelated levels: workplace, work organisation, society and socioeconomic system. Our case studies would be undertaken at the level of work organisations (plant/enterprise), but would also include information about individual workplaces as part of the overall division of labour inside the enterprise. The socioeconomic system and the national level form the larger context of the enterprise, provisionally defined by us in terms of property relations, organisational strategies, technological climate, education and industrial relations. It was assumed that a case (as a constellation of findings at the enterprise level) is embedded in a macro-context by which it is influenced (and which it also influences in turn). We assumed, in other words, that there is always an impact of society on the enterprise and we 'only' wanted to know in what sense and how this takes place. The issue of generalisation therefore loses much of its relevance for our purposes. It changes from a question of statistical or reasoned representativeness to an intellectual exercise in conceptual thinking.

Against this background, then, the two answers to the generalisation question do not have much relevance for us. Our position necessitates, however, a continuous movement between the level of the case study and the macro-level of society and consequently also a continuous re-analysis of the case-study findings in order to elaborate their relations with the social context. Such a procedure is only possible if one has the opportunity to confront a certain national case with cases from other countries. This again implies that the international comparison itself is seen as a creative process rather than as a mechanical act that is undertaken at the end of the research.

As a matter of fact, we have applied a type of case study that falls outside the traditional classification but has gained considerable popularity in international comparative research: matched cases. The argument can be derived from our research hypothesis.

Since we question the autonomous and universal influence of technology and assume, instead, the existence of societal and system effects, our findings would be more convincing if referring to similar technologies. This is why we decided to investigate only specific technologies and preferably in comparable enterprises.

However, although we adopted the principle of matched-case comparison, the reality of our respective research situations forced us in practice to make a number of compromises. The biggest problem was that some of the teams, for different reasons, did not really have the possibility to choose their cases according to the agreed criteria. Some of our criteria appeared to be nation-specific, as for instance the size of enterprises. There were also system-specific influences concerning the type of product and batch size, the specific organisational structure and division of labour in industry. Besides, there were also a number of practical reasons for the fact that not all researchers were able to strictly adhere to the selected criteria. Some participants had already finished their empirical work in other types of firms before joining our international project; some had definite obligations to do their research in specific enterprises, while others had problems with getting access and had to turn to 'second choice' enterprises. Nevertheless, criteria for ideal cases were elaborated and it was agreed that whenever it was not possible to adhere to them, a clear description of the investigated enterprises in terms of these criteria would be given. For the CNC cases, enterprises should be selected with the following characteristics:

- the production process should involve complex metal-cutting;
- production should be in small batches;
- factories should be medium- to large-size, depending on national criteria;
- stand-alone machines and preferably not machining centres should be used;
- and there should already exist some experience with operating them.

For the Process Control cases it was not really possible to match all of them: preference was given to oil refineries, but in the end paper and aluminium factories were also included.

The general contents of the case studies have already been sketched. A comprehensive topic list was established in order to guarantee that all teams would look at and report on the same phenomena. No detailed standardised research instruments were worked out, however, leaving it to the professional responsibility of the individual teams to find adequate ways of collecting information. An additional argument for this was that our prime interest was not in comparing individual and isolated data (like individual responses to questionnaires or scale positions) but in comparing more comprehensive problem situations. Most teams applied the whole gambit of research techniques ranging from intensive interviews with key persons, to observations, the study of documents and even limited surveys.

This is what we had in mind when we started our common work. A certain pragmatism, or maybe rather flexibility, was needed on our route from conception to realisation in order to find *ad hoc* solutions for the many problems that we would encounter during our work. In the following section a detailed description will be given of how we have proceeded in practice.

From design to reality or the realisation of the research design

Between May 1982 and April 1987 seven general meetings were organised and a number of smaller meetings took place. In between, numerous bilateral contacts were taking place between the co-ordinator and participating teams and between individual participants. Especially in the second half of the period, when we were working on the comparative analyses, the importance of small meetings was considerable.

The first general meeting, held in Velm (Austria), was devoted to an exchange of information about participants' finished, ongoing or planned research in the field of work and technology. In this sense it was also a kind of selection moment. Participants had been invited to this meeting from among the group of researchers that had taken part in the Automation and Industrial Workers project, from the group of experts that had been consulted in the preparatory phase and from the network brought in by the co-ordinators. The two initial criteria for selection were quite simple: a geographical coverage of Europe and research experience in the field.

The meeting was also used to 'test' the project proposal in terms of acceptance of the basic research dimensions, methodology and organisational structure. By and large this was indeed the case, though some scepticism appeared concerning the strategy of comparative analysis, which some participants considered not to be elaborated and clear enough. In addition, although in general technological determinism was rejected by most of the researchers, some raised objections to an all too absolute rejection of the autonomous role of technology and warned about falling back to other forms of determinism. As a matter of fact, these views were a manifestation of the existence of a wide diversity of conceptual and theoretical approaches. No need was felt at this stage to force all teams to reach theoretical consensus, but a continuous debate about theoretical aspects of the problematic was asked for.

Figure 1.4: Coverage of Research Dimensions by Country in Initial National Proposals

	Case					
	1	2	3	4	5	6
CSSR	X	X	X	X		
Finland			X	X		
FRG		X	X	X		
GDR	X	X	X	X		X
Great Britain	X		X	X		X
Hungary		X	X			
the Netherlands		X		X	X	
Poland			X	X		
USSR			X	X	X	X

1 - decision-making on introduction
2 - organisation of work
3 - work content
4 - qualifications
5 - work culture
6 - industrial relations

Figure 1.4 shows for the CNC and Process Control part which research dimensions were covered by the various teams in their own research projects. The overview reflects perfectly the fact that most teams had conceptualised their research within the framework of mainstream discussions of the late 1970s and with an almost universal focus on issues of qualification and work content. In contrast, the decision-making process only rarely received systematic attention. Even the studies from Czechoslovakia and the German Democratic Republic were actually not so much concerned with this, but rather with the process of implementation of new technology in a number of pilot enterprises, the experiences of which should be used in future large-scale introduction. Also the dimension of organisation of work received attention only in a few cases, reflecting the orientation of most studies to the micro-level of individual workers and workplaces.

The acceptance of these two dimensions as the very core of the international research therefore meant more than just a simple extension of the various national research designs. Indeed, it implied a thorough reconceptualisation of the contents of some studies. This proved to be more easily said than done, indicating also the wide gap at the time between changed general theoretical notions (anti-technological determinism) and their translation into empirical research designs. In addition, none of the national research projects had been designed as part of an international comparative project, which not only had conceptual and methodological implications but also created practical problems of a financial and organisational nature for many teams (some teams had to cancel their participation for these reasons). A predictable consequence of this situation was that a real integration of the national studies into the international design would only be possible in the course of the project when, after many discussions, a kind of agreed and internalised frame of reference would be developed.

A first step towards developing such a common framework was discussing explicitly the different research interests of the participating teams, and this was the main aim of the second general meeting, which took place in Visegrad, Hungary, at the end of 1982. It turned out that the research interests were in fact very diverse and nationally specific (reflecting also differences in national research funding). One of the British teams, for instance, was preoccupied with new technology and industrial relations and union responses, a question hardly shared by any of the other teams. The teams from Czechoslovakia and the German Democratic Republic, as mentioned earlier, were part of a national programme of introduction of new technologies and their research was defined in these terms.

Also there appeared to be a lot of ignorance and stereotyped thinking about other countries, which caused quite a problem since one of the core issues of the international analysis had to do exactly with the relationship between enterprise case studies and the

22

national context. Obviously the project had some educational functions to fulfil as well.

A concrete problem for the research design was then to define those national characteristics about which information should be collected and presented to the other teams. This problem had two aspects: it had to do with a lack of basic information about the participating countries, but at the same time it also referred to the national characteristics that would be relevant for the international comparative analysis. While there was, indeed, an acute need for some basic information, it was also realised that really relevant national characteristics would only become clear during a later stage of 'confrontation' of different case studies, and that even these would not necessarily be the same for all countries.

We decided to proceed in the following way: From available comparative studies we knew about the relevance of a number of national characteristics for the introduction of new technology and organisation of work at the enterprise level, like the educational system, the industrial relations system, the 'technological culture' and the market position of the enterprise. Information on these topics would be immediately useful for the other participants as background information when reading the case studies. Each team, therefore, agreed to prepare a national background paper which at this stage would have primarily an informational character. In a later phase these national papers should be amended on the basis of our discussions and be integrated with the enterprise case studies. The latter would then also change their character and become national case reports, integrating micro- , meso- and macro-levels of analysis. It was clear to us that such national case reports could only be the final result of a process of comparative analysis. It was not so clear, however, how this comparative analysis was to be organised. Roughly, the procedure we had in mind was a stepwise process including the following stages:

- preparation of informative national reports;
- preparation and discussion of enterprise case studies followed by an analysis of differences and similarities of any of the research dimensions between case studies from different countries;
- trying, through a more intensive 'confrontation' of the cases, to 'understand' these similarities and differences as 'typical' in their own right and to analyse which national or system characteristics could explain them;

- this would result in 'national case studies', in which national reports and case studies would be integrated, and also in a number of separate comparative analyses.

Since there was some scepticism as to the feasibility and fruitfulness of such a rather open approach, it was suggested that each team should already at an early stage propose concrete issues for comparative analysis. This, however, proved to be a rather unsuccessful alternative. Clearly, the point was that most participants were not ready to think in comparative terms, occupied as they were with their own national research. It was in fact not before the last meeting but one that a definite agreement could be reached about topics for comparative analysis.

At the third meeting (Berlin, German Democratic Republic, 1983) first national background reports and enterprise case studies were available and were used to discuss the problem of comparability. The case studies showed the importance of being exact about the type and character of the technology studied. In industry especially the distinction between stand-alone machines and complete systems of interrelated technology proved to be crucial, while the very existence of these two types of new technology also indicated differences in strategies of technological innovation. The latter types, for instance, dominated in some socialist countries and in large engineering enterprises in some of the capitalist countries, the former appeared to be more typical of the smaller and medium-size engineering enterprises in the West. (We needed, however, the concrete research reports to realise this.)

These first discussions, therefore, somehow confirmed that the procedure chosen for the project would be fruitful. From the presentation and subsequent discussion of this first series of papers a number of issues emerged that also popped up again in later discussions and became in the end the hard core of our comparative analysis. These were issues that proved to be of general concern and most of the following meetings were devoted to their further elaboration.

In the case of the CNC studies, it appeared that this technology was used in East and in West European enterprises both in a centralised and in a decentralised way. The question that arose was: Why is this so? Is this the result of certain choices? Is this already a stable situation or merely typical of the first stage of implementation? Is this the result of a change in work organisation or was the work organisation like that already before?

Second, in many cases we saw old and new technologies side by side. This obviously posed specific user problems of planning and manning which were different from when a whole new integrated system had been introduced. But also in the latter case we found that the integrated systems were connected with separate machines of various technological ages that were not part of the system. Why is this so? What are the patterns of co-operation that develop under such conditions and what are the constraints and/or possibilities offered by a specific technological constellation?

A third issue was related to the division of work. We found across all the cases differences between the official and the real division of work. In some cases operators were not supposed to program their machines, but they did so. In other cases they were allowed to, but did not do so. In some cases there was good co-operation between operators and programmers, in others not. This raised the question of qualifications and selection criteria for operators and programmers. And this again touched the problem of the creation of these qualifications and their availability in the enterprise or on the labour market, but also led to questions about the very content of programming for CNC machines.

From the available Process Control cases (from the paper and aluminium industries in the German Democratic Republic and in Hungary) it became clear that there were still considerable technical restrictions for a fully computerised control and that there was still a firm place for human intervention. Also fundamental differences between these two socialist countries appeared with respect to the existence of an overall and elaborate system of social planning. Such a system was absent in the case of Hungary.

First indications of different roles and responsibilities of trade unions in capitalist and socialist countries with respect to the introduction of new technology became clear as well. In the latter, trade unions were involved in the principal decision-making process, being part of the enterprise power structure. Their main task in the implementation stage was securing the co-operation of the workers involved, by protecting them from negative consequences.

These points were taken up again during the fourth meeting in Italy (Firenze, May 1984). A few more case reports were available, and an attempt was made to systematise the discussion on comparative analysis and to go beyond the mere listing of interesting similarities and differences. The starting point for this was a remark made by several authors that their cases should not be considered as typical or representative of their national situation.

Other authors maintained, however, that what they had written could also be found with other cases from their countries. Although the problem of representativeness had been discussed earlier and judged to be of little relevance for our methodological approach, it was no surprise that it came back again. One obvious reason for this is that in the Vienna Centre type of projects, national teams tend to consider themselves very easily as representatives of their country, rather than as a group of researchers coming from a certain country. It is an interesting phenomenon how different concepts of representativeness are applied in different situations.

The discussion proceeded to the question of what to compare, and two positions were taken. The first stressed that it was necessary to define in advance comparative research interests and to select those dimensions that would have priority for comparative analysis. The second position was a bit more pragmatic and favoured focusing on those dimensions that would emerge from first critical confrontations of case studies. The main argument was that at that moment differences between participants would be too big to reach a workable consensus. It was understood, however, that a clarification of the various theoretical positions was necessary, if only for understanding the type of questions posed by the different teams.

So far, except from discussing the basic rationale of the project, the work had mainly focused on the solution of various technical and organisational problems (like the restriction of research dimensions, the elaboration of a topic list, the selection criteria for the cases, the module working procedure) and on a review of the first case-study reports. There had been hardly any occasion for a thorough theoretical debate. While there was certainly no illusion that such a debate would solve all the problems connected with the existing theoretical heterogeneity, it was expected to make this at least explicit and by that prepare the ground for the next comparative stage. This was, indeed, becoming an urgent matter since any comparative analysis would only be possible through the intensive co-operation between the research teams.

It has to be said, though, that it proved rather difficult to organise a 'theoretical discussion' (even on such a well-defined theme as technology and work) not related to concrete research questions and/or interpretations of research findings. We had at our disposal two papers with overviews of the Western (basically the Anglo-Saxon) and the East European research traditions respectively.[15] While most of us indeed recognised the main approaches and could identify with them or were able to add some others, especially from the French and German traditions, the identification issue was obviously not the most important one. What did matter, in fact, was to find a point where these different approaches could meet fruitfully: a kind of convergence point that would make it possible to 'make use' of the existing variance rather than to attempt to unify it.

Such a convergence was actually developing in social sciences and could, as we have seen, be located in attempts to develop a multi-level approach and to relate the analysis of micro- , meso- , and macro-levels (workers' attitudes, group strategies, enterprise structures, societal institutions). While such attempts varied very much and practically ranged from rather eclectic to very original and comprehensive approaches, they could function for us as a theoretical horizon.

With respect to our paradigm of anti-technological determinism, the overview of research approaches once again showed clearly that in the socialist countries technological determinism is mainly contested at the mega- (= system) level, while the macro- (= country) level has been highly neglected, and sometimes a firm technological determinism can be found in empirical studies, i.e. those mostly focusing on individuals and workplaces. Most of the recent Western literature that takes a critical stand towards technological determinism seems to be limited to micro- and meso-levels of analysis. Not surprisingly, these differences also clearly recurred in the case studies. Some of the socialist countries' cases initially firmly suggested a direct connection between basic characteristics of the socialist system and implications of the introduction of new technologies, the individual countries being almost taken as archetypes of socialist societies. On the other hand, most of the Western case reports either presented the enterprise as a reality in itself, isolated from the societal context, or suggested the existence of a kind of 'logic' of capitalism in operation in all the capitalist countries in a similar way.

The discussions of those approaches gave us enough confidence to make two other decisive steps. It was decided that the national case studies should attempt to relate the various levels of analysis, avoiding, of course, merely ideological statements. Secondly, we agreed that the comparative chapters should be written by international teams of authors and preferably even by East-West teams.

With the adoption of these principles the need arose to finally come to more concrete agreements on the contents of comparative analysis. That was the agenda of the fifth general meeting (Nieborow, Poland, spring 1984). We started to talk on the basis of the assumption that a publication had to be prepared for which each participant would take partial responsibility. The whole problem was now, basically, how to integrate into a well-structured book the comparative potential of the initial research design with the concrete interests of the individual participants and the available empirical material. In addition, a format for the individual chapters had to be elaborated. Since the project as such had been based on a number of clearly defined theoretical and methodological premises, these obviously had to become the leading principles for any publication that would result. In other words, all chapters would have to be conceived as contributions to the development of an anti-technological deterministic paradigm and be based on a comparative analysis; furthermore the work should be collective. Given such high demands, it seemed appropriate to introduce also some limitations to make the thing work. Each chapter should only cover one of the research dimensions of the initial research design, while the latter should more or less define the frame of the book as a whole. Not all contributions would necessarily have to include the information on all countries. Thus, we also adopted a kind of module approach for the final stage of our work.

To start, each of us agreed to prepare a short outline about how and why to deal with one particular research dimension. A small group would be convened to have a look at the individual suggestions and would try to make a proposal for regrouping them in terms of chapters and teams of authors.

Due to some organisational problems the whole group could only meet again in May 1985 (Amelia, Italy). In the meantime all the national case studies, except one, had become available and an agreement was reached to prepare them for publication as well. Furthermore, the study of all suggestions for comparative analysis received resulted in a proposal to choose a limited number of issues, each of which had the theme of an on-going debate in social sciences, and that participants should join on that particular theme which was closest to their own interest. Each comparative chapter was to contain three sections:

-   a resumé of the on-going debate around the topic chosen as an explication of its theoretical relevance;

28

- a confrontation of the major hypotheses or arguments from this debate with the empirical material from our case studies;
- finally, conclusions on the basis of comparative analysis for the validity of these arguments.

It was at this stage of the project that most of the bilateral contacts and meetings took place, although less than hoped for and far less than necessary. Obviously, practical problems of East-West co-operation on this level had been underestimated a bit, especially from the point of view of their financial and organisational implications. It was also true, though, that other obligations of participants began to receive higher priorities, which was also due to the fact that practically nobody had guaranteed finances and working time to engage in this phase of international comparison. In a number of smaller meetings and a final general meeting (Prague, Czechoslovakia, April 1987), the concrete contents of the publications were agreed upon.

This book contains the results of the first phase of our work, the national case studies dealing with various CNC and process control technology. Both the comparative analyses and the case studies on office automation will be published separately.

* * *

It is certainly not merely an act of courtesy when I conclude this introduction by saying that it is thanks to the active involvement and dedication of all participants that we have finally succeeded in finishing our work in a relatively short period. We are, of course, very grateful to all those institutions that have made it possible for us to do the research and to meet and discuss together, and we do hope that the results of our work as presented in this and other publications justify all the money, time and energy that has been put into it. We as the participants know very well that such results go far beyond what can be written down at a given moment, but we also realise that our readers will only judge our work on that basis. For us, the process of understanding of what goes on in our own and in other countries has not finished with this publication. As a matter of fact, it has only begun, and all we can hope, therefore, is that what has been collected in this volume will be worth reading for others.

29

Notes

1. Austria, Belgium, Czechoslovakia, Finland, German Democratic Republic, Federal Republic of Germany, Great Britain, Hungary, Italy, the Netherlands, Poland and Soviet Union.

2. The results of this study have been published in Forslin *et al.* (1979 and 1981) and in Adler *et al.* (1986).

3. It was, for instance, impossible to locate new technologies in administrative settings in any of the socialist countries, and up to the middle of the 1980s we could not find any colleague doing research in this area.

4. See for overviews of the discussions in various countries Child (1986), Düll (1975), Francis (1986), Hoss (1986), Kulpinska (1986), Maurice (1980).

5. One could place the Sociotechnical System Approach (see Butera and Thurman 1984) and the Labour Process Debate (see Wilkinson 1983, Thompson 1984 and Wood 1982) in the West, and the approach of Scientific Work Organisation in some of the East European countries (see Autorenkollektiv 1980) in the first group. In the second group one can place above all the traditional Marxist approaches that assume the existence of capitalist and socialist 'logics', and, secondly, the 'societal effect' approach that has been developed by Maurice and his team.

6. See Braverman (1974), Benz-Overhage *et al.* (1982) and Richta (1969); for the societal effect approach see Maurice *et al.* (1984) and Rose (1985).

7. Thus, the American Office of Technology Assessment (1984) concludes in its report on Programmable Automation (computer-aided design; computer-aided manufacturing; computer-aided management techniques and computer-integrated manufacturing) that all of these technologies are still in their infancy and have only recently been implemented in a very reluctant and careful way by enterprises. Some of the potential technologies are only in the stage of laboratory experiments, but much will become available during the 1990s.

8. Some authors argue even that new technologies, because of their complexity and sensitivity to failure, require, in order to be effectively used, a non-Taylorist work organisation that is based on learning rather than on control. See, for example, Hirschhorn (1984).

9. A French qualified worker is not the same as a German qualified worker; Maurice *et al.* (1982), Sorge *et al.* (1981), Eyraud and Rychener (1986) and Maurice *et al.* (1986).

10. See, for example, Burawoy (1985), Dubois and Makó (1980), Hoss (1984).

11. The additional complications are mainly due to the fact that there are more researchers engaged, each of them with her/his own theoretical approach and professional experience; there are more units for analysis (how to make them comparable); there has to be consensus about research design and instruments (exact translations, similar codings, etc.); and above all, there is a need for co-ordination and control of the research process itself.

12. See also Brossard and Maurice (1974).

13. However, a closer look at some of the alternative approaches indicates that the acceptance of context-boundedness can have unexpected 'dogmatic' or 'ideological' implications. There is more than one international project in which the following argumentation can be observed: The systems involved in the comparative analysis are different in a number of fundamental respects; from this follows that (lower-level) social phenomena - because of the very system-boundedness - are (or

30

rather should be) different as well. The argument is latently present in many comparative East-West research projects and sometimes functions to show 'how good our system is' (and how bad the other one, of course). The example is given to indicate that, in our view, it is an empirical question how lower and higher levels are interrelated and that ICR should be considered as a methodological help to find an answer.

14. There has, indeed, been a striking convergence in the use of quantitative research instruments of the survey-type despite clearly opposing theoretical views.

15. These papers have been published in Child (1986) and Kulpinska (1986).

References

Autorenkollektiv (1980) *Wissenschaftlich-technischer Fortschritt und Inhalt der Arbeit. Ein Beitrag zur Theorie und Praxis der Arbeitswissenschaften* (Scientific-technological Progress and Work Content. A Contribution to Theory and Practice in Science of Work), Berlin

Adler, F., B. Koval, P.E. Jacob, V. Jez, S.C. Mills, J. Rehak and G. Wieser (1986) *Automation and Industrial Workers. A Cross-National Comparison of Fifteen Countries*, volume 2, parts 1 and 2, Oxford, Pergamon Press

Benz-Overhage, K., E. Brumlop, Th. von Freyberg and Z. Papadimitriou (1982) *Neue Technologien und alternative Arbeitsgestaltung. Auswirkungen des Computereinsatzes in der industriellen Produktion* (New Technologies and Alternative Work Organisation. Effects of Computerisation in Industrial Production), Frankfurt/Main and New York, Campus Verlag

Braverman, H. (1974) *Labor and Monopoly Capital: The Degradation of Work in the Twentieth Century*, London, Monthly Review Press

Brossard, M. and M. Maurice (1974) 'Existe-t-il un Modèle Universel des Structures d'Organisations?', *Sociologie du Travail*, no. 4, pp. 403-426

Burawoy, M. (1985) *The Politics of Production. Factory Regimes under Capitalism and Socialism*, London, Verso

Butera, F. and J.E. Thurman (1984) *Automation and Work Design. A Study Prepared by the International Labour Office*, Amsterdam, New York, Oxford, North Holland

Child, J. (1986) 'Technology and Work: An Outline of Theory and Research in the Western Social Sciences', in P. Grootings (ed.) (1986) *Technology and Work. East-West Comparison*, London, Croom Helm, pp. 7-65

Dore, R. (1973) *British Factory - Japanese Factory. The Origins of National Diversity in Industrial Relations*, Berkeley/Los Angeles, University of California Press

Dubois, P. and C. Makó (1980) *La Division du Travail dans l'Industrie. Etudes de Cas Hongrois et Francais*, Paris, Groupe Sociologie du Travail

Düll, K. (1975) *Industriesoziologie in Frankreich. Eine historische Analyse zu den Themen Technik, Industriearbeit, Arbeiterklasse* (Industrial Sociology in France. A Historical Analysis of the Topics Technology, Industrial Work and the Working Class), Frankfurt/Main, Europäische Verlangsanstalt

Eyraud, F. and F. Rychener (1986) 'A Societal Analysis of New Technologies', in P. Grootings (ed.) *Technology and Work. East-West Comparison*,

London, Croom Helm, pp. 209-230

Forslin, J., A. Sarapata and A.M. Whitehill (1979) *Automation and Industrial Workers. A Fifteen Nation Study*, volume 1, part 1, Oxford, Pergamon Press

Forslin, J., A. Sarapata and A.M. Whitehill (eds.) (1981) *Automation and Industrial Workers. A Fifteen Nations Study*, volume 1, part 2, Oxford, Pergamon Press

Francis, A. (1986) *New Technology at Work*, Oxford, Clarendon Press

Gallie, D. (1978) *In Search of the New Working Class: Automation and Social Integration within the Capitalist Enterprise*, London, Cambridge University Press

Grootings, P. (ed.) (1986) *Technology and Work. East-West Comparison*, London, Croom Helm

Grootings, P. (1986) 'Technology and Work: A Topic for East-West Comparison?', in P. Grootings (ed.) *Technology and Work. East-West Comparison*, London, Croom Helm, pp. 275-301

Grootings, P., B. Gustavsen and L. Héthy (eds.) (1987) *New Forms of Work Organization in Europe*, New Brunswick, Transaction

Hirschhorn, L. (1984) *Beyond Mechanization: Work and Technology in a Post-industrial Age*, Cambridge, the MIT Press

Hoss, D. (1984) 'Technologie et Travail dans les Pays de l'Est: le Cas de la Hongrie et de la République Démocratique Allemande', *Sociologie du Travail*, no. 4, pp. 548-557

Hoss, D. (1986) 'Technology and Work in the Two Germanies', in P. Grootings, B. Gustavsen and L. Héthy (eds.) (1987) *New Forms of Work Organization in Europe*, New Brunswick, Transaction, pp. 231-271

Kern, H. and M. Schumann (1984) *Das Ende der Arbeitsteilung? Rationalisierung in der industriellen Produktion* (The End of the Division of Labour? Rationalisation in Industrial Production), Munich, Beck Verlag

Koistinen, P. and K. Urponen (eds.) (1984) *New Technologies and Societal Development, Research Reports in Social Policy and Sociology*, no. 2, University of Joensuu, Faculty of Sociological Sciences, Joensuu

Koval, B. and M. Nochevnik (1986) 'Automation and Industrial Workers: the Preparation and Implementation of an International Project', in P. Grootings (ed.) (1986) *Technology and Work. East-West Comparison*, London, Croom Helm, pp. 185-205

Kulpinska, J. (1986) 'The Concept of Technology in the Sociology of Socialist Countries', in P. Grootings (ed.) (1986) *Technology and Work. East-West Comparison*, London, Croom Helm, pp. 67-101

Lutz, B. (1976) 'Bildungssystem und Beschäftigungsstrukturen in Deutschland und Frankreich. Zum Einfluß des Bildungssystems auf die Gestaltung betrieblicher Arbeitskräftestrukturen'(Training Systems and Employment Structures in Germany and France. The Influence of Training Systems on the Formation of Manpower Structures) in ISF München (ed.), *Betrieb, Arbeitsmarkt, Qualifikation*, Frankfurt/Main and Munich

Lutz, B. (1984) 'Technik und Arbeit: Stand, Perspektiven und Probleme industriesoziologischer Technikforschung' (Technology and Work: Present State, Perspectives and Industrial-Sociological Problems of Technological Research), in P. Koistinen and K. Urponen (eds.) *New Technologies and Societal Development, Research Reports in Social Policy and Sociology*, no. 2, University of Joensuu, Faculty of Sociological Sciences, Joensuu, pp.

59-87

Maurice, M. (1980) 'Le Determinisme Technologique dans la Sociologie du Travail (1955-1980). Un changement de paradigme?', *Sociologie du Travail*, no. 1, pp. 22-37

Maurice, M., A. Sorge and M. Warner (1984) 'Societal Differences in Organizing Manufacturing Units: a Comparison of France, West Germany and Great Britain', *Organization Studies*, no. 1, pp. 59-86

Maurice, M., F. Sellier, and J.J. Silvestre (1982) *Politique d'Education et Organisation Industrielle en France et en Allemagne*, Paris, PUF

Maurice, M., F. Eyraud, A. d'Iribarne and F. Rychener (1986) *Des Enterprises en Mutation dans la Crise. Apprentisage des Technologies flexibles et Emergence de Nouveaux Acteurs*, Aix en Provence, LEST

Mokrzycki, E. (1982) 'What to Take into Account When Comparing? The Problem of Context', in M. Niessen and J. Peschar (eds.) *International Comparative Research*, Oxford, Pergamon Press, pp. 45-55

Niessen, M., J. Peschar and C. Kourilsky (eds.) (1984) *International Comparative Research. Social Structures and Public Institutions in Eastern and Western Europe*, Oxford, Pergamon Press

Noble, D. (1979) 'Social Choice in Machine Design: the Case of Automatically Controlled Machine Tools', in A. Zimbalist *Case Studies on the Labor Process*, New York, Monthly Review Press, pp. 18-50

Nowak, S. (1977) 'The Strategy of Cross-National Survey Research for the Development of Social Theory', in A. Szalai and R. Petrella (eds.) *Cross-National Comparative Survey Research: Theory and Practice*, Oxford, Pergamon Press, pp. 3-48

Office of Technology Assessment (1984) *Computerised Manufacturing Automation. Employment, Education and the Workplace*, Washington

Piore, M.J. and C.F. Sabel (1984) *The Second Industrial Divide. Possibilities for Prosperity*, New York, Basic Books

Rantalaiho, L. (1986) 'Case History of a Research Project on Work and Technology: a Participant Interpretation', in P. Grootings (ed.) *Technology and Work. East-West Comparison*, London, Croom Helm, pp. 141-184

Richta, R. (1969) *Civilization at the Crossroads. Social and Human Implications of the Scientific and Technological Revolution*, Prague, International Arts and Sciences Press Inc.

Rose, M. (1985) 'Universalism, Culturalism and the Aix Group: Promise and Problems of a Societal Approach to Economic Institutions', *European Sociological Review*, volume 1, no.1, pp. 65-83

Sabel, C.F. (1982) *Work and Politics. The Division of Labour in Society*, Cambridge, Cambridge University Press

Sorge, A., G. Hartmann, M. Warner, and I. Nicholas (1981) *Microelectronics and Manpower in Manufacturing: Applications of Computer Numerical Control in Great Britain and West Germany*, IIM/LMP 81-16, Berlin, Wissenschaftszentrum

Szalai A. and R. Petrella (eds.) (1977) *Cross-National Comparative Survey Research: Theory and Practice*, Oxford, Pergamon Press

Thompson, P. (1984) *The Nature of Work. An Introduction to Debates on the Labour Process*, London, Macmillan

Ussenin, V. and M. Nochevnik (1979) 'The Experience of the International Comparative Study', in J. Forslin, A. Sarapata and A.M. Whitehill (eds.) *Automation and Industrial Workers. A Fifteen Nation Study*, volume 1, part 1,

Oxford, Pergamon Press, pp. 17-30

Von Thienen, V. (1983) *Technikfolgen-Abschätzung und sozialwissenschaftliche Technikforschung. Eine Bibliographie* (Technological Consequences - Assessment and Social Science Technological Research. A Bibliography), Berlin, Wissenschaftszentrum

Wilkinson, B. (1983) *The Shopfloor Politics of New Technology*, London, Heinemann

Wood, S. (ed.) (1982) *The Degradation of Work? Skill, De-skilling and the Labour Process*, London, Hutchinson

Zimbalist, A. (1979) *Case Studies on the Labor Process*, New York, Monthly Review Press

2

Flexible Machining Systems in the Czechoslovak Engineering Industry

Jaroslav Jirásek

Introduction

In 1948 the Czechoslovak people embarked on the path of socialist development. During the years of socialist reconstruction the country underwent a major socioeconomic transformation. It built up a rather powerful economic potential by far outweighing its demographic scale and based on a system of nationalised means of production (90 per cent state and 10 per cent co-operative enterprises); one-third of its national income depends on foreign trade.

Slovakia, once an agricultural country, was transformed into an industrial territory. Its industrial output surpasses that of the whole pre-war Czechoslovakia. Industry, the main branch of the economy, accounts for about 60 per cent of the national income and 38 per cent of employment. Since 1948 industrial output has risen eleven times, with the fastest growth shown by the engineering industry (28 times) and by the chemical industry (32 times). Engineering alone accounts for 30 per cent of total industrial output. The combination of up-to-date technology matched by traditional craftsmanship enabled the country to cover a large and demanding production programme, the heterogeneity of which is now even considered to be a major barrier to further dynamic growth.

New technologies in machine-tool shops

The machine-tool industry

The machine-tool industry pertains to the traditional branches of the engineering production sector.

35

After two rounds of nationalisation in the late 1940s (1945 and 1948) separate metal-working factories were put together into one single joint corporation, Továrny Obrábecích Stroju (Machine-tool Factories), for brevity called TOS, a national corporation and almost monopoly producer of metal-working machinery and instruments.

Attached to the TOS-Corporation are several research and development institutes, among which there is the Institute for Cutting Machine Tools and Methods (in Prague), servicing all companies with cutting procedures. The institute has approximately 1,000 employees, including specialists and workers in the research laboratories, development departments, testing departments etc. The services are paid either by governmental bodies (to subsidise principal innovation), by the General Directorate of the TOS-Corporation (if the innovation has a broader field of application) or by the companies using the services themselves. In addition the institute is entitled to make use of 10-15 per cent of the budget according to its own estimations.

The production programme of the TOS-Corporation began to serve broad demands for metal-cutting, forming and tooling. It covered turning lathes, milling, boring, drilling and grinding machines, gear shaping machines, presses, forging machines, shears, sawing machines, bending machines (all of them including automated and versatile types) and different kinds of tools, jigs and fixtures. Thanks to the consolidation of several parallel factories the TOS-Corporation in the early 1950s was able to introduce an advanced level of specialisation and concentration of production. Each factory developed a specific line of machinery and/or tools and many common parts were centralised in only one factory, supplying all the others (spindles, gears, chucks etc.).

The advantage of centralised planning and organisation was manifested in a rather dynamic growth of production as is shown in Table 2.1.

After the late 1960s the accent was transferred from unit growth to the sophistication of design and improvements of production methods. The average annual output of units remained constant but the value of production continued to increase.

Now the metalworking industry keeps its above average position among the many industries (as many as 796 individual branches) of the whole industrial sector. The machine-tool industry supplies important commodities for foreign trade. In 1982 Czechoslovakia ranked twelfth in the world machine-tool production and eighth in the world machine-tool exports (American Machinist 1983).

Table 2.1: Growth of Production of Machine Tools, 1937-80

	1937	1948	1950	1960	1970	1980
Cutting machine tools units	5,496	11,270	12,910	30,233	35,186	36,876
Forming machinery units	-	4,094	4,962	5,476	9,156	8,500*

*Change in the definition of a unit (since 1975)
Source: Statistical Yearbook of the CSSR, 1982.

Table 2.2: Share of Machine-tool Industry in Total Production and Total Employment*

	Of the total production in per cent		Of the total employment in per cent	
	1975	1980	1975	1980
Cutting machine tools	5.17	6.47	10.90	11.53
Forming machinery	2.06	2.31	2.98	3.72
Total	7.23	8.78	13.88	15.25

*According to the statistical nomenclature of industries
Source: Statistical Yearbook of the CSSR, 1982.

First steps in automation

The historical trend of the engineering way of production tended towards 'producing automated machines by automated machines'. The TOS-Corporation was involved in this revolutionary change and had to pay more attention to advanced levels of automation.

The main striving for comprehensive automation started in the late 1950s, when 150 NC machines were installed and the first two fully automated transfer lines were introduced in the car industry (for the fabrication of engine bodies and crankshafts). From the very beginning this new machinery was individually evaluated from the technological, economic and social points of view to establish a comparative basis for further improvements in the design or technological utilisation (Rápos 1982: 212-217).

In the 1960s the TOS-Corporation proceeded to a higher level of automation. Another 60 automated transfer lines consisting of NC machines and versatile spindle machining units were put in operation in the engineering industry. One of them was provided with remote control at a distance of 45 km. The company delivered the same type of automation to a couple of its own factories (Rápos 1982: 212-217).

The automation drive was accompanied by several socioeconomic problems. In the fore of them was the expensiveness of the machinery. Machine tools equipped with NC devices were delivered for an almost double price compared to traditional machine tools. Some of them did not pay off for the users. The operators had to be retrained for extra expenses (regular vocational training started only later) and the traditional system of work supervision and control had to be reassessed. The amount and content of work changed as well. Fewer operators were needed but in the climate of almost permanent shortage of labour this hardly provoked any problem. However, in many cases the operator found himself with only minimally demanding work tasks, deprived of his craftsmanship (which was transferred to the engineer-programmer) and his wage was at issue as well. Sometimes not an upgrading but a degradation of work was the outcome.

In the 1960s a competing line of solving technological problems was developed. The introduction of the so-called standard (group) methods made it possible to unify the fabrication of parts with similar configurations and decrease the demand for sophisticated technology and intricate resetting of machine tools. In the leading TOS-Corporation factories the economy of work grew by up to 30-40 per cent, thus challenging the high cost of flexible NC machinery (Rápos 1982: 156-157).

Towards flexible machining systems

In the 1970s automation reached the level of machining centres and automated shops. Comprehensive automation covering nearly all basic cutting/forming operations was introduced under the title 'integrovany vyrobní usek, or IVU' (the Czech acronym for integrated manufacturing systems - IMS). There are already as many as 40 in operation and some 30 under design and construction.

An American report recently described the trend in development of automated batch manufacturing systems in Czechoslovakia as an outspoken trend 'toward extreme flexibility' and evaluated it as a 'true job-shop environment that is typical in the US and other Western countries'. The report especially appreciates the IVUs (IMS) at TOS Kurim, ZPS Gottwaldov, Kovosvit Sezimovo Usﾞí and Povázské Strojírny Banská Bystrica insisting that they have all fundamental features of flexible manufacturing systems (FMS) (American Machinist 1985).

The new IVUs are characterised by the following technological advancements:

- grouped NC machines;
- tool machining centres;
- pick and place manipulators;
- palletised move with auto-loading;
- automated material-handling carts;
- automated storage/retrieval magazines.

They are designed for 24-hour operation regimes with only one shift tended by humans.

The 'brain-trust' for these technological breakthroughs is the Research Institute for Cutting Machine Tools and Manufacturing, attached to the General Directorate of the TOS-Corporation in Prague. Teams of experts from factories and external institutes are invited to develop projects with this institute. All projects are negotiated with independent evaluators, with the trade union organisation of the factory and in sessions with the top management.

The first introduction of any new machinery is usually not expected to give the full yield on invested capital. But it serves as a 'school' for further experience, as a training centre for employees from other factories or as a show-room for future clients. Expert teams of economists, sociologists and ergonomists collect information for socioeconomic assessment. Some projects are subsidised by the Federal Ministry for Technology and Capital Construction[1] (if they represent a breakthrough that can be diffused), in which case governmental experts are involved as well.

The process of introduction of new technology

A higher level of automation was the target of a new project developed under the auspices of the Ministry of Light Engineer-ing. Those participating were four research and development institutes and seven factories (all of them widely known as pioneers of advanced technology). The project consisted of 24 tasks (distributed among the participating institutes or factories) and covered several automated flexible transfer lines for box-shaped parts of up to 1250x250x1250 mm and round-shaped parts (shafts) of up to 320x500 mm. The plants were situated in different places, all of them being middle-sized and leading in their production field.

Our analysis is based on the following cases:

IVU Model	Pilot plant	Short description	In operation since
400	ZPS Gottwaldov (South Moravia)	8 machining centres, programmed transfer system (along the working places), computer (off-line)	1974
1250	TOS Kurim (near Brno)	5 machining centres, 4 NC machine-tools, programmed transfer system (in the middle), computer (off-line)	1977
200 (box) 200 (shaft)	TOS Hostivar (Prague)	two joint automated production systems, each consisting of 5 machining centres with an automated transfer system in the middle, computer (off-line)	1981
500 (wheel)	Kovosvit Sezimovo Ustí (South Bohemia)	5 machining centres with an automated transfer system, computer (on-line)	1981
1200 (box)	Kvosvit Sezimovo Ustí (South Bohemia)	5 machining centres, 4 NC machine-tools, automated transfer system, computer (on-line)	
VS 43 (wheels and shafts)	Skoda Plzen (Western Bohemia)	3 fields with an automated transfer system of which one field is fully automated with 12 NC machine-tools, computer (on-line)	1982

All flexible machining systems have many common features. They use a central transfer system to operate the working places. The parts are moved on pallets that proceed automatically from one working place to another, turn around the pivot, are placed or displaced in the magazine and are prepared for two to three shifts a day, so that the work may go on almost without human tending in the second or third shift.

The main technological problems are provoked by the transfer systems. They are partly delivered by domestic firms, partly imported, but usually they need a certain time to achieve full reliability. Flexible pallets are probably the most rewarding result of domestic engineering work. Their capacity to be stored for multi-shift work has significantly contributed to the economic advantages of the flexible machining systems. Direct connection between the transfer system and the working place is executed by different programmed manipulators. In the beginning some of these also caused reliability problems.

The first two IVU cases (in ZPS Gottwaldov and TOS Kurim) started as only semi-flexible systems, but they were later converted into full flexibility with on-line computer control. The case of TOS Hostivar with several IVUs was the first attempt to build up an automated plant. It did not go so far but at the same time it served as a starting point to further breakthroughs. The first 'unmanned factory' entered operation in TOS Olomouc (North Moravia) in 1985; the number of workers was reduced from 150 to 27.

Most cases were (with the exception of TOS Hostivar) introduced with delays of one to two years and achieved the projected production level one year later. In the case of TOS Hostivar automation was forced with exceptionally concentrated forces and means. All the cases were undertaken as pilot projects to collect experience and to make use of this in later applications. The economic results (expressed as capital savings in the first year after the introduction) were

IVU Model	Capital savings (1 year in million crowns)
200	0.7
400	1.6
1200/1250	2.4

The long-term plan of flexible machining systems in the Czechoslovak industries makes provisions for the following number of IVUs:

IVU Model	Number of units by 1990
200	100
400	95
800	55
1250	18
320	160
Total	428

The TOS Hostivar case

TOS Hostivar is a medium-sized plant, the main deliverer of grinding machine tools. It employs some 3,500 people, of whom approximately half are workers. The plant is situated on the eastern boundary of the capital of Prague (on the territory of the former village of Hostivar).

The production programme covers different kinds of grinding machinery. Especially well-known are grinders for gears and centreless grinding. The majority of the production is exported, two-thirds to socialist countries and the rest to capitalist and developing countries. Some of the exports are whole grinding departments for industrial plants abroad.

The project of flexible automation was undertaken with governmental assistance in the years 1976-82. The first years were filled with research, general design and evaluation, to find out the optimal and at the same time realistic solutions to problems. Three research and development institutes were involved at that time: the branch institute of the Ministry of Light Engineering, the Institute for Machine Tools and Metal Cutting (of the TOS-Corporation) and the Design and Rationalisation Institute (of the TOS-Corporation).

TOS Hostivar has 13 production departments, four of which are for the time being subject to flexible automation. The basic principles laid down in the foundations of the automation project are:

- centralised production control by a central computing system (on-line) that makes all the decisions to start, proceed, check the iterative operations, feed the transfer lines and store the finished parts;
- centralised transport system connecting the working places (transfer lines with parts on pallets);

- manipulator taking the pallets from the transfer line and positioning the part in the machines (as an operating device of the transfer line);
- automated carts (moving according to induction lines on/under the surface of the floor) to operate the transport between the production departments;
- machining centres and NC machines, some of them with fully automated feeding, others combining automation with manual operations.

One production department is automated for small box-shaped cast iron parts up to the size of 250x250x250 mm and 30 kg of weight. The department produces 100,000 parts per year in 300 different configurations. It makes, on average, 3,600 production batches per year.

Another production department is automated for wheels and shafts up to a diameter of 160 mm and a length of 398 mm. Parts may be of steel, cast iron or other metals. The volume of production may be indicated as 300,000 units per year of 750 different configurations accomplished in 2,500 production batches.

The basic technological principle of both departments is similar and they differ almost only in the selection of technological machinery. The control and transport systems are equal, with one exception: in the second department the round parts are handled in specially shaped transport boxes.

The third production department is provided with automation for larger round parts, i.e. wheels of up to 500 mm and shafts of up to 798 mm. Their weight may go up to 60 kg. Their substrate may be steel, cast iron or aluminium. The dimensions of production are: 64,000 units per year in 1,300 production batches. The average number of production operations is eight. In the middle of the production department there is a steel hardening device (with an intensive air ventilation). The material handling between the transport system and the machines is operated by hand and, if the weight exceeds 15 kg, by pneumatic hoists. Otherwise the technological pattern is again the same as in the two production departments for smaller parts.

For better insight, a scheme of the production department is presented in Figure 2.1. The oiling and cooling fluids are supplied automatically. The waste is carried away under the floor.

In the fourth production department automation had to solve production problems of the processing of box-shaped parts with dimensions of up to 1,200 mm and as heavy as 400 kg. Per year 21,500 units are produced. They have around 100 different configurations and are divided into 960 production batches. All other technological characteristics are similar to those in the third automated shop.

Figure 2.1: Scheme of Production Department at TOS Hostivar

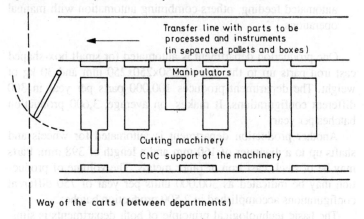

It is evident that the basic advantage has been achieved by the centralised system of production control watching the whole movement of the work in progress. The actual level of automation at the working place may be expressed as semi-automation. The main operations are fully mechanised, while auxiliary ones are done by hand. Smaller parts are handled by the operator; larger parts are handled with the help of pneumatic hoists and heavers.

The number of worker-operators has decreased to one-third. But at the same time the production of the plant has grown, so there was no other reason for this decrease than replacement. Workers in material handling, who formerly represented more than one-fifth of the shop workers, have almost disappeared. Some workers have been transferred from the material-handling jobs to the so-called preparatory department, where raw material together with the necessary tools is placed on pallets or inserted into the transport boxes.

Human tending of the general part of the production department with six CNC machine tools, as presented on the scheme, consists of one man per shift. An additional two to three workers are available in the first shift to prepare in advance the work for the afternoon and night.

The centralised computer control department has ten engineers and technicians in the first shift and one in the two other shifts. One man is permanently at the control desk, following the process on the screen. Others take care of the program bank, preserve the documentation on the magnetic media, are on the alert when a program is tried for the first time, and help the methods engineer and technicians to improve the programs. (The control department services not only the four automated shops but also nine other production shops.)

Workers at the TOS Hostivar plant are rather well paid; at the NC machine tools they get some 4,500 crowns, which is 1.5 times above the average in the economy and, for instance, more than the basic pay of the majority of engineers. It is no wonder that they have been concerned to keep their economic level. When many workers were reluctant to join the automated shops, management approached young workers. For them the improvement in wages was rather attractive and they were the first to work in the automated shops. The attitudes of other workers changed soon and there was no deficiency in skilled workers for the automated shops later. On the contrary, the interest was sometimes higher than the available places and the opportunity to select the best people increased. A retraining programme enabled the careful preparation of engineers and workers in time. But there was and still is an open problem with the accuracy of the execution of tasks. Automation asks for a most reliable and precise performance of work tasks. The worker does not tend only his machine tool but supervises and services a broader area of the shop. To a certain extent he combines the duties of a supervisor (foreman) and the former operator. His impact on the whole performance is incomparably higher. At the beginning it was necessary to help the workers to understand their new responsibilities, the interaction of man and machinery, and the complexity of the system. It was necessary to understand the shop not only as a set of production and transport or other tools, but at the same time as a functioning model (that is theoretically). Workers in the automated shops were expected to understand the interrelations of the technological, organisational, economic and social aspects of the automated systems.

The project was put into reality more or less according to the objectives, only some technological expectations were not - at least in the beginning - mastered in full compliance with the plans. But social conditions of a high-performance workplace became far more complicated and comprehensive and provoked the necessity of further workers' education and training together with an increase in wages for broader responsibilities.

Workers' role in an automated shop increases also due to a wider participation in reconsidering the technological or organisational solutions. In many cases it is the workers who dispose of a broad immediate experience in the shop, have a close knowledge of how the automated system works, which cannot be easily substituted by others (for instance by engineers who do have a deeper knowledge but only a fragmented close experience).

The ZPS Gottwaldov case

Závody presného strojírenství (Precise Engineering Works), abbreviated as ZPS, in Gottwaldov, a district town in South Moravia (famous as a centre of mass shoe manufacturing) is a leading company in the framework of the TOS-Corporation.

According to the production programme adopted long ago, ZPS Gottwaldov manufactures primarily lathes and semi-automated lathes (NC lathes, lathe machining centres). The plant in Gottwaldov has some 5,800 employees, half of whom are workers (two-thirds of them direct production workers, one-third auxiliary workers).

The origin of the ZPS plant goes back as far as the establishment of the Bata Shoe Corporation. It was a conglomerate with its own engineering production. However, as to the size, there is no comparison with the rather small former plant. The trade-mark 'ZPS' is now known not only in the country, but abroad as well.

The ZPS has a research and development department, and engineering services (for design, methods, maintenance and repair, energy, material handling etc.). Engineers and technicians represent one quarter of the total workforce.

The introduction of automation started in two production departments. The company was assisted by the Institute for Cutting Machine Tools and Methods, by another in-firm Design Institute of the Machine-tool Industry (also subordinated to the headquarters of the TOS-Corporation) and an in-firm Training Institute. Important assistance was provided by the Ministry of Light Engineering through its Research Institute for Technology and Economics of the Engineering Industry (in Prague). This is a branch institute participating in many cases of automation in the engineering industry. The institute has 1,200 employees, of which some 60 are in charge of general research and development in automation and many others have different specific tasks in high technology.

In one of the production departments an automated integrated production system (IVU 400) for manufacturing box-shaped parts was implemented. The conversion of the department started in 1974. Now it is enlarged and stabilised. It consists of three conventional machines, two NC machines, eight machining centres, and one desk for precise measurements. The movement of parts to and from individual working places is performed by a transporting system controlled by a central computer.

In the TOS-Corporation groups of departments to be automated were invited to visit already automated departments in other plants. Such was the case in ZPS Gottwaldov. Foremen, setters and workers visited between two and four plants with more advanced automation.

The structure of employment in the automated shop is presented in Table 2.3.

Direct production workers were selected among the best workers on conventional machinery. However, not everybody agreed to change from the beginning and a part was made up by young workers (who had passed their vocational training at least partly on NC machinery). All workers for the automated department were promised they would not lose their wages, on the contrary they were granted a ten per cent bonus to the basic wage. As long as automation was being implemented, any minus difference in their wages was compensated.

Workers receive wages according to the class of their skills. The scale (ladder) of skills is divided into eight or nine classes. A worker with completed vocational training (three or four years) usually is in the fourth or fifth class, while the work in the automated department is graded as equal to the eighth class so that they would at least keep their previous wage level. A worker gets a basic wage per hour according to his class, then a bonus for the fulfilment of the objectives of the whole shop. In addition he may get other bonuses for excellent quality, high individual activity, economy of materials etc. The wage schemes have to be approved by the labour union of the plant. Usually 75-80 per cent depend on the worker's skill-class or piece-rate and the rest on different bonuses. The average wage in the plant was 3,600 crowns. In the automated shop it was improved by a ten per cent bonus. As a matter of fact this was no substantial increase, but better work conditions later proved to make recruitment into automated shops attractive.

Table 2.3: Structure of Employment in ZPS Production Department

Direct production workers, total	28
at conventional machines	6
NC machines	4
machining centres	16
measurement desk	2
setters	4
material handling workers	4
quality inspection	2
foremen	3
production planning	1
auxiliary technician	1
operators	2
programmers	5
total	50

The production workers' educational level was generally vocational training (three years obligatory) plus a supplementary training for automation. Four workers had an accomplished secondary education. Programmers had the highest level of education (three were technical university graduates, two had passed a technical high school).

Setters and key workers usually came from the development departments of the plant. They were already tested on the NC machinery and were the core of the workforce in the department. The formation of an experienced core was of great importance for the future consolidation of the work. For this, however, not only education is relevant, nor the curriculum ('nothing that usually stands in the certificate'), but some predisposition which could be indicated as 'personal culture'. In the Gottwaldov plant it was assessed that among the most desired personal qualities were natural intelligence, reliability, flexibility, and co-operativeness. The manager for personnel affairs insisted that the selection of workers should take into account first of all a high feeling of responsibility, ability to co-operate and flexibility. Preferably workers should be middle-aged, not too young, neither too old. Since the machinery was very expensive, it had to function without break-downs and therefore needed most of all reliable tending.

Some workers had learned how to improve the programs. They observed the execution of the operations and easily discovered delays, unnecessary times for motions of the instrument etc. Often they contacted the programmers and together implemented corrections of the programs for the machinery. Workers can partly manipulate the programs themselves if they see, for instance, that they may repeat the program for a larger batch (and thus save the preparatory time). They are not entitled to modify the programs themselves, but some of them - if allowed - could already do so.

In conventional manufacturing the workers have one machine, while with NC they have two or three of them. In automated shops such multiple tending is common place. At the beginning, management step by step increased the responsibility for multiple tending. The workers used to ask for wage increases each time their responsibility was enlarged (though it did not involve much additional strain). Later it was adopted to start with multi-machine servicing from the very first day.

In the course of time, workers began to be bored when nothing happened as the machine was operating automatically. The research institute suggested installing recreation (rest) rooms with calculators, displays, plotters etc. to enable the workers in the intermission times to study the work and make suggestions. First experiments are on the way and it seems that they may be rewarding (either improving the workers' working conditions or leading to a higher number of suggestions). Other workers prefer to read, improve their physical fitness or play competitive games.

Problems have occurred with the foremen, for whom the change in the content of work has been drastic. The foreman used to be a 'dispatcher' of work tasks, now he is supposed to understand the whole system, take immediate and responsible decisions, and keep the shop socially on a high level of collectivism. The foreman's responsibility has grown far above his actual training. He has to know more about the technological system, its sequences and links, about sociology and group psychology.

The management in ZPS Gottwaldov - according to a long tradition - comes mostly from the ranks. The production manager and the technological manager both had university education and enjoyed a long work experience. The workers - when asked anonymously - appreciated the knowledge, experience and personal qualities of the managers (the share of negative responses did not exceed 10 per cent).

The managers in charge of automation rather often appear

among workers to discuss the problems and find a right solution. A permanent form of workers participation are the so-called 'shop meetings' ('production meetings') organised by the labour union organisation to discuss openly the plan, its fulfilment, disruptions of the deliveries, quality deficiencies and all other topics of life in the plant. Managers and foremen are invited to present explanations. They are obliged to answer questions by the workers in due time (at the next meeting). In questions of wages, bonuses, standard times, work security and hygiene the trade union must not only be asked but has to give its consent (one-sided decisions of management are not valid).

The mutual understanding between management and workers is considered good and efficient. Not only during working hours, but also outside the plant people of all professions meet. As the differences in pay are not excessive, they find many common interests.

The Kovosvit Sezimovo Ustí case

The Kovosvit Machine-tool Company has acquired a leading position among machine-tool manufacturers. Its production programme covers, first of all, advanced boring machinery (including automated machining centres). The plant is located in the town of Sezimovo Ustí in South Bohemia (at the Vltava river).

Before its nationalisation in 1946 the company was a part of the Bata Corporation, one of the outstanding shoe producers, delivering shoe-making machinery for in-firm shoe factories all over the world. According to the later delimitations of the production programme within the machine-tool industry, Kovosvit focused on boring techniques and boring machinery (excluding only heavy boring machines).

Approximately 300 employees of Kovosvit live either in the town of Sezimovo Ustí or in the nearby villages. All of them are closely connected with the fate of the company; there is scarcely any other adequate opportunity of industrial jobs. The company procures dwellings for a substantial share of its employees (more than one-third) and assists the town committee in improving general living conditions.

The young management of Kovosvit is broadly known as conceptual in the field of technological progress and has accumulated a remarkable experience in advancement of modern technology.

The implementation of a flexible machining system (IVU 320) for small wheels and shafts in this factory has been evaluated among the most successful ones. As a matter of fact, the plant has many times been recommended as an example for similar technological breakthroughs. The production department to be automated had some 80 workers, one-fifth of whom were workers with higher skills (NC operators, setters) and one-fourth were engaged in material handling. The project envisaged a reduction of the workforce to some 20 operators.

The IVU 320 consists of 25 CNC machines linked together by an automated transfer system. The transporting devices are pallets or boxes moved automatically from the preparatory magazine through the cutting operations up to the ready-made (finished) parts magazine. The movement of parts is controlled by a computer centre. The basic machinery has been supplied either by Kovosvit itself or by other domestic manufacturers of machine tools and transporting devices. The central computer is a Soviet-made production control unit (M 6000).

A sizeable advantage was gained by the fact that the management was much in favour of automation and promoted the project from the very beginning up to the stabilisation of output. Thanks to this positive approach of the top-management, the transformation from the conventional to the automated way of manufacturing was rather smooth. However, several social problems emerged and had to be delicately tackled.

While nobody's further employment was endangered by the automation, workers were afraid to lose their social status in the shop. As people had no previous direct experience, they asked many questions about their future jobs. The project was rather carefully discussed with everybody involved and the explanations proved to be broadly acceptable. It was confirmed as a very valuable prerequisite to inform people in advance of what was going to happen. This social information was heavily assisted by several research investigations by the industrial branch research institute. Detailed information was collected on the physical conditions of work, attitudes and behaviour of the persons, interpersonal relations, supervising and performance etc.

At Kovosvit the conversion to automation was implemented almost without any increase of wages. The average wage was some 3,200 crowns, before and after automation (compared with TOS Hostivar it is some 600 crowns less). This is to be explained by the fact that in the town of Sezimovo Ustí the living expenses are lower and there is less labour turnover because of fewer job offers in the locality.

Automation did introduce, however, deep changes in the division of labour. This was probably the most influential source of social problems during the implementation (and continues to be so after that). The individual performance of the worker is now subsumed in the output of the automated production system as a whole and the collective performance of the working group. This asks for a certain *esprit d'équipe*, which was less necessary in conventional manufacturing (and had a different pattern). Not only has the worker to supervise several interconnected machines, but he has also a new impact on the final results by either keeping the process within the prescribed limits or operatively changing the combination in compliance with the central controlling bureau. Also the experiences in this plant proved that the worker has to know more about the process 'as a working model'.

What matters under automation is less a worker's ability to operate the machine tool and his ability to overcome physical stress, but his concentrated attention and his capacity to quickly find out what is wrong. Before, the level of knowledge and length of practical experience were important in the job evaluation. Now many other personal features are of great importance, such as a high level of conscientiousness, individual discipline, mutual assistance. The problem has, however, another side. Workers with exceptional high individual output sometimes cannot show their full performing capacity. They can feel 'lost' in the technologically determined production system. In such cases it proved to be better to enable them to be promoted to other jobs. At Kovosvit it was possible to promote a small number of workers (three or four) to other technical jobs (if they showed willing). Other workers were transferred to the instrumentation and repair departments. Most of them, however, went to the preparatory department to feed the transfer lines with parts, and tools.

Problems have also here merged in connection with the job. The shop foreman formerly distributed work tasks among the workers (working places) and checked the finished operations. Now his job content differs remarkably: he has to control the whole working process, ensure unity between the objective and subjective factors, make immediate and flexible decisions, and provide for a co-operative spirit among the working group. All foremen proved suitable for the new tasks. There were four at the beginning and only one quit (because he refused to accept the increased shift work). However, there are continuing complaints that they are still not fully proficient in their jobs. They have only gradually overcome the inertia of their old habits to act according to the complexity of the process. For instance, it happened that the automated supply of parts broke and the foreman tried to save the continuity by carrying boxes and setting the machine tools by hand. Sometimes they regained the stability of the process but often the disturbances accumulated instead. Obviously they needed training for this kind of emergency situation.

Less expected were the social problems that occurred in the group of technicians and engineers. In the end there was more hesitation, discontent and dissatisfaction here than among workers. Some technicians did not cope with the new comprehensive tasks and quit the production department in spite of the fact that there was rather generous support for retraining. Some of the older technicians had been educated without an intimate knowledge and special know-how of the sophisticated machinery and instrumentation or computer-supported manufacturing and programming tasks. It happened that they reconsidered the demands for more advanced education and training essential for continuing their old jobs. The social sample at Kovosvit was not a large one and the generalisations cannot be overestimated but combined with other observations they testify that usually it is education, not age, that is the most problematic social limit to advanced automation.

One of the practical demands has been to design the incentive wage and bonus scheme with a well balanced impact on individual as well as collective performance. The problem is still under discussion and it cannot be said that a definite solution has been found. A fruitful tendency seems to be to negotiate the tasks not with individuals but with the group as a whole and to provide room for self-management within the group.

At Kovosvit the conversion to automation was carefully calculated to increase the return on invested funds. The machinery was therefore concentrated on a small floor. As a result this same advantage entailed an increase in noise. According to industrial standards the upper limit is 80 db, but after the automation had been accomplished, the level of noise went up to 85-90 db and it was necessary to install some noise-reducing walls. Noisy work also appeared among the most disturbing sources of fatigue. According to some on the spot investigations 80 per cent of people got tired for mental and 20 per cent for physical reasons. This is just the opposite as compared with conventional manufacturing. As a result the working hours were divided by short breaks when people left the shop and came together in special rest-rooms. In general, the architecture of the working-rooms will probably be one of the challenges of automation. While the working environment gets burdened with noise, the work itself asks for concentrated attention, quick decision-making, exactitude of human tending etc. At Kovosvit the problem was partly relieved by establishing so-called 'social zones' adequately equipped for human comfort (rest, refreshment, games etc.).

Some problems - not only of a social kind - are the inevitable consequence of the fact that automation has been introduced in only some of the production departments. For the time being, automated shops are something like an enclave within conventional manufacturing. People from outside look at the workers of the automated shops 'waiting and seeing'. The work is visibly easier and invites further workers to join. On the other hand, the implementation of automation is hampered and limited by the old-type manufacturing. Sometimes it is difficult to achieve desired compatibility. This can only be solved by spreading out the principle of automation and covering the whole of manufacturing.

At Kovosvit workers in the automated shops after a time showed some unexpected positive attitudes. They were asking for more technological information and for more organisational knowledge. They were most cost-conscious and interested in optimising the function of the machining system. As a whole, they became more participative. As a result the production capacity of the plant grew to an extent which surpassed the internal needs of the company. Some 30 per cent of the production is now sold to external clients throughout the country. Automation paid off quickly, therefore, and encouraged further diffusion of automated technology.

General experiences from the cases

The basic lesson of the Kovosvit case, to 'begin with the people', has also been used in other automation cases, most consistently in the automation of Motorlet in Prague (manufacturer of airplane jet engines) which is just beginning.

It is mainly the Research Institute for Technology and Economics of the Engineering Industry where the results of social studies are preserved.

Implementation of the IVUs positively changed the general pattern of the plants. In comparison with the conventional way of production, automation increased the productive performance while saving physical resources:

physical changes:		improvements (limits):		
labour productivity	+ 92	-	740	per cent
number of workers in the shop	- 33	-	60	per cent
production time (average cycle)	- 50	-	85	per cent
production area	- 44	-	83	per cent

Social problems did not represent a substantial obstacle. Nobody was afraid of losing his job but, of course, many people hesitated whether, they should work with the new technology. They expressed their uncertainty as to the effect on their position in the shop, craftsmanship and wage. As soon as the automated shops started to operate and the work was obviously attractive and better paid, such attitudes changed and most people were willing to join the automated shops. Surprisingly enough, workers, not only young ones, but also those in their fifties and sixties were applying for retraining and passed with almost no visible difficulties. Retraining was necessary in all cases. The TOS-Corporation (Headquarters for TOS Kurim, ZPS Gottwaldov, TOS Hostivar) opened an in-firm training programme offered by its own institute for training and retraining.

In the beginning the presumption was falsely accepted that the worker has no or hardly any (in any case, no important) impact on the machinery. Very soon this view had to be revised; workers' influence on the general performance proved to be not negligible at all. Wages were then combined with bonuses for such activities as careful preparation of the pallets, operating, supervision and tending of the machinery.

After a relatively short time the first workers asked for training in the programming department and were able to write programs as well as service the machinery. As a matter of fact, some workers therefore switched from the genuine worker's profession to a technician's profession. It turned out that rather a lot of workers had capacities for such further development.

The consolidation of the automation in the plants took a certain time and involved workers and engineers in many unprecedented problems. In many cases groups of engineers, technicians and workers were invited to solve the problems together. Working groups were formally instituted, the task was identified and a bonus promised as motivation. Often such working groups (called 'rationalisation brigades') grew spontaneously and suggested their contribution to the management.

People involved in shift work receive an increase in wages (usually a fixed sum) and are entitled to a few additional days of holiday. The IVUs are directed towards multi-shift work of the machinery but reduced shift work of the people. Human tending is allocated in the first shift, while the second and third shifts need supervision only. However, workers got almost the same allowance for shift work as before.

Some minor problems arose also among the auxiliary personnel. While material handling have mostly disappeared, cleaning work and other simple tasks have become more demanding, mainly because they need more punctuality and discipline. Problems have been reduced after a small increase in wages.

In all cases management put the project up for discussion. The trade union organisation of the plant was invited to express its opinions as to the social aspects of the whole undertaking. By law the trade union organisation has a legal consulting power on such changes and has to approve all re-shaping of jobs. Mutual consultation between management and trade union was repeated before any further step of the project in progress. In fact the Minister of the industrial branch had presented in advance the long-range programme of automation to the Minister of Labour and to the Central Council of the Trade Unions. As a result, the union organisation of the plant was provided with the consensus on the central level and a recommendation by the Central Council of Trade Unions (via its branch central committee). The discussions between management and trade union organisation were active and demands were presented by each part. The union organisation - in the name of workers, technicians, engineers, and clerks - asked usually, first of all, for assured training, improvement in wages, and adequate replacement of workers and employees displaced by automation. After these problems were settled, the committee of the trade union organisation would recommend that union members (in all cases more than 85 per cent of the labour force) should participate actively in the introduction of the automated shops. Management in some plants stressed the fact that since the cost of one machining hour had increased (direct costs from 35 up to 200 crowns per hour), and the machinery was very expensive, more diligence and discipline was needed. In some plants this problem has not yet been satisfactorily settled.

There are some examples of initiatives of the Socialist Youth Union when young workers and engineers suggested that they should take the first burden of the innovation and get involved in some complicated tasks. In one case a 'youth shop' operated only by young people was established. All such projects were observed from the very beginning by the plant organisation of the Communist Party, taking responsibility for the compliance of the project with the general technological and socioeconomic strategy of the Communist Party of Czechoslovakia. Members of the organisation were asked to assist in overcoming the difficulties of innovation. In the case of TOS Hostivar, the newly introduced automated shops were shown to the delegates of the XVIth Congress of the Communist Party of Czechoslovakia in 1981.

These and similar experiences of the pilot plants are collected and evaluated by the TOS-Corporation and its research institutes. They serve for further promotion of flexible automation systems not only in the framework of the firm, but through distribution to everybody who needs a similar body of knowledge. For every case there is full documentation from the beginning to the end. The institutes are obliged to repeat the evaluation of the process and results after some time. They are also obliged to offer consulting and implementation services.

Socioeconomic impact of flexible machining systems

The main economic advantages of IVUs result from the following technical-organisational characteristics:

- increase in speed and continuity of operation;
- fabrication of parts with intricate configurations;
- multi-shift operation (with limited human tending);
- multiple control by one operator of several machine tools;
- lower break time and unproductive use of power and machinery;
- lower waste etc.

It is still an open question, however, how to determine the economic effectiveness of automated machinery at the enterprise level. Capital expenditures seem to be high in comparison with the substituted labour cost. In Czechoslovakia, however, direct wages do not cover by far all labour expenses. A substantial proportion of the real social labour costs is remunerated via social consumption. This can make up as much as one-third to half of the total labour costs. This phenomenon induces the false impression of labour being cheap. Therefore, additional costs have to be added to the calculated wages.

Automation generally multiplies the fundamental social impact of the machinery while transferring work from the hands and brains of men to the technological means and thus decreasing the direct work factor of production. As long as machinery is adopted to increase productivity, it involves changes in the character and content of work and also diminishes the share of direct work. Automated machinery gives a new momentum to this old rule. It is obvious that we are dealing with an economic law of work change and labour displacement. That law is bound to the use of machinery (its existence is socially independent) but differences in socioeconomic environment specify the actual form of change and its manifestation.

For the first time Czechoslovakia faces these changes, in a situation where demand for labour is more or less satisfied (saturated) and a certain surplus of labour is perceived. While the possibilities exist to distribute labour fairly in the economy, this social problem has to be solved together with the economic objective of increasing productivity and output.

In the particular case of the TOS-Corporation there was no fear of unemployment at all, but several people were unsure as to their further professional outlook and the level of future remuneration. In some factories the problem was not solved satisfactorily and this led to minor unnecessary delays. As a lesson, a prospective reform of social planning (in use in all enterprises since the early 1970s) is being accepted which includes:

- identifying the critical spots of work change and labour displacement;
- informing about who will be concerned and what shall be the challenge and contingency;
- accomplishing programmes and facilities for retraining and replacement of workers (and also technicians or engineers);
- stimulating participation with higher wages (on the future workplace);

- offering rewards for prompt implementation.

Social problems of automation are of increasing importance. Sometimes it is the social side of the technological innovations that frames their full breakthrough and quick diffusion.

Among the set of social problems, the following were analysed and improved:

- as long as people did not fully understand the change, their behaviour remained reserved;
- complementarity of enterprise and individual interests was to be attained;
- the example of the most advanced and respected colleagues was essential;
- some time to get accustomed to the new work situation and mutual assistance were of tremendous importance;
- the shift from physical to mental and emotional strain occasionally called for patience;
- the shift from direct touch of the machine tool to digital signals and pushing buttons asked for more understanding of the 'theory' (model) of the process (involved a certain intellectual training);
- only a few individuals felt a deterioration of their professional status and wanted to preserve their old work content and craftsmanship.

None of the IVUs introduced so far has been without social problems. They have caused some defects and delays, but finally have not prevented the technological breakthrough. On the contrary, a new social know-how has been collected to make future ventures in automation easier and smoother. The societal environment is capable of overcoming emerging social problems. But the challenge lies elsewhere: not to apply only defensive social measures but to incite a new social activity.

Note

1. Since 1983 the State Commission for Scientific and Technological Progress and Capital Investment.

References

American Machinist, volume 1983; 1985

Jirásek, J. (1984) *Vedecke premeny vyroby* (Scientific Transformation of Production), Prague

Rápos, J. (1982) *Integrovane vyrobni useky* (Integrated Machining Systems)

Statistical Yearbook of the CSSR (1982), SNTL, Prague

3

The Introduction of New Technology in Industrial Enterprises of the German Democratic Republic: Two Case Studies

Georg Assmann, Detlev Nagel and Rudhard Stollberg

Social objectives related to the use of new technology[1]

Scientific-technological progress is considered to be the main factor in the intensification of the national-economic process of reproduction. Its economic effects, first of all the increase of productivity, construct the base for solving the main task, i.e. the 'further raising of the material and cultural standard of living'.[2]

This general orientation is valid for all of the different economic units and branches and, above all for the centrally led industrial trusts, where scientific-technological progress at present is going on most quickly. In empirical investigations we find the following reasons for introducing new technology:[3]

- the application of cost-decreasing technologies in order to economise materials, energy and working power and - as for the workers - to better use the social working capacity;
- the creation of new products for the satisfaction of inland and export needs;
- the necessary increase of production corresponding to the actual needs;
- the improvement of the working and living conditions in the given production spheres.[4]

It has to be noted that the direct economic aspects should always be connected with changes in the working and living conditions of the factory workers. The management of the trusts together with the workers are in the first place interested in eliminating physically hard or difficult work by new technologies. But this is only one factor of immediate influence on the workers. It is widely held that the scientific-technological progress is modifying the character of work, that the elements of creativity in work are growing, that the level of qualification and responsibility of the workers is increasing, and that new collective forms of work are arising.[5]

When in the German Democratic Republic one speaks of the 'unity of economic and social policy', this refers above all to the close interrelationship between economic, technological and social problems and their solution. In other words: scientific-technological progress should have all-round *social* effects, should not only increase prosperity, but influence the social processes, too.

If a trust is planning important technological modifications which will exert a great influence on the living conditions of a large number of workers (for instance, quantitative and qualitative modifications of the working places), then the trust management, together with the trade unions, prepares a so-called socioeconomic programme which contains all the measures for the best possible realisation of the modifications. Such programmes reflect the unity of economic and social policy at the level of factories.

First of all such a socioeconomic programme is based on the economic aims of the trust. Because the trade unions continuously participate in establishing the economic aims of the five-year plan, it is guaranteed that the direct interests of the workers are respected. Corresponding with legal orders it guarantees to protect the wages of the workers paid hitherto, in case their work is modified. The given legal orders are concretised in detail in the so-called works' collective argument (*Betriebskollektivvertrag*) concluded between trust management and trade union.

Starting from this the socioeconomic programme deals with the modifications caused by the introduction of new technologies for the workers. Such modifications are, for instance:

- the change of the work, working collective, vocation or factory;
- qualification for a higher degree or training for a new vocation;
- modification of the working conditions;
- modification of the wages.

The sociopolitical programme contains the principles of the disengagement and re-engagement of the workers. It includes also information about volume, time and reasons for the necessary modifications and changes and determines the responsibilities of the trust management and trade unions.

It is well known that the social status is varying as a result of the above changes. Considering these changes in their macro-social sphere, one can see - as a rule - that they indicate a social advancement. The changes in the character of work, the higher qualification demands, the greater tasks which the 'innovators' movement (*Neuererbewegung*) is faced with the new forms of co-operation between different groups and the higher demands on collective forms of work give the working class, too, a new profile; its influence on the social structure is continuously increasing.

Research makes evident that the behaviour of workers whose situation has changed as a result of technological innovations is influenced by considerations concerning the social status in the microsphere. First of all the change of working collective is considered to be an undesirable attendant circumstance. With regard to this fact the socioeconomic programme shows how to plan the changes so that

- the worker really and consciously understands the macro-sociological meaning of the given changes, and that
- the changes go on without any essential impairment of the worker's social welfare.

We shall analyse the introduction of new technology in more detail in two cases: the one concerns the introduction of process control in an aluminium factory; the second case is about the introduction of NC and CNC technology in a machine-tool factory. In both cases the fundamental principles sketched in this introductory section will be illustrated. We shall focus our analysis especially on the process of introduction and on the changes that have taken place with the introduction of new technology.

The introduction of process control in an aluminium foil factory

The factory that we studied has existed since 1950 and is located in an industrial region together with two large chemical combines.

A high percentage of all working people is employed in these two combines. The factory itself employs 640 workers and produces different types of aluminium foil. It covers the main part of the inland needs and also exports part of its production. In 1983 the yearly output was 10,000 tons; in the year of its foundation the factory produced only 76 tons. At present it mainly produces three types of foil: bright foils for the dairy farming, food and electronic industries; coated foils for the food, the refrigerating and the electronic industries; and grill foil, aluminium package, wall paper and gift foil for the consumer goods market.

The workforce is predominantly male, about 30 per cent are women. The latter work mainly in the consumer-goods sections. The heart of the production process is the cold rolling of foils in rolling mills. The factory started in 1976 with the introduction of two computer-controlled rolling mills, which became operational in 1979/80. Rolling speed, band drive and optimalisation can be controlled by a microcomputer. The installation presents the latest technology in aluminium rolling.

After rolling, during which the input material of 0.4 mm thickness can be reduced to 0.005 mm, the foils are cut to the required width for further processing. The new rolling mills not only can produce bigger size foil (1.5 m wide as compared to a maximum of 80 cm on the old rolls), they also have a six times faster rolling speed. In addition, the factory is now working in a continual shift system (including Saturdays and Sundays), in which one shift lasts twelve hours and workers have a free period of 72 hours after every three shifts. This system is one that has been taken over from the chemical factories in the area. Before the introduction of the new technology the factory had been working in an interrupted three-shift system (eight-hour shifts with Saturdays and Sundays off).

The factory has a large core workforce which shows a remarkably low turnover. This is the case above all for the foil rolling mill. One important reason for this is that the majority of the workers are skilled metallurgists who will not easily find a job according to their qualifications elsewhere in the region. But it is also true that the working conditions and the social relations in the factory are rather good. It fulfils its plan tasks in an exemplary manner and has been honoured for this several times. The management is a young dynamic team that takes up new tasks with energy and maintains good relations with the workers.

Reasons for introducing new technology

The introduction of the two new rolling mills has had two main reasons. First of all the need for aluminium foil, above all in the processing industry, had drastically increased. Before 1975 the factory could not satisfy the inland need and was also scarcely able to fulfil any export tasks. The situation of the balance of payments demanded therefore an increase in production. In addition it would also become possible to produce more for the consumer market.

A second reason was compatibility with the producer of the base material. As a result of the introduction of a new wide-band rolling technology in the foundry factory also belonging to the same combine a high production capacity had been created. With the subsequent introduction of the new rolling stands it became possible to use this production capacity and to close the technological gap. The new rolling mills were also supposed to improve the working conditions (noise, disturbances, physical work) which is, as pointed out before, a basic principle for any technological innovation. The introduction of the new technology in this single case also has to be understood against the general political background. Since the 1970s Party and government have been oriented towards a policy of intensification of production, which implies that increases in production should be reached primarily through investments in latest technology.

Participation in the change process by the trade union and the workers

As indicated, the technological changes in this factory had their origin basically in productivity reasons of national relevance. This is also the reason why the problem was taken up by institutions competent for the realisation of such projects, i.e. the relevant Ministry (of Ore Mining, Metallurgy and Potash Industry in cooperation with the State Planning Commission) and the managements of the combine and the foil factory respectively.

The new mills were imported from France and installed together with GDR companies. Such import of new plants is a matter of national economic trade and generally trade unions do not exercise any influence on such decisions. However, the implementation of such new systems forms part of different plans (mainly of the plan on science and technology) that are drawn up and discussed every year at the enterprise level. Since these plans can only be decided upon and sent to the Ministry with the consent of the trade unions, this project had also to be approved by the unions. This consent was based on the general support that trade unions give to rationalisation strategies increasing social welfare and therefore for the benefit of everybody. It was also expected that the claims of the unions for further improvement of working conditions (at least for some workplaces) would be honoured. At this level it was especially the regional section of the IG Bergbau, which is responsible for the whole combine, that has been active. But also the union leaders at the factory level supported the project.

A more intensive involvement of the production workers took place with the implementation of the technology. This was done by the rationalisation department of the combine together with the management of the factory. In general meetings and during consultations at various levels the workforce was acquainted with the project. The goals of the changes were explained and the future workplaces were demonstrated with the help of pictures of the technology.

In the preparatory stage every two weeks some workers (engineers and skilled workers) were sent to a factory in Czechoslovakia where a similar technology was in operation. At the same time foremen (*Meister*) were trained to prepare production workers for their new tasks.

Workers from the traditional mills were offered work at the new machines after their installation. Despite the problems connected with such a change (change of work collective, necessary further qualification) more workers than were actually needed were willing to change. In fact, management therefore had the opportunity to select and prepare the best workers. This was done in consultation with the union leaders in the factory, who were as much interested in an effective solution to the change as the management.

Almost all workers that we interviewed had participated in the discussions about rationalisation in their work collective. More than half of them even actively co-operated in the innovations group. A little less than half also contributed with concrete suggestions for the realisation of technological change. Only a minority though participated in the Scientific Work Organisation (WAO) collective.[6]

There was in general high involvement of those workers who remained at the old workplaces and this indicates that the management and the union tried to engage the whole workforce. It has to be added, though, that it was not altogether clear at the beginning who would change to the new machines.

About half of the workers, however, did not feel very well integrated in the innovation process. Half of them stated that the changes were performed without involving the workers. An equal number also related this feeling to the fact that they had never worked in this field before. Only few saw the reason in lacking qualifications on their part and only ten would say they were not interested.

These data would suggest that not enough had been done to stimulate all workers to participate in the reorganisation. Expert interviews and the analysis of documents, like reports of meetings, however, prove that there have been ample opportunities for this. If one takes this into consideration then it has been the less engaged workers who see the reasons for their rather passive behaviour in management's policy. There was also some contradiction with other statements. So for instance, more than three-quarters of the workers confirmed that there had been discussions during meetings and on other occasions about scientific-technological progress; the majority of those working at the machines felt well informed, in particular about the technical innovation.

If one looks at the motivation of those who are now working at the new machines for changing their workplace, one can find some overlap between workers' interests and the interest of the factory. Most important are work-related motivations; personal problems or problems with former colleagues hardly play a role.

One can expect that replacements cause a certain opposition because the social status could be negatively affected. It has been mentioned already that this did not play a big role in this factory since more workers than necessary were willing to be transferred. And while the change of working collective was the least important motive for changing the workplace (see Table 3.1), problems were rather encountered with the new task, the new working process and the acquisition of new qualifications. The problem of new working collectives was not very relevant since most workers knew each other fairly well. There were no problems with wages either, since the management had offered workers at the new machines higher pay. This does not mean, however, that all workers were satisfied with their pay and we shall return to this later.

Table 3.1: Reasons for Agreeing to New Working Place (in per cent, n = 49)

	fully applies	partly applies	does not apply
I wanted to have another job	30	20	50
I did not want to stay in my work team	4	0	96
I wanted to qualify myself	39	12	49
The change-over was necessary for the interest of the factory	52	8	40
I received the order	28	2	70
I wanted to support the realisation of technical innovations	40	18	42

For an understanding of the change process it is also important to see how the workers judge the whole process of reorganisation. In Table 3.2 an overview is given of the main problems experienced by the workers on the new machines.

Table 3.2: Problems with Change-over to New Technology from the Point of View of Workers Concerned (in per cent, n = 49)

knowledge and abilities of the workers were not sufficient	41
organisational faults by management	24
inadequate information of the workers	30
the technology was not mature	9
insufficient quality of the raw material	78
the colleagues had difficulties with the change-over	52
the new technology brings the workers only a few direct advantages	26
other problems	7

Changes in work content and working conditions as experienced by workers

The Merseburg Aluminium foil factory includes a foil rolling mill, foil refinement and consumer goods production sections. Only the first of them was investigated. The structure of this factory is shown in Figure 3.1.

Figure 3.1: Structure of Aluminium Foil Factory

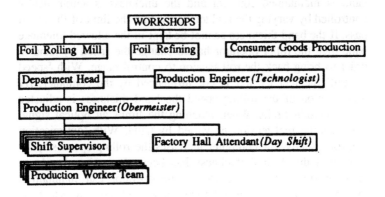

The production takes place with old and new machinery. The difference between the two is that the former have two rolls for rolling, the latter four. The new machines are equipped with automatic control. They can roll aluminium bands of a thickness of 0.4 mm to 2 times 0.009 mm and up to a width of 1,600 mm.

A quick work-roll change device equipped with automatic spindle control allows a work-roll change including all additional works to be performed in less than 20 minutes (standard value). The Control System automatically controls the band thickness and records the rolling process. The roller feeds the values for the adequate rolling program (roll number, band number, nominal thickness and so on) on a keyboard and controls the input data on the monitor. From the given technological values the microcomputer selects the best rolling program. After automatic calibration of the thickness gauge the thickness measurement begins when the roller starts moving.

If control is performed by hand, the given primary data are only registered by the computer. An intervention by hand is possible at any time even when the system is switched on. After having started the band by hand and as soon as it has reached the desired thickness the operator can switch over to one of the three automatic control systems; retraction control, speed control and optimisation control. In 'retraction control' the rolling speed set by hand is maintained constant and the thickness is automatically controlled by varying the reel tension within the limit of the given pass. If the band thickness cannot be kept in the allowed tolerance band then the roller operator has to change the speed by hand in order to bring back the roll tension to control range. With 'speed control' the reel tension is not influenced by the computer. By modification of the rolling speed the band thickness is adjusted within certain limits. When reaching the limits an optical signal demands the reel tension be varied by hand. With 'optimisation control', finally, the computer increases the rolling speed step by step until the desired thickness has been obtained and reduces simultaneously the reel tension. The operator can maintain a maximum speed and a relatively low reel tension which is confirmed by an optical signal. Another signal indicates the reel tension being near the minimum. In that case the computer lowers the rolling speed.

Rolling and cutting at both the old and the new machines still imply a certain number of manual operations. During that time the machines stand still and the worker is entirely engaged with such activities as:

- changing the raw material at one or two bands;
- repairing band cracks;
- putting the band into the roll gap,
- eliminating scrap work;
- setting the rolling stand;
- adjusting and setting cutting knives and separator;
- changing finished bands and inserting new winding rolls;
- changing work or back-up rolls and cutting knives.

Since the level of automation and mechanisation differs between the two production lines, the share of manual work is different, too. It amounts

- at the narrow band (old) to about 35 per cent, and
- at the wide band (new) to about 24-27 per cent.

The most essential differences with regard to manual activities are: While old technology requires installing the reel by hand, with new technology the reel is installed with a handling device. Using old technology, rolling parameters are set with the help of mechanical reels, while with new technology the program is fed on a keyboard.

While manual work on the new machines decreases there is a considerable increase in required attention. The team at the rolling stands has to follow the whole rolling process and especially also to interpret the signals from the monitor. This results in them being tied to their workplace, that is to say the operators cannot leave the mill (all at the same time). Due to the fact that changing finished bands and installing new reels happens about 20 times per shift and every now and then band cracks have to be repaired, the work has a relatively high degree of complexity. The increased responsibility of the workers is caused by the greater material value of the machines and by their higher productivity: one lost working hour is far more expensive than at the old machines.

The social relations have not changed very much. The rolling teams (three workers at the entry rolls and two at the finishing rolls) always have eye contact and can - if necessary - also speak with each other, which is not always easy given the noise of operating rolls. In addition there are occasional contacts with workers at other machines in the same production hall. The need for co-operation within each team is very high, each member has to rely on the other and in case of band cracks or starting up all operations have to be well timed. The working conditions are characterised above all by the long twelve-hour shift, by oil, dust, noise and sometimes also draft. The first two are within permissible limits, while at the new machines there is less noise than at the old ones. All workers at the new machines have received 150-200 marks net more than before, which means an increase of about 20 per cent.

The workers are qualified as 'forming metallurgists' which is a skilled worker's occupation. Job titles at the roll stands are 'foil roller' and at the cutting machines 'winder and cutter'. Some workers work as transporters. The head rollers are responsible for the work of the whole team and have a *Meister* qualification. They are highly qualified workers who have more detailed knowledge of their machines than thé shift foremen. They receive therefore also higher wages. The factory managers suggest that the work of these foremen is rather characterised by stimulating the rollers to work autonomously than by regimenting them by orders. Co-operation between foremen and rollers is generally good.

Many of the changes that we have mentioned are also contained in the workers opinions about their new workplaces (Table 3.3).

Table 3.3: Workers' Estimation of Modifications Caused by Change to New Rolling Stands (in per cent, n = 48)

	yes	no	I don't know
work became physically easier	56	40	4
work became mentally less exerting	19	66	15
work became more responsible	75	21	4
work is connected with higher qualification demands	58	40	2
work became more diversified	68	21	11
work is connected with greater autonomy	66	30	4
controlling activities became more frequent	85	15	0
working results are essentially higher	86	6	8
workers are more tied to their working place	75	21	4
there are more agreeable conditions in the working environment	41	55	4

The introduction of NC and CNC in a machine-tool factory

Characterisation of the enterprise

The second study was carried out in an enterprise of the machine-tool and machine-construction industry. The major product of this enterprise is the manufacture of toothed-gear grinding machines which are preferably turned out for export. With some 2,000 workers this enterprise is one of the structure-determining enterprises in the region. As the parent firm of a combine consisting of eleven individual enterprises, this enterprise maintains important leading functions within the combine.

The sequence of production in the enterprise in question includes: research, development and design; technological preparation for manufacture; component manufacture; and assembly.

The department studied has the task of manufacturing all small component parts of the machine tool. For this purpose metal-cutting machining processes are almost exclusively used. The range of manufactured items comprises about 5,500 different components with a lot size of 5-30 pieces per order. Thus it is a pronounced small-batch production. Even single-piece manufacture may be required for individual orders or to comply with special wishes of the customers. The efficiency of this department or section determines the success of production within the entire enterprise. That is the reason why it received the majority of investments for rationalisation and extensions, with the consequence of the increasing use of NC machine tools.

Technological development in the engineering industry

In 1981 some 280,000 metal-cutting machine tools were in operation in the metal-working industry of the German Democratic Republic, with the share of NC machine tools accounting for some 1,700. This was a rate of 0.6 per cent. With reference to the type of machine, lathes (60 per cent of all NC machines used) and milling machines (25 per cent of all NC machines used) predominated.

The further qualitative development of the use of NC machines is increasingly orientated towards the introduction of so-called 'Technological Units'. These are complexes of production lines which are noted for the control-side connection of

- NC machine tools;
- industrial robots for feeding the NC;
- storing device for workpieces;
- measuring station for the automatic control of dimensional stability.

The controls used in the majority of NC machines require the manufacture and provision of corresponding information carriers (punched card, punched tape, magnetic tape etc.) and permit the machine operator to make corrections in the program only within very limited margins.

In 1979 the control mechanism CNC 600 was the first freely programmable control developed in the German Democratic Republic on the basis of microprocessors. This control makes it possible to correct and to completely change the control commands by means of an operating desk without the need of changing the information carrier. The control CNC H 600 is a mechanism which is in the stage of development and enables simple programming by the operator.

The implications for work coupled with the introduction of NC machines will be analysed on the basis of the following cases:

Conventional machine tool	replaced by NC/CNC machine tool
Horizontal drilling and milling machine	Machine programming centre with NC 470
Vertical drilling and milling machines of different types	Machine programming centre with CNC 600

In the case of the replaced conventional machine tools the control of the machining process (longitudinal and/or cross feed, cutting speed) as well as the change of tools (twist drill and thread cap, countersink, milling cutter etc.) was largely done manually. With the introduction of NC the functions of control and tool change were largely automated.

The machining centres are equipped with NC used for machining complicated prismatic components. The tool-changing device with a storage facility of 20 tools and 40 tools makes it possible to carry out a great number of machining processes without the need for the operator to change the tool. The existence of four, or three, axes of motion ensures a minimum of workpiece clamping operations.

The production process after introducing new technology

Work preparation

Planning the production times for the components, i.e. the moment when the workpieces have to be available at the workplace, and the sequence of the machining operations is done on the basis of technology and the timing of orders. All the data are processed by a computer which will supply the corresponding control data for the provision of workpieces and for the technological documents required (drawing, order card, programming documents, wage calculation receipts) and will inform the enterprise section on the time, place and kind of tools, testing instruments and clamping devices to be made available.

The technological process of preparation for production to be covered by technologists includes the following tasks:

1. Decision on type of production.
2. Decision on conventional or NC/CNC processing.

3. Specifying the sequence of operations.
4. Preparation of description of sequence of operations.
5. Specifying the tools, testing instruments and clamping tools to be used.
6. Computer-aided or manual preparation of operating periods.
7. Decision on scope of controls.
8. Determination of wage group.
9. Operative attendance at the production process. This time serves for clarifying the technological problems in co-operation with the workers. Operative attendance is gaining special importance in the case of NC/CNC machining.
10. Elaboration of NC/CNC control programs, establishment of data carriers and testing of programs at the machine tool (in conjunction with the operator).

The data prepared under items 1 to 8 are stored by the machine and are printed out in the form of an order card for the corresponding parts of a job order. The NC/CNC programming documents (punched tape and programming-step printout) are filed and, if required, attached to the production order.

The division of labour existing in the enterprise in question within the department responsible for technological production preparation is essentially technique- and thus machine-oriented. For this reason the scope of activities of a production technologist comprises all sub-items, as indicated in the breakdown. (Tasks 1 and 2 are, however, within the competence of the department chief.) The technologists usually have a college or university education in mechanical engineering (engineers, certified engineers).

Due to the technical development (transition from NC to CNC controls, use of electronic computing and drafting aids) and under conditions of constant production parameters, the share of programming activities is expected to become smaller. Thus the time required for the establishment of a control program will be cut by some 70 to 80 per cent upon transition from NC to CNC control.

Direct production

When an operator receives a production order he has to make himself acquainted with the job order and the related technical documents and he has to check whether he has received all necessary parts. This means that he has to be able to read the technical drawings, to control the sequence of the machine operations as well as to check whether the program covers the job order in terms of type and number of workpieces to be machined. He then has to prepare the machining centre, to equip the tool storage according to plan and to fasten the workpiece on the clamp table. Next he has to read in the punched tape with the control program. He machines the first workpiece stepwise and compares the movements of the machine with the program. The technologist/programmer has to be called in case of any deviation. If everything is all right he finishes the whole lot number, fills in the pay receipts and returns his completed job order.

Quality control

The observance of the quality parameters is ensured by a number of control systems that are independent of each other.

The technological documents contain stipulations on intermediate controls required as independent operations. The integration of these intermediate controls into the sequence of the technological flow of production as well as the scope of controls are laid down by the technologist. Control is done at a separate test workplace by independent quality controllers.

The production worker stipulates the scope of his own control activities on the basis of the experience gained. If he is not convinced of the quality-conform machining of a workpiece, he can call for the quality controller responsible for his workplace.

The management of a section each month selects the number of production workers who are obliged to present to the quality controller every first and third workpiece machined according to the job order. This applies above all to such production workers who lack sufficient experience in vocational practice, have a scrap and rejects rate that is above average, or have an insufficient qualification.

Service and maintenance

Every operator is responsible for the servicing and maintenance of the NC machine put into his hand. This involves: cleaning of the machine workplace; regular removal of chips and regular refilling of coolants conforming to grades. The elimination of mechanical, electrical and electronic damage or disruptions, however, is exclusively within the competence of specialised maintenance personnel.

76

The job situation of operators

Scope of activities

The scope of activity (complexities of jobs) at an NC machine comprises the following range of functions:

- programming;
- pre-adjustment of tools;
- setting;
- operating;
- feeding the NC machine with workpieces;
- attendance;
- maintenance;
- controlling.

The real scope of activities depends upon the degree of labour division within the production range. The structure of labour division differs between enterprises depending on the kind of production (small-, medium- or large-series production), the type of NC used, the conditions of the structure available for the labour force etc. In one-third of the workplaces in the plant studied, the scope of activities is covered by the functions of setting, operating, feeding and servicing. In 14 per cent of the cases the scope of activities is confined to operation, feeding and servicing.

Although the programming activities are not an integral part of the job and thus not part of the work to be paid, the operators of CNC-controlled machines, in particular, are concerned with these activities to a differing extent.

The idea is to correct faulty programming sets as well as to optimise the cutting parameters rather than to establish complete programs. These programming activities, although the operators do not possess an adequate qualification or authorisation, are tolerated both by the management personnel and by the technologists competent for programming. The reason for this is to ensure a more effective course of production.

Job requirements

By and large, the requirements correspond to those with conventional technology. Only in the field of visual perception, due to the reading of alpha-numerical symbols on the display unit will an increase in the requirements have to be met.

The highest intellectual requirements exist in the NC machining centre as compared to conventional, NC-controlled and CNC-controlled machines. The reason for this is the need for adjusting the complicated workpiece on the clamping table in correspondence with a zero point fixed by the technology. This zero point serves as the reference point for the calculation of the wave lengths to be programmed in the various motion axes. The operator must take this zero point from the technical drawing, identify it theoretically and virtually duplicate it intellectually in clamping the work-piece. Only if the defined zero point corresponds with the practical one (and this has to be accomplished in the dimensions of 10-2 mm) is it possible to proceed to the machining.

This partial function of zero-point adjustment of the workpiece is automatically done by the CNC-controlled machining centres. The operation of NC requires thinking in more abstract categories as compared with conventional machine tools.

The automatic tool changing reduces the amount of heavy physical work. In shaping the work process it is assumed as a principle that labour intensity shall not be increased (i.e. the degree of intellectual and physical labour spent within a definite period).

The periods arising as non-productively usable down-times are compensated for by transitions to two-machine operation. In pursuance of the above principle the worker is entitled to reduce the number of NC machine tools to be operated by him without any loss of his wages in the event of extremely short machining periods and thus increased physical stress (more frequent feeding of the NC machine, more frequent changing of tools), i.e. in our case to revert to one-machine operation. This is also made possible as operating the new machinery is less strenuous because the machine operations are controlled by the software rather than by the machinist. Increasing requirements emanate from the co-operation with the technologist. The machining of the workpiece in accordance with time and quality requires:

- the persistent information of the technologist on programming errors or faulty or non-optimum technologies by the operator ;
- the support of the operator by the technologist for clarifying the problems in connection with the process of machining.

The effectiveness of this co-operative relationship both under the aspect of production optimisation and in the sense of approximation of members of different social strata is substantially determined by the kind of comradely relationship and mutual assistance that is necessary when working with NC machines.

The technologist, viewed under the conditions of conventional technology, is, among other things, responsible for the calculation of the machining times for the various components which, in turn, provide the basis for assessing the individual work performance of the production worker. It was the case once that a CNC-production worker for different, yet temporary, reasons deemed it necessary to have a higher machining time than what was possible to concede him on the basis of the technologist's calculations. This was a cause for tense relations between these two colleagues. With the receding influence of the production worker on the immediate operating process due to NC/CNC machining, the calculated machining-time expenditure loses its behaviour-determining effect, the 'assignment of guilt' to the technologist for a temporary non-fulfilment of norms is deprived of its sense, so that the barrier preventing the development of positive relations has been eliminated.

In this context, however, another problem emerges in relation to the technical changes and the alteration of the co-operative relations with regard to the programming activity. In line with the scope of activities the operator, when inadmissible machining tolerances emerge, would have to call for the technologist to eliminate any possible programming errors. This would lead to a source of additional loads on the shoulders of the technologist. Since the NC operator has a higher income, on average, than his 'technological partner', such an approach could possibly disturb the development of positive relations. This potential conflict was solved in such a way that the programming in the above manner by the NC operator was accepted to a limited extent, with mutual understanding among the operator, foreman and technologist. However, this understanding was reached outside the officially stipulated task division. It was only reached since it complied with the interests in a smooth flow of production of all persons involved, though for different reasons.

However, a change of the co-operation conditions between the operator and his super-ordinate manager or head will be the result, and there will be a change in the conditions for implementing important management functions for the foreman.

Since the programming activities arbitrarily assumed by the production worker cannot be approved officially by the management personnel, the effective functioning of the reproduction process as to programming is solely dependent upon the goodwill of the operator, provided that he has the abilities and skills. If this goodwill is subject to changes due to the exchange of the operator or the emergence of conflicts between operating personnel and management, the increase in effectiveness appears to be no longer guaranteed on the basis of this informal consensus. Thus the necessity for a modified way of guaranteeing the relationship of authority between foreman and skilled worker has resulted from this situation.

Another example demonstrating the change of social relations due to the use of NC was observed in the metal-cutting section. There the necessity of a parallel use of conventional and NC/CNC machine tools led to an analogous differentiation within the collective in the sense of informal groups. The reason for this differentiation was the view held among the lathe operators of conventional machines that NC/CNC machining would make no great demands upon the abilities of a lathe operator. A typical remark: 'A CNC machine is only operated by those who cannot earn their money as a normal lathe operator'. This difference in opinion will affect the content of the relations to be put into reality.

The responsibility to be exercised by the NC operators will have to be considered from two aspects:

- Responsibility can be assessed on the basis of the amount of damage caused by faulty operation at the workpiece and the NC machine tool; and on the basis of the amount of production loss caused by the damage. Since the NC machines are expensive and highly productive this will be reflected in the great demands upon responsibility.
- The probability of subjectively caused damage increases with the widening of the scope of activities. The greater the complexity of tasks, i.e. the sum of all functions to be executed by the operator, the greater his influence on the quality-conform machining of workpieces and the functioning of NC and thus his responsibility. A measure of the responsibility to be assumed would be obtained only if both these aspects were linked with each other.

With continuous attention of great intensity needing to be paid by the operator of a conventional machine during machining of a workpiece, the operation of an NC machine will require intense attention only upon the setting of machine and workpiece. Of course, it is necessary to constantly observe the automatic machining process (the operator is not allowed to leave his workplace), but the degree of intense attention permits, as a rule, the exercising of other functions (such as the setting of a second NC machine, cleaning works etc.) and recreation (coffee drinking, reading a newspaper etc.).

Qualifications of operators

Some 150 production workers are employed in the section under study. The average age of the almost exclusively male workforce is around 30, that of the NC operators is 31 years. The latter show a small variation within the age structure.

Prompted by the transition to the three-shift system the effect of rationalisation, coupled with the introduction of NC machine tools, did not lead to a release of workers.

All production workers have certificates as skilled workers. Up to the introduction of NC they were exclusively skilled workers for the different metal-cutting technologies. But with the advent of NC there was the need to employ also skilled workers of other lines (in the case studied there were also machine fitters). However, in this group of skilled workers it became obvious that despite their formal command of mechanical engineering, their performance was worse compared to the group of lathe operators. There is no well-founded knowledge available on the reasons for this difference in performance.

Generally, it is possible with simple NC and a low complexity of tasks to instruct skilled workers of other lines to the extent of acquiring the basic routines, but nevertheless this does not, as a rule, lead to utilisation of all machine- and control-oriented performance potentials inherent in NC equipment. To make this possible and, in addition, to create performance-stimulating approaches, it is required to aspire to a high measure of complexity of tasks. A foremost requirement is to provide a training orientated towards the NC used as well as towards the machining technology.

In the enterprise the qualification requirements for production activities are determined by means of a uniform scheme of identification and evaluation. The qualification requirements evaluated on a system of points provide the basis for the qualification groups to be established and thus for fixing the hourly wage. The documentation worked out as a result of studies has to be confirmed by the enterprise manager, the technical director and the enterprise union management.

Table 3.4 contains the deviations of qualification requirements for NC machines compared with conventional technology. After assessing all qualification criteria, there is an increase in the qualification requirements for NC by 109 per cent compared with the conventional technology. However, this difference does not have any consequences according to the qualification groups.

Particularly great qualification requirements must be met for the activity of programming. However, programming activities are not, as a rule, part of the tasks of the NC operator. In fact, the CNC operators do have some knowledge on free programming in the test field and they also apply this knowledge, although it has no effect on the qualification of groups and accordingly is 'not paid'.

Table 3.4: Changes in Qualification Requirements at Machining Centres

Criteria of evaluation	Difference to conventional technology
Design structure of the working media	+ 12 %
Design structure of subjects of labour	- 50 %
Complexity of measuring procedure and of measuring and testing means and instruments	- 50 %
Knowledge on material classification	- 50 %
Intellectual capacity, including increased attention with multi-machine operation	+ 250 %
Possibility of influence on production results	+ 300 %
Scope and level of manual dexterity	- 50 %

In a representative study on NC qualifications it became obvious that 60 per cent of operators possessed ready-for-application knowledge on programming, with only 6 per cent of them having received adequate training.

These facts are indicative of the lagging behind of enterprise work organisation with respect to the activities of the workers and their need to use them.

Role of the trade union during the introduction of new technology

The general objective of the socialist process of rationalisation is derived from the continuation of pursuing the main task, the unity between economic and social policies. The fundamental goal is to raise the material and cultural level of the people on the basis of a high rate of development of production. To increase the effectiveness of the reproduction process, especially by means of scientific and technical progress is, in the final analysis, a means for the steady improvement of the material and cultural needs. This incorporates also the consistent improvement of working conditions and the formation of more demanding work tasks. To make use of the important preference of socialist rationalisation, i.e. the fact that the carriers of rationalisation measures at the same time carry out the material reproduction process, it is necessary to show the basic conformity of interests between all groups involved in the process of rationalisation.

The changes in the material, social and economic conditions of work coupled with the introduction of new technology affect considerably the interests of workers. In particular this is the case when changes in the shift system are required due to measures of rationalisation; workers are released from previous jobs and changes in work standards have to be put through.

The immediate partner of the state management is the enterprise trade union organisation with its corresponding organs. The enterprise trade union executive represents all workers employed in the enterprise, independently of their affiliation to definite trades and craft groups.

The provisions of socialist labour law, as laid down in the Labour Code, provide the basis for concrete union activities. Accordingly, the trade union has the right

- to take part in the elaboration of plans;
- to exercise influence so that the measures of increasing labour productivity are coupled with improvements in the working and living conditions;
- to take part in determining the formulation of wage conditions (i.e. work standards [norms] and other parameters of work performance are only allowed to be put into force with the consent of the enterprise trade union). To this end, the following statutory provisions have to be observed: Wages are not permitted to fall owing to the introduction of new technology/technique. Payment of an extra compensation is possible in the event of the transition to multi-machine operation and measures to stimulate shift work become effective with the transition to three-shift operation. In this stage of vocational

adjustment (six months as a rule) changed work standards are set up. The greater responsibility coupled with new technologies is not allowed to lead to greater deductions from pay if quality parameters are not observed. Thus with the intervention of the trade union executive it was prevented that refinishing works and rejects were sanctioned by wage cuts;

- to take part in determining the work-time and vacancy planning;
- to control the supply of workers and the construction of social amenities;
- to organise mass control over the observance of socialist legality;
- to exercise influence on the adherence to labour safety and health protection;
- to take part in determining the preparation, conclusion and modification of labour contracts;
- to exercise control on the preservation of the rights of workers;
- to ask for information from the enterprise manager or the leading executives and to render account of it;
- to demand retribution from the supervisory management in the event of insufficient fulfilment of tasks, the violation of socialist legality and disregard for the rights and proposals of workers by the state management of the enterprise.

In the case of rationalisation measures the trade unions bear great responsibility for the fulfilment of these tasks. In this context a number of statutory regulations under the labour laws were passed, ensuring the workers their basic interests. These legal regulations include:

- guarantee of a workplace for all workers in line with the social requirements and the personal qualification;
- planning the necessary measures for training and further education, so that the qualification required for a new or modified activity is reached;
- enterprises are obliged to create the material, personnel and financial preconditions for the successful implementation of qualification measures;
- enterprises are required to pay the costs of study fees, travel expenses, literature for study, or personal working media to the worker in the process of qualification;
- enterprises have to create the preconditions for the required

84

qualification of workers to be done largely during the working time;
- obligation by the enterprise to render help for the procurement of housing and for moving if it is necessary to resume work at a different location;
- conclusion of new work contracts at least three months prior to the beginning of changes;
- transitional payment of an amount of money equivalent to the annual provisional reduction in pay if the previous pay cannot be maintained at the new workplace.

The Enterprise Collective Contract to be concluded between the state and the union management serves as an instrument in the process of establishing a far-reaching consensus of interests between enterprise and workers. In this Contract the enterprise manager and the enterprise trade union executive oblige themselves to fulfil

- the tasks of the plan;
- the tasks for the permanent improvement of the working and living conditions;
- the tasks for the development of a high cultural and educational level (including the measures for the technical training and further education required).

The Draft Collective Contract is subject to consultations with all workers and has to be presented to the panel of elected trade unionists for decision-making. 'The enterprise manager and the executives, on demand of the enterprise trade union management have to render account of the fulfilment of their obligations.'[7]

This shall be exemplified by a brief excerpt from the Enterprise Collective Contract valid in the enterprise where NC/CNC was introduced.

In the above-mentioned sense there is an obligation by

- the director of the enterprise to create the preconditions for effective and personality-promoting work, for the provision of corresponding working conditions, for the creation of efficiency-stimulating parameters of work, for the improvement of working conditions at 170 workplaces, for the provision of manifold material incentives upon transition to three-shift operation, for the additional provision of wage funds for extended tasks as a precondition for the saving of workers, for the redistribution of wages and salaries thus saved to the amount of 25 to 75 per cent;

- the enterprise trade union committee to exercise influence on guaranteeing the incorporation of workers in the preparation for and the implementation of measures of socialist rationalisation, to exercise influence on the contribution towards socialist rationalisation with a view to improving the working and living conditions.

These obligations refer to concretely mentioned enterprise projects and they have to be controlled at any time for their observance. Thus the trade unions exercise their influence on the preparation and implementation of rationalisation measures via the work of so-called rationalisation collectives or WAO collectives.[8] These collectives are composed both of technicians and workers that belong to the section subject to rationalisation. This co-operation ensures a high measure of consideration of the interests of the workers operating the new machines or equipment.

The connection between enterprise and trade union interest on the basis of valid statutory provisions guarantees a great measure of concurrence of interests. Thus it is understandable that with the introduction of new technological processes or new machines and equipment no conflicts arise due to the incompatibility of interests. Therefore, with the introduction of NC no instances of opposing attitudes were observed. This is quite understandable when realising that apart from the economic effect coupled with the introduction of new technical production means there has been an improvement of the material, social, and even the financial conditions of work.

Notes

1. By the term 'technology' we understand technology in its widest sense, including the machines used (technology in a narrower sense) as well as production engineering (*Produktionsverfahren*).

2. See *Programme of the Socialist Unity Party* (SED) (1976), p. 20.

3. One of the authors is the leader of a sociological research collective concerned with the introduction of new technologies in a great industrial trust.

4. About the motivation of the scientific-technological progress in socialist countries see also G.S. Grudoznik (1974) *Wissenschaftlich-Technischer Fortschritt - Sozialistische Arbeit - Persönlichkeit*, p. 122.

5. About the interrelations between scientific-technological progress and

the character of work see also W. Fitze *et al.* (1976), *Wissenschaftlich-Technischer Fortschritt - Sozialistische Arbeit - Persönlichkeit*, p. 20.

6. Suggestions as to how to improve working places need not only be made spontaneously and then be given to the innovators' office. In order to solve certain tasks, workers can conclude innovators' contracts with the factory management. This is a planned and organised possibility to change the production process. In both cases those involved receive a bonus according to the usefulness of their suggestions.

7. *Labour Code of the GDR* (1976), 29, section 3, Berlin.

8. Scientific work organisation (WAO) teams are temporary working teams consisting of production workers and specialists of the department of scientific work organisation, in order to seek optimum solutions for certain rationalisation measures, especially measures for the reorganisation of working places. Scientific work organisation intends to create working places which simultaneously raise productivity, diminish load and promote personality development.

References

Fitze, W., N. Paulick and H. Schleiff (1976) *Wissenschaftlich-Technischer Fortschritt - Sozialistische Arbeit - Persönlichkeit* (Scientific-technological Progress - Socialist Work - Personality), Berlin, Dietz Verlag

Grudoznik, G.S. (1974) *Wissenschaftlich-Technischer Fortschritt - Sozialistische Arbeit - Persönlichkeit* (Scientific-technological Progress - Socialist Work - Personality), Berlin, Akademie-Verlag

Labour Code of the GDR (1976), Berlin

Programme of the SED (1976), Berlin, Dietz Verlag

4

New Technology and Work in Hungary: Technological Innovation Without Organisational Adaptation

Katalin Nagy

The socioeconomic context for technological change in Hungary

The management system and state of the economy

In the past two decades we have witnessed considerable progress in the Hungarian economy. Political stability made it possible that in 1968 the previous management system based on centralised planning was replaced by one based - partially - on market mechanisms. In every sphere of the economy the role of money incentives has gained in importance. A marked improvement in the level of consumption and living standards of every stratum of the society can be felt. The importance of foreign trade has grown and the country has become more open to economic and political influences both from the East and the West. A second economy has developed, first in illegal rather than in legal forms.

In the mid-1970s, however, the favourable tendencies of the early 1970s stopped. The energy price boom and other negative terms of trade developments were a major strain on the country's balance-of-payments and debt position. Foreign trade problems impeded economic activity in a period when the conditions of the proper functioning of the economy were changing anyway; extensive labour resources, cheap raw materials, investment resources etc. were all running out.

Tensions were aggravated by the fact that the reform of the macro-economic management system could not speed up to a degree sufficient to change things radically. The unchanged firm-level organisational and management system and the network of previously existing personal connections were mainly responsible for that. A process of regression has thus emerged in which profit motivation and other formal elements of firm independence peacefully coexist with disguised plan instructions (Antal 1982).

This 'mixed' management system gradually substituted market mechanisms by centralised directives which pursued the aims of resource (labour, material, energy, import, investment etc.) allocation, export promotion and integration into the world market. This centralised management system was not very instrumental, however, in transmitting world economy developments to the firms. In an era of resource scarcity squandering was a widespread phenomenon and production did not adapt to demand (Tardos 1982).

This non-adaptiveness was 'compensated' first by foreign credits and later by domestic investment resources. From the late 1970s the real income of the population was also restricted along with investments. Diminishing real incomes and investments have improved the country's balance-of-payments position but cannot be a lasting solution considering their adverse effects on economic growth and living standards, and their endangering of social stability, which has been after all the main achievement of the Hungarian political system.

Policy-makers see a way out of this impasse in the further deployment of the reform process. Several favourable developments occurred in this respect in the early 1980s: the legalisation of the shadow economy, the promotion of small ventures, the restructuring of central management organisation, the strengthening of the collective nature of firm management etc. Further and more radical developments are not only a matter of firmness and resoluteness of the government but also of social consensus and interests.

The present state of the economy and the necessity for radical change compel facing up to the problem of technical progress. Investment resources have considerably decreased since the beginning of the decade and they have been frequently tied to export promotion or import substitution programmes. Investment loans now are mostly short-term, with high interest rates, and often prescribe the employment of home-made equipment. The chances of employing modern technologies with higher resource and/or hard currency requirements and a lengthier adaptation period are worse today than they were some years ago. Short-term interests favour those investment projects which are low-cost, have short pay-back periods and whose products can be promptly exported (Szabó and Szöllösi 1984).

In the present situation the further diffusion of new technology will mainly depend on changes of the economic conditions at the macro-level and on the government's initiatives.

Employment and wages

In the Hungarian economy there is practically full employment, which means job security for almost every worker.

Until lately the labour market was characterised by constant excess demand, but nowadays, in the era of slow economic growth and stagnating wages, signs of excess supply are gradually appearing. Excess labour demand caused wage inflation, large-scale abandonment of some occupations, the strengthening of employees' market position and lower achievement phenomena, which posed almost unsolvable problems for management. With excess supply, a new regulation problem arose: labour force allocation had to be implemented in such a way that the productivity of labour be raised and - at the same time - full employment be secured (or at least not seriously impaired) (Galasi 1982).

Characteristic of firm-level labour policy is hoarding and squandering the labour force whatever the state of the labour market. Some reserve labour - for use in peak periods - is always present. Moreover, labour is relatively cheap and if a firm employs more low-wage workers - with the overall wage level held constant - worker groups who are in key positions can have better pay.

The relative cheapness of labour and the constraints imposed by wage regulation are often a hindrance to the introduction and utilisation of advanced technologies. Because of investment resource scarcity firms prefer labour-intensive technologies to capital-intensive ones. (If labour is abundant this preference is backed by social considerations, too.)

Full utilisation of advanced technologies, on the other hand, is often prevented by the lack of skilled labour. Workers who change for new technologies want better pay as a compensation for their retraining and taking bigger responsibility. As the full utilisation of high value, high productivity machines is a prime concern of the firm, these higher wages are usually paid. But labour force procurement for old technologies is also a problem, these constituting a large - often the largest - part of all capacities. Firms want to keep their employees working on old technologies, therefore they have to narrow wage differences, and work on new technologies must lose some of its appeal. In some cases because of the inadequacy of the wage system firms did not have enough labour to run a factory even in one full shift (Balázs 1984, Nagy 1984). The causes of such worker and management behaviour are to be found in the macro-level regulators and in wage policy.

Government has a tight control over wage level and wage differentiation although theoretically firms are free to choose their own wage policy. In practice, however, they have only a very limited choice, therefore wages are considerably levelled off, and links between wages and performance are weak. The compressed wage structure is an obstacle to incentive wage differences. Performance is therefore withheld, full utilisation of labour is attained only in peak load periods. Wages in the 'legal' economy - their minimum assigned by labour market relations and their maximum by government regulation - are relatively low compared to the cost of living and consumer aspirations (Héthy 1984).

Advantages of a central wage policy are that it takes into account some socially accepted wage criteria such as education, seniority and working conditions, narrows inequalities through wage levelling, holds back inflation and contributes to the elimination of reserve labour (partly by transferring it 'inside' the firm) (Héthy 1984). Social costs of this wage policy are the weak incentive effect of wages and the impossibility of material advancement on the workplace. This is the main reason why the second economy is gradually gaining ground - and 70 per cent of industrial workers enjoy some income originating from this field.

The second economy meets demand in industries where the government sector fails for some reason or another (inflexibility, constraints on field of activity, lack of motivation etc.). Wages in this sector are tied to performance and are much higher per hour than in the government sector. That is why workers hold back their performance in state-owned firms, which has a negative effect on labour productivity. The possibilities of earning an extra income differ greatly, however, between groups of workers (Héthy 1984).

Skill levels and job structure

One of the most spectacular changes in the Hungarian labour market in the last decades was a sudden improvement in the educational structure. In 1980 half of those in the 50-54 age bracket had no finished basic education, the figure being 4 per cent for youth entering work. Five per cent of the group leaving work had received higher education, while the figure was 10 per cent for those entering. Behind this high formal level of education (attested by diplomas and certificates) the real level of knowledge was not high, the cause being the rapid extension of mass education.

Demographic change has thus had a positive effect on the educational structure of the workforce. The job structure, however, has not matched this process. This phenomenon has several - mainly systemic - causes: socialist industrialisation created low-skilled jobs in great numbers and this forced job structure survived; investment policy pursued quantitative goals, which was easier to fulfil by automating the main production process, while neglecting auxiliary ones; labour is under-priced against capital, which hinders automation etc.

The educational system prepares to an ever higher extent for skilled jobs but the labour market cannot match this. This incongruity between educational and job structures is most felt in the case of manual work. It is caused (besides the slow evolution of the job structure) by the vertical organisation of the school system, which 'forces' 90 per cent of the youngsters at the age of 14 (too young for work but also for choosing a career) to enter vocational training. The source of unskilled labour is thus drained but not the demand for it. Shortage has raised the prestige and the wages of unskilled occupations, which now have appeal also for skilled workers (Frey 1985).

Capacity constraints and long-range planning limit effectively the number of high school graduates but not the number of those entering vocational training. This latter form of education is regulated by short-range operative plans reflecting the actual interest of firms. As a result of excessive global demand on the labour market, more skilled workers are produced than the economy effectively needs. This notwithstanding there is a standard shortage of skilled workers (apart from some very popular crafts) because an important and growing part of skilled workers choose an unskilled or semi-skilled job. No special tension arises out of this situation because unskilled jobs have a high prestige (and high wage too) and the knowledge behind a skill certificate is low. This 'over-educated' worker stratum has such a low level of general education that it is sometimes insufficient even for unskilled work. The training programme has too much professional knowledge and little general education. The horizontal departmentalisation of training, its adaptation to the daily needs of production, has resulted in a rigid structure of manual labour. The school gives no convertible knowledge (Frey 1985).

Structural relationships of the economic model and investments

Technical innovation in the Hungarian economy is closely connected to investment. The connection is not reciprocal, however: new investments do not always embody new technology in the sense of being 'up-to-date' or 'more sophisticated than the others'. This phenomenon can be explained by general social and economic determinants of the investment process which are also manifest in the case of technical change.

We describe the mechanism and socioeconomic environment of a firm's investment activity using J. Kornai's descriptive model of the traditional socialist command economy (Kornai 1980).

Let us start the presentation of the model with its social side. The model is explicit only on those elements of social relations which are closely related to economic phenomena, namely the relationship between the state and the production units. In traditional planned economies the relationship between the state and its firms is paternalistic, the state being the parent who takes care of its children and the firms - being dependent - seeking this caretaking. Caretaking or dependence may turn up in different degrees but it never ceases to exist. A firm which goes bankrupt, for example, is always given assistance.[1]

As a result of this paternalistic relationship, financial resources do not limit the firm's activity: the budget constraint is 'soft'. Neither the state's nor the firm's behaviour is determined by efficiency criteria, the firm does not face a genuine risk. Not a firm's income or efficiency but power relations, personal connections and traditions decide on who can invest and who cannot. Thus it is not a firm's finances but its ability to bargain with the state and to obtain new resources which determines the quantity of its output. This is the very mechanism which makes an economy 'resource constrained' as Kornai puts it.[2]

In a resource-constrained economy firms led by an expansion drive and facing soft budget constraints tend to 'syphon-off' the market and to buy up every product they can use as an input. Permanent shortage is the result which is felt also in day-to-day production. With the budget constraint being soft, shortage does not lead to the rationalisation of the production process but to an in-flated demand for shortage goods, to stockbuilding: This results in a self-perpetuating process: shortage adds to demand and demand adds to shortage. Demand is 'almost insatiable', suction spreads over every market. In a resource-constrained economy firms are geared towards expansion. Investment expansion is an all too 'natural answer' to the problems of bottlenecks and other deficiencies in the production process within the firm and outside it or to yet unfulfilled demand for its products.

Growth is also motivated by management's identification with the organisation, because its power, its prestige, its material and moral incentives all depend on 'size'. Concerning management's identification with the firm there is yet another motive which is working against prudence in firm-level investment decisions and this is the fact that managers' fate is tied to the firm (Laky 1982). The reasons for this are the high level of concentration in Hungarian manufacturing (sometimes a firm is a whole industry), the seniority system and the general housing shortage. Besides these objective factors there are a good number of organisational and personal causes which practically block managers' mobility unless they change positions or professions. Due to this 'forced' attachment, management has a uniform attitude towards investment, every member of it accepting the role it has to play in the battle over resources.

A further cause of the steady greed for investment is the softness of the budget constraint, since it sets investment demand free from the fear of loss or failure. The only constraint on investment demand is the quantity of available resources, which - being always less than demand - is perforce always binding. In a shortage economy where no efficiency criteria prevail every growth objective is justifiable (on the very basis that it reduces shortage) and so the demand for investment resources is almost insatiable.

Some characteristics of the decision-making process on investments

According to this model the most important events of the investment decision process occur not within the firm but on higher levels of the allocative hierarchy, which is also demonstrated by several empirical findings (Laky 1982). The investment decision process of the firm was in most cases pointed outwards: as if advantages of the project had to be demonstrated not for the company itself but for those higher instances that allocate resources. Firms were inclined to consider as useful every development objective that was already approved - and consequently financed - by some higher authority if it promised some investment for them, whether it was really important or not.

The ordinary ranking of 'means' and 'ends' was thus reversed. 'Getting the money' had become the primary aim of the firms, and in order to better place themselves in this fight for central investment resources they were ready to invest in anything, whether the action conformed to the firm's strategy or not.

With resources being transferred from some higher allocative levels and with the ensuing attitude of 'seizing the opportunity', the decision process within the firm gradually became reduced to the sole task of how to obtain money. As the benefits of the investment had to be proved only to those allocating the resources, the number of those participating in the process was limited. For proving something to the 'outside world' it is enough for a small group of - mainly technical - leaders to participate, using information readily at hand plus some 'expert judgment' to assess the data needed by the higher authorities. Discussions were avoided in order not to reveal weak points (Laky 1982).

One would expect that the firm is more rational, more prudent if it invests from its own resources, but the research mentioned above and some other case studies have proved the contrary.

The firm's own resources are as limited relative to demand as those of the central organs. The different departments and professional groups within the firm have the same reasons to fight for them - professional ambitions, the desire to be 'big' - as has the firm in its relation to the centre. They use the same tools in influencing upper management in their favour - limited factual information, bold guesses - as does the firm. Who gets the investment depends primarily on intra-firm interest and power relations, on each department's ability to influence the allocative process.

Technological level and utilisation of new investments as a consequence of the decision-making process

Analysing the many factors which together make out the interest in investments, we find that the backing of an investment in general is much stronger than that of some special mode of its implementation, involving predetermined technical parameters. Every firm is glad to use top technology, and raising the level of technology always figures among the first on the list of investment objectives. But the need 'to invest at whatever cost, the sooner the better', often neglects considerations concerning the level of technology, the latter being rather of a long-term character. If sticking to an up-to-date technology would jeopardise a project or substantially delay its implementation, the firm tends to accept or - as our experiences have demonstrated - even suggest some less advanced solution which is easier to implement (Nagy 1982).

It is certainly an objective of central organs to raise the level of technology in firms. In making their choice, however, they have no guidance nor any economic control. The home market is in a state of suction (shortage economy), everywhere there are bottlenecks so every available technology needs development. Impulses from the capitalist market are felt very faintly - they are suppressed - and no market impulses come from the Council of Mutual Economic Aid (CMEA). Central organs are thus compelled to select among interest groups those representing 'the strongest bottlenecks' and 'the most promising trends of technical change', considering their relative strength, as well as state-level CMEA agreements, but not objective economic needs (Greskovits 1986).

Summing up we can state that the technological level of new investments is determined in a 'haphazard' manner, almost independently of the firms' - and partly of the allocative organs' - original intentions.[3]

The efficiency of new technologies in a similar manner is strongly influenced by the constituents of investment behaviour. The scarcity of investment resources and the decision process itself lead to a pronounced tendency to leave out of the calculations the cost of auxiliary facilities - or in other words lead to the building up of 'labour-intensive variants of capital-intensive technologies'.[4]

As a result of these deficiencies in investment decision-making, new bottlenecks arise in production processes that have only recently been automated, a phenomenon amply illustrated by case studies on the introduction of new technology (Balázs 1984, Nagy 1984).

The list of these typical economic and technical constraints, ordered according to their relative frequency and taken from an inquiry comprising 327 machines, 30 per cent of them NC and CNC, by Parányi (1983) is the following:

1. There are not enough workers for multi-shift runs.
2. The quality of raw material is not adequate.
3. The worker is not interested in working on the intensive technology.
4. Tooling and instrumentation is inadequate.
5. Capacity of old machines is sufficient.
6. There are no high-quality technical instructions.
7. One has to spare the machine because repair is difficult.
8. There is much standstill during work.
9. Commission work is not profitable.
10. Workers are inexperienced.
11. Production costs are higher than on old equipment.
12. Work allotment is inadequate, does not fit in with machine capabilities.
13. Machines must be spared because there is no money to replace them.
14. Technological discipline cannot be secured.

Some features of work organisation

Characteristic of the content and technical level of work in Hungary is the fact that the role of manual work in manufacturing is dominant, its share being 60 per cent, with mechanised work amounting to less than 30 per cent and conveyor belt work to only 10 per cent. Of all workplaces 3-6 per cent are automated and altogether 90 robots are working in the whole country (Héthy 1984).

Work organisation in production is developed mainly by management's initiatives and its aims are determined by productivity considerations rather than by workers' claims. The crisis of the traditional Taylorist work organisation in the developed countries and the ways and means to overcome it have therefore a special connotation in the Hungarian environment.

The basic question is whether Taylorism exists in the Hungarian economy or not. In our opinion Hungarian practice is rather to be called quasi-Taylorist. While formal features of Taylorism are present (like technical division of work, hierarchification, payment by results, assembly line) they are severely modified by the reality of the production process. The daily problems of supply of materials and tools make a painstaking prescription of workers' tasks obsolete; create in reality a factual need for multivariance (not always recognised in the classification); cannot fix the worker to his working place; cause continuous changes in work rhythm; modify the role of the hierarchy and leave considerable autonomy to the worker in the execution of his work. It is under such circumstances that certain key groups can develop powerful positions and do resist major organisational changes (Grootings *et al.* 1986).

Another source of the strong position of some worker groups is to be found in the peculiarities of Hungarian investment policy. As already mentioned, 'labour-intensive variants of capital-intensive technologies' were favoured, i.e. up-to-date, high-productivity machines were bought without appliances, spare parts etc. necessary to their optimal (or even 'normal') functioning (Köllö 1981). This investment policy was pursued in order to attain maximum output with minimum investment. Technologies which have emerged in this way are vulnerable, their running is possible only by workers who know perfectly local circumstances, bottlenecks etc.

Hungarian research on the effects of technological change on the working process has registered a strong resistance to such change (Makó 1983). The strongest resistance comes from those workers who have played a decisive role in the old work process and thus belonged to the core of the old work organisation. Every change - be it of a technical or organisational nature - that could possibly weaken their position is fiercely opposed by them. Because members of the core contribute to the stabilisation of management's power, a natural alliance emerges between them with the aim of preserving existing social relations within the organisation.[5]

It will be clear by now that the characteristics of the socioeconomic context (both at national and enterprise level) create very specific conditions for the introduction and use of new technologies. We shall illustrate this by two - in our opinion - not atypical cases. The first case describes a paper factory introducing computerised process control and the second concerns a machine factory introducing CNC machines.

Computerised process control in a paper mill

The paper mill

The Paper Industrial Enterprise where we have done our research includes all the production units of the Hungarian paper industry, namely 13 mills and a research institute. The workforce of the Enterprise amounts to 14,000 persons.

The basic task of the firm is the possible full supply of inland consumption. Its production on average corresponds to two-thirds of the requirements. The export of the industry is insignificant, its import, however, is much more considerable due to the scanty inland raw-material basis. The paper mill examined is the second largest of the Enterprise. In 1980, 32 per cent of the paper industry production was made here. The stock of its production means is much more modern than the average, which is indicated by the fact that the above-mentioned one-third of the total production is accomplished with only 17 per cent of the total personnel of the industry.

The organisation of the paper mill and its management structure can be seen from Figure 4.1.

The paper mill employs nearly 2,300 persons. The ratio between blue- and white-collar workers is 90:10, with 56 per cent skilled workers, 32 per cent semi-skilled, and 12 per cent unskilled workers.

The base-material (cellulose) and paper-manufacturing workshops work in four shifts. Due to the high number of shifts, and especially to the continuous working order, the paper mill has since the 1970s had a constant lack of labour.

Impact of the new technology on work

Traditional work and its organisation

We have to give a picture of the traditional technology of paper manufacturing in order to understand the importance of the new technology.

The mechanised technology of paper manufacturing works is in brief as follows: the raw material of production is wood cellulose dissolved physically or chemically; wood-ground and some filling substance (e.g. kaolin) is added and mixed with water, then the paper pulp is formed. Water is removed from the paper pulp on the screen of the paper-manufacturing machine and a wet paper sheet is formed. This raw paper is then dried on hot rollers. Manufacturing of the paper is done by a paper machine, which produces the paper in an endless band of 1 to 10 m width. The main parts of the paper machine are: the screen section (for the felting and dehydration of the paper pulp), the pressing section (for the further dehydration and pressing of the paper band), the drying section (for the complete drying of the paper), the smoothing machine (for the smoothing of the coarse surface), and the winding part (for the winding of the paper band).

Figure 4.1: Organisational Scheme of the Paper Mill

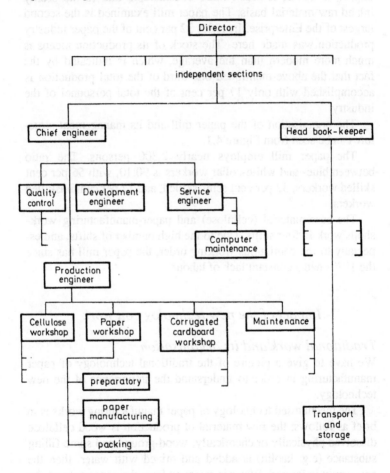

This simple listing of paper-manufacturing technology covers a very complex, sophisticated process. Its 'black box'-like feature is the result of the complexity of the base material as well as the production method and equipment. This is why the main trend of the

100

development of paper machines has always been the extension of the feasibility of measurement and control of the manufacturing parameters. In this manner computers could gain a considerable role in the paper industry already in the early stage of the industrial application of computer technology.

Short history of the application of the new technology

In the second half of the 1970s new qualitative requirements occurred for the paper industry, in addition to the quantitative ones. The printing industry underwent a considerable reconstruction in that period and installed a new, up-to-date stock of machines which demanded paper of a new quality and in an increasing quantity. New administrative technologies and computerised data processing also required a better quality of paper.

The foreign trade situation of the country called for a higher quality as well. In order to decrease the payments in foreign exchange, imports had to be decreased in such a manner that the foreign paper of high quality should be replaced with inland products. For the realisation of new quality standards the management of the Enterprise decided to use computerised process control - on the basis of western examples.

The installed AccuRay system measures and controls three basic interconnected parameters. Regulation is done on the basis of a dynamic model, which in case of any intervention takes into account the interactive effects of the three characteristics. Several special programs belong to the system and give a wide range of information.

The operators and maintenance personnel of the computer were trained by the firm AccuRay. Operators of the process control were mainly the former key workers of the traditional organisation of the paper factory. No selection was made, since AccuRay claimed that the operation of the system would not exceed the capabilities of an average skilled worker. The production management did not want to change the traditional organisational order either, since it wanted to introduce the new technology with the minimum of conflict and to keep the core workers.

According to calculations, the production increased by ten per cent, while the consumed cellulose decreased by three per cent and steam energy by six per cent. The qualitative parameters of the manufactured paper improved by 50 per cent. Speaking about economic results, it can be stated that computerised process control has fulfilled the expectations.

Computerised process control as one type of innovation in the paper industry

The two paper machines of the factory work side by side in the same hall. The computerised process control was installed on the paper machine No. 1. Direction of the two machines is done by a foreman. His task is to obtain the maximum from the machines and to help in the remedy of any accidental trouble.

For the operation of both machines six persons are needed and in case of manpower shortage the common personnel of the two machines may not be less than nine persons.

The members of the six-person group work on a separate section of the machine and are responsible for their section. Women work on the wet section of the machine, men on the dry one. The subordination is hierarchical; everybody is responsible not only for his (her) work, but also for the work of the subordinate. On the lowest level there are the helper III and the felt-maker. They are mainly semi-skilled workers, while all the others are skilled. In case of absences everybody has to be able to do the work of his (her) superior as well.

Except for the lowest posts, experience gained on a lower position is also needed in addition to formal skills. The possibility of promotion depends on a higher post being vacant. Since there are considerable differences in wages for the various positions, promotion is an attractive possibility, which, however, does not occur too often. Since the skills of the paper industry cannot be used in other works, there is only a low labour turnover.

Paper manufacturing is said to be implicitly 'practical', as the skills can only be learnt by practical experience. In addition to periodically measuring the paper quality and observing the instruments, the operators feel the visible, audible and tangible characteristics of the machine and the paper, with a high degree of 'intuition'.

An important further characteristic of paper manufacturing is that it is group work. The workers are responsible personally for their own work, and for each other. The operation of the technology supported by practical experience and group work brings about a considerable autonomy of the group.

The demand on physical and intellectual resources varies. According to a foreman, 'in normal operation it is 10:90 per cent, in case of trouble the other way around'. Trouble - paper break - occurs generally unexpectedly and can be due to many reasons, therefore the workers are always under stress. In addition to this stress, the working conditions are burdened with noise, vibration, and the accident-prone continuous working order.

In spite of these unfavourable conditions, the workers do like the work and are satisfied. Indeed they tend to stress the possibility of solving problems and unexpected situations as well as their responsibility for making the work varied, interesting, and even 'challenging'.

The workers are also strongly bound to the mill: for the majority it is actually the first working place. This relation is to a large extent forced, since the skills tie the workers to the place and, vice versa, the paper mill cannot exist without their skills.

Figure 4.2: Organisation of Paper Manufacturing

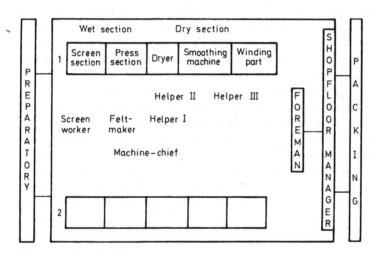

New technology and work organisation

With the new technology the task of the machine operators became more varied. By means of constant measurement and regulation and the display on a screen, defects became visible which had not been thought of before, and new solutions were needed for the remedy of defects. This increased at first the physical load and stress. With the consolidation of the system both effects decreased again.

By rendering the changes in the production process transparent the complexity of work decreased also. The process could thus be better followed and handled as a whole.

The personal autonomy of the operators has increased in certain respects and decreased in others. It has increased due to the fact that defects can be observed by any member of the group who can then warn the machine chief. At the same time the work of everybody has become more controllable and the machine chief has more time for inspections. Defects in the process are unambiguously shown by the computer and therefore responsibility can easily be traced. While the responsibility of work has increased, the perception of this, however, has differed among the workers.

The structure of the new skills required for the use of process control differs considerably from the traditional ones. The traditional skill is based on empirical experience and local knowledge and requires basically synthesising work. This is done now by the computer while the process demands from the operators more abstract analytical work. The traditional experience and skill has lost part of its value.

Speaking about working conditions, two factors have to be mentioned: the change of the wage system and the possibility of promotion. Task wage was introduced for the paper machines after the introduction of process control. Different norms were stated for the two machines due to the different quality and quantity of the products. This resulted, however, in differences in payment, which was objected to by the trade union. As a result the separate norms have been terminated and the task wage depends today on the common production, with wages being the same on the same position at each of the two machines.

From the description of the traditional organisation it is clear that the possibility of promotion is very restricted. Differences in the ability to learn and operate the computerised process control increased for a time the possibility of promotion. (For example, a young educated helper who had learnt every trick of the system could advance fast to become a machine chief, and then foreman.)

External relations of the workshop with the group of service workers increased with the application of process control. The career of this group demonstrated the connection and the 'bargaining' between new technology and the traditional work organisation. The group belonged first to the chief engineer and stood in the organisation above the paper workshop. Information given by the computer was directly accessible to the management of the mill. The computer operators at the beginning tried some checking and interfered with the manufacturing in case of any deviation from the computer program. The machine chiefs objected to this by saying 'no computer technician should direct a worker who has been working here for 30 years'. The management of the production also did not push; it was essential for them that the paper was of good quality - it was not so important how it was made. Thus the computer technicians stopped interfering. Later the group was placed under the service engineer and thus stood on an equal level with the production management. In the meantime their number had also decreased by half; they became overloaded with increasing maintenance work, while at the same time they received fewer spare parts due to import restrictions. Finally, the group came under the control of the production management in spite of its formal independence. Placement of the computer beside or under their control was not objected to, however, since in this way production information would not get directly to the higher management. (It is another question why the latter did not demand this.)

By keeping to the old organisation problems with the foremen occurred also. The foreman should know and understand the process control. When he appeared not to be able to do this, the operators were arranged in such a way that at least two men who were able to work well with the computer would be present in each shift. No foreman was exchanged for the computer, since the necessary professional experience of working with both machines could not be dispensed with.

Another problem was caused by the traditional style of shop management. It became obvious after the installation of the computer that a rigid form of management would decrease the efficiency of the system. The chief foreman kept for himself the adjustment of the process so the machine operators could only interfere secretly since the computer itself was not able to perform the programmed results. This way of management changed only after the old chief left and the acceptance of process-control tasks by the machine chiefs, as well as economic and qualitative results, improved considerably.

In the traditional work organisation on the paper machine, replacement of the workers played an important role, and this aspect remained. Basically this system of mutual replacement promoted training in working with the computer for everybody. On the level of the workshop, however, the replacement possibilities became slightly restricted. The operators of machine No. 2 did learn in practice the essential part of the new system, but - as one foreman said - 'they do not know the details and so cannot be efficiently transferred'. Nevertheless, the division of labour within the group became more overlapping. On the screen on the operator's desk everybody would see the manufacturing process, and defects could be observed by anyone and repaired jointly. The visibility of the manufacturing process increased at the same time through the autonomy of the group, since the screen would be observed not only by the members of the group, but by anybody, including the managers.

Impact of new technology breakdowns

At the time of the introduction of the system, the group of main-tenance workers insisted they were suitably prepared. The enter-prise made no maintenance contract with AccuRay, only some spare parts were provided and a framework was given for some predetermined repair work. No problems occurred with the com-puter during the first three or four years; after that, however, the natural wear became more obvious. Due to import restrictions the supply of spare parts was not secured, the number of maintenance workers decreased as well with the result that the computer often did not work, or became totally unreliable.

The failing of the computer meant a new 'hazard-factor' in the manufacturing process. According to a foreman: 'This is as if all the instruments disappeared from a car during running'. The situa-tion without the computer was more severe than before, since the workers were no longer accustomed to the traditional routines. According to a helper: 'To work without process control means to work blindly. In spite of knowing the machine, where the neces-sary things are, I am uncertain, I am nervous'. The failing process control implied that for operating the process and repairing the de-fects much more time and effort were needed. Due to this the stress and physical load again increased considerably.

Acceptance of the new technology

Decisions concerning the computerisation of process control were made on several management levels of the enterprise and of the paper mill. Participation of the workers only took place during training. This also aimed at the acceptance and understanding of the changes, however - in the absence of practical knowledge - the workers could not get answers to their basically practical doubts. It could not be made clear whether the computer would free them from the earlier tasks; operators also were afraid of the computer, which they thought would 'peach' them and increase the pace of working. On the other hand, some people were expecting 'miracles' and the solution to all problems by the computer.

While in the course of operation such misunderstandings were cleared, it became obvious that the computer is 'no God' and by itself could not manufacture any paper; it was a means, though more important than the others. Everybody was actually able to learn to operate the system at the level of 'pressing the buttons'. Some workers did not understand the theory of the trend or the histogram. All they knew was that 'one is good, when it is flat, another, when there are large peaks'. Operation proved, though, that the computer could not be left alone, it had to be controlled as well.

The acceptance of the new technology was promoted to a large extent by inserting it into the traditional organisation. Although this solution decreased the utilisation and potential capacity of the new technology, the computerised process control brought about considerable results also in this way. According to the organisational traditions, the basic operation was learnt by everybody, while the more sophisticated special programs that would demand a higher level of attention and would make possible a greater control of the operators' work were not pushed through. In this way most of the controlling and accounting program was left out from the everyday practice. The operators themselves did not want a new control over their work and production management did not want to lose any of the key workers, so nobody insisted on this part of the programs. In fact, traditional production accounting was also retained. The precise records that the computer was able to give were used practically by none of the managers.

Summing up

It must be stressed again that the effects of the computerised process control have been influenced by the conditions of its introduction and by the traditional organisation of work.

The persons immediately concerned were left out from the introduction. They could affect only the operation. The technical optimum of the computer and that of the new control system were in conflict with how the transitional technology and control system were organised. In the bargaining process that followed, the traditional relations of the organisation proved to be stronger.

With regard to the qualitative characteristics of work, the effects of the new technology and traditional working are separated. Part of the traditional features (responsibility, team work, complexity etc.) were enhanced, while other features (professional skill, autonomy) decreased slightly and former work burdens (physical load, stress) did so considerably. Further effects of the new technology will depend upon changes in the organisational and technical features, and it can be concluded safely that the new technology so far has played only a limited role in initiating such changes.

Similar experiences can be reported from other cases of the introduction of new technology, as the second case study on the introduction of CNC machines shows.

CNC innovation in a machine factory[6]

The factory

The factory of our second case study specialised in the production of large-size and heavy-duty equipment for power plants. The early 1970s up to 1977 were the golden days of the factory; the introduction of the CNC machine park began also in this period. The power plant equipment amounted to 40 per cent of the total output. Unique machines and production lines for the chemical and canning industries, and boilers, were produced as well.

By the end of the 1970s it became obvious that due to the general economic restrictions the expected power plant investments and other industrial orders failed to come in. The decrease in demand affected practically all products of the enterprise. Things were made worse by the failure of two risky product innovations which led to an unhealthy increase in the factory's stock.

In the early 1980s the personnel consisted of 1,950 persons; 650 were manual workers in production, 500 were manual workers in other spheres of activity (maintenance, unskilled work), the rest were clerical staff.

The enterprise has two factory units, one in Budapest, the other in the country, the latter being rather a small unit with a personnel of about 200. The enterprise is headed by a general manager, two managers under him are responsible for technology and for business. Quality control, personnel policy, legal questions, organisation and administration are departments directly controlled by the general manager. The introduction of any new technology is the task of technical departments within the factory (see Figure 4.3).

Figure 4.3: Organisational Scheme of the Enterprise's Technical Departments

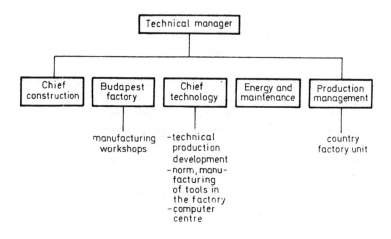

The introduction of NC/CNC technology

The enterprise had bought the first two NC machines for the Budapest factory in 1974, in the period of the economic boom. Their application had been recommended by the National Committee of Technical Development, a ministry-like body called upon to spread technical culture in industry, with funds of its own to support enterprises and grant credits. In this case the Committee had granted favourable credits so that another four machines arrived in 1976. The whole development concept relied on the expected orders for power plant equipment; it was hoped that the modern machines suitable for processing large-size equipment would increase productivity and shorten production time.

The introduction of new technology was motivated also by the increased mobility of manpower. It was expected that with the CNC machines capacities would be so flexible and productive in all bottlenecks that they would compensate for the problems of manpower fluctuation.

Although CNC innovation had started in the period of the market boom it did not stop despite the change in economic conditions, the last machines arriving in 1982. Only minor economy measures indicate the changing conditions: some complementary equipment to the machines has not been purchased. This, of course, makes their future optimal utilisation doubtful.

Organisational experiments in the first phase of CNC innovation

When the first CNC machines were purchased, operators were unprepared for the new technology. For years these machines were used as traditional machine tools, controlled by hand. In 1978, when two valuable CNC machines arrived, an experienced engineer who was familiar with the CNC technology was appointed chief technologist. During a few years the CNC machines were exclusively controlled by this specialist rather than by the workshop. At the same time the recruitment of skilled workers was started. The chief technologist organised a course in the factory where CNC operation and some basic knowledge about computers and programming were taught. Some 25 persons volunteered for the course but only 16 started to work on the new machines.

The independent CNC group received its orders directly from the management of the factory unit. Five CNC technologists worked out the program of these machines, first with the help of manual programming, and after the arrival of a computer exclusively with machine programming. Apart from programming, the technologist had to work out the plans for component parts and tools and determine the preparatory time as well as the standard time/production time (piece); the technologists controlled also the running of the program.

After some time the CNC machines were put back into the workshop, i.e. under traditional control. Three foremen were appointed but they soon left. For one year the machines worked without the direction of a competent foreman. The CNC technologists helped but nevertheless the foremen became dependent upon

110

skilled workers. For a while one of the CNC technologists worked as a CNC foreman but owing to the shortage of technologists he soon returned to his original job. Today, foremen are familiar with the new technology to the extent of understanding the tasks and being able to give professional advice but they do not understand the soul of the machine, the programs.

Changes in qualifications

There are only CNC technologists and machine operators for handling CNC technology. In the other fields (for instance quality control or maintenance) there are no CNC experts, indeed there are no such specialists in the important preparatory phase of CNC technology itself.

The technologists are mainly young experts who have acquired the necessary knowledge for programming and computer utilisation. In the beginning their inexperience resulted in many defective programs. Since the introduction of the computer there have been fewer faulty programs but there are still technical disputes, basically because the technologists have no experience in metalworking. ('They don't know how to turn on a traditional lathe'). Hence the worker must often reverse the order of operations in the program.

The CNC machines are operated by the most experienced, most intelligent skilled workers competent in the traditional technology. The operators of the largest and most up-to-date CNC machines are greatly respected because of their expertise. It would be difficult to decide whether these people are skilled workers or technicians. Learning the CNC technology has increased their professional knowledge and enlarged their horizon. (Among the 14 machines there are only two simpler drillers which are operated by semi-skilled workers.) Today only those who have become fans of their technology are working on these machines: turnover was 20 per cent in four years.

Operators find CNC processing physically easier but intellectually more demanding. Due to the piece production and special features of work organisation (we shall come back to this later) they do not suffer from the pace dictated by the machine, while their defenceless exposure to the machine and the stress effects of speed are not yet significant.

This change in the level of qualification and in the nature of work can be explained by the specialisation of the division of labour on the CNC technology and the piece-production character of manufacturing. Thus the preparatory phase which separates the technologist-programmer and the machine operator is lacking, that is, preparation is also done by the operators, 'enriching' in this way their work and skill. The work-pieces are single pieces (series are made rarely) so that preparatory work is required almost for every single piece.

The impact of the lack of structural innovation

At present the CNC machine park functions in the traditional enterprise organisation, among traditional machines and in structural conditions introduced several decades ago. The machines and their operating agencies did not come up to expectation. True, the products manufactured with the CNC technology are much more accurate but productivity has not increased in the same measure as the value of resources. Dissatisfaction with the economic impact of the new technology is justified but the blame should not be put on the CNC technology but on the receiving factory environment. On the one hand there are the shortcomings of the factory's traditional structure and work organisation, on the other hand, CNC technology has not received special treatment.

The placing of new technology

In the past the factory had a production-cycle attitude; later workshops producing component parts and assembly workshops were established. The placing of even the traditional machines was determined by historical contingencies. No analysis was made of the stream of material when the workshops and halls were developed.

In the case of CNC machines special management, technology, provision of tools, measuring and control would have been required in establishing a special workshop; instead the scattered placement of the machines makes their operating more difficult, while there are also other negative circumstances. The machines are spaced so densely that it is impossible to accumulate (prepare) by their side the basic materials and the finished products; there are indeed machines where the shortage of space causes much difficulty to the cranes in hoisting the basic material to the machine. As a result of careless placing, for instance, one of the large-capacity machines has been put into a hall where the crane above

112

the machine can transport only one-third of the mass the machine is able to process.

Work flow and production organisation

The enterprise uses a ten-year old technology-standard system including a design documentation recorded according to some 100,000 designs. The task of this department is to identify the components which occur repeatedly and establish a documentation for the new pieces.

This procedure does not take into account the changes of the machine park. So the work-piece is either put on the CNC machine on the basis of the old documentation, or the possibility that these machines can perform the task better does not even arise. Whether a work-piece gets on a traditional or a CNC machine is decided in the technological department, hence the design department cannot even take it into consideration.

The design and the production run on the basis of a production number; this number is given to the product when the factory accepts the order. So it happens frequently that the same standardised piece of work gets into the manufacturing process several times, independently of the other (one NC operator, for example, produced 14 pieces in four instalments within a six-month period). In the case of CNC machines new measuring and adjusting involves a loss of time even if the previous programs can be used.

Production is organised according to the logic of classical piece machine production in workshops otherwise manufacturing fixtures and in assembly halls. The work is organised on the workshop basis. The foreman gets the documentation and material of the products scheduled for the next month or the next ten days from the production department. The material remains in the workshop until the arrival of the complete CNC program. Owing to the construction number system to which production is adapted it is, for instance, impossible to exploit the CNC flame-cutter adequately. This machine is really efficient if it cuts the maximum number of work-pieces from a given plate in a single phase of work. With the existing organisation of work this is impossible: from the material arriving at the workshop only the pieces needed for the actual product are cut and the remaining material is transported back to the store-room.

Together with his job the operator gets the complete documentation of the piece of work: its design, its technological description with the program, the time voucher with standard time and the materials to be used. However, he must supply the necessary tools himself. This involves, even in the case of the expensive CNC machines, that the worker leaves his place to fetch tools, or to have them made. There are not enough special tools, so the workers keep snatching them from each other and carrying them from one machine to the other.

Production therefore begins often with some additional work: either the tool has to be made or - what happens frequently - the size of the material does not correspond to the order (for example the plates are thicker). In this case the suitable size must be produced by manual control on the CNC machine before starting the program.

Earlier processing used to have two phases: rough cutting and levelling. Rough cutting means the planing of the inaccuracies of the cast. This has been left out from the present technology, so roughing is also done on the CNC machine. The non-homogeneous mould pulls and knocks the machine about, and damages are frequent.

Maintenance and quality control

In maintaining and repairing CNC machines the biggest problems are caused by the lack of expertise. Nobody in the maintenance department has been trained for this. The shortage of spare parts does not make things easy either. Servicing Western European machines and the purchase of spare parts are very costly, and due to foreign currency restrictions, some machines stand still for weeks.

Quality control faces similar problems. The appearance of the CNC technology has not influenced its process in any manner, it is being done with traditional technical means. Statistical means of control are unknown, control does not extend to machine-programming or to position-measuring.

The wage system

The basic reason for introducing the NC/CNC machine park was the shortage of skilled manpower. The factory sent its own skilled workers on a CNC course within the plant itself. First reluctance

114

was so great that 25 per cent of the trainees dropped out. They were then replaced by skilled workers lured away from other enterprises. However, this did not stop turnover. Initially all machines worked in two shifts; now there is not enough personnel for this and, indeed, today there are more machines than operators.

Aversion to the CNC technology has not disappeared in the course of the years. Even higher wages could not compensate for the increased stress, which is mainly caused by the inadequate application of CNC machines and the inadequate conditions of production, the intellectual burden and the much greater responsibility owing to the greater financial value of the machines. This work, although physically easier, demands a special way of thinking. The operator must see the process of work in advance, understand the program and be able to find the faults. The skilled workers fear mostly that 'they haven't got that feel of the machine as with traditional machine tools'.

In the first phase of the innovation CNC operators received a 15 per cent higher hourly wage, justified by higher professional expertise. Later a special wage system was introduced which allows for higher monthly incomes. The system is a progressive efficiency wage combined with a bonus for quality: 90 per cent of the wage is guaranteed (in case of a performance below 90 per cent); every one per cent above a 100 per cent output entails a five per cent wage-plus.

Performance, however, does not depend only upon the workers' abilities but also upon the quantity of work, the prescribed standard time and the number of work-pieces. But, as we have learned from the foregoing, there is not always work for these machines. Besides, the standard time is always debated.

The time given for manufacturing a piece consists of the preparatory time and standard time. The technologist follows the principle that the CNC machines are four to five times more productive than traditional machine tools. This, however, is true only in the case of standardised production. In the case of one- or two-batch production the total processing time may be even longer because of constant re-adjustment and preparation. The technological department does not take this into consideration, and grants only fragments of the old standard time. The technologists have a vested interest in proving the efficiency of the CNC technology because the computer serving it is attached to their department and they have an exclusive right to it.

Under such conditions it is very difficult to produce over 100 per cent but nevertheless the income must be ensured owing to the shortage of skilled manpower. So the 'normal' wage is established with different supplements and 'manoeuvres'; the enterprise and the worker are mutually at each other's mercy. The enterprise fears turnover, the worker wants to keep the higher income which he can get on the CNC machine.

The role of the trade union

The introduction of the CNC machines has caused tensions right from the start. The shortcomings of labour organisation became more perceptible in production, and the tightening of the wage scale was also felt strongly. In the investment period the trade union had a bad relationship with the enterprise management. Management did not allow being influenced in questions pertaining to work organisation or the placing of machines.

In the early 1980s the enterprise received a new manager; the trade union approached him in the matter of CNC machines and their operators right after his being appointed. At that time the wages of those who worked with the traditional and those who worked with the new technology were spectacularly different, to the great advantage of the latter. The trade union defended the interests of those who worked on the old technology and achieved a substantial rise in their hourly wage, in making it come close to the wages of CNC operators. The dispute lasted for six months. From April to September the trade union did not ratify the wage increase of CNC operators before there was a decision about the wages of the others. The trade union's action was justified (particularly in view of the inflation in Hungary), yet it is ambiguous with regard to the utilisation of the CNC technology because the relatively high wages were the only hope for eventually returning to two or three shifts on these machines.

The economic impact of CNC innovation on the enterprise

Since 1976 the economic indices of the enterprise have been deteriorating continuously. Economic problems and market recession appeared in the enterprise parallel with the introduction of CNC. In the beginning it was expected that the new technology would increase productivity, decrease production time, improve quality, reduce costs, save labour, ensure the continuity of production and returns from sales, and improve technological work discipline. CNC technology was considered as a magic device but the miracle did not happen.

Technical experts still say that although CNC did not bring the expected results, without it the factory would have gone bankrupt. (True, CNC enabled them to accept some valuable orders for high-precision equipment.) Today the CNC machine park means to the management of the enterprise at least as much trouble as it brings advantages. Its preservation (amortisation, tool consumption, energy) costs 500 million forints per year. One machine can produce 200-300 forints per hour but its standing idle costs the same - and these machines are often at a standstill. The average number of shifts is 1.1.

The high costs of repair and maintenance increase expenses further. It seems that the traditional machines keep up the CNC technology rather than of the other way round.

The way out from this situation could be a change in the range of manufacture or commission work with the CNC machines but this, by itself, cannot bring a solution. With the present organisational structure, work organisation and control system it is impossible to operate the CNC machines efficiently. Computerised innovation has not been accompanied by the organisation's adaptation to the new technology, but further procrastination can lead only to the failure of the CNC technology.

Notes

1. The new economic mechanism introduced in 1968 'hardened' the budget constraint to some extent, but basically - it can be proved - the systems characteristics did not change much.

2. If the budget constraint is 'hard', the firm's activity is the function of its income. Output is constrained by profitability and market considerations. This model is called 'demand-constrained'. In this model firms are competing in how to loosen the constraints of demand, how to enlarge their markets: with cost reduction, quality improvement, product development etc. In this economy the market is in a state of 'pressure'.

3. There are some other considerations that 'simplify' decisions concerning computerisation, namely the embargoes of capitalist countries and the scarcity of (convertible) foreign exchange. These mean that from the late 1970s practically nothing but CMEA Riad computers were to be introduced. The opinions on Riad computers are mixed. I do not want to decide the question. But I am

inclined to say - based on my own and other research on computerisation - that their capabilities as for use value, quality and reliability are limited (Nagy 1984, Tamás 1983). This is one 'built-in' factor of the unreliability of new technology. However, to look into the causes of this is not our topic here.

4. During socialist industrialisation 'labour-intensive variants of capital-intensive technologies' served the threefold aim of quantitative, extensive growth, full employment and cheap investment (Köllö 1981). Under the new circumstances (intensive growth, labour shortage etc.) the old investment practice is further pursued.

5. This rule is involuntarily manifested by management's practice of giving preference to young newcomers or volunteers in filling posts on new technologies (Héthy and Makó 1981). This practice is usually explained by 'openness', flexibility, and other characteristics which are certainly relevant for adapting to new technologies. But an even more important factor may be the fact that social and interest relations are underdeveloped in these very worker categories. Both their position in the organisation and their ability to assert their interest being weak, they cannot lose much with a change. On the contrary, they may expect some advantage from it in the long run, which is why they are more ready to accept it.

6. This section is based on a case study done by Katalin Balázs.

References

Antal, L. (1982) 'Gazdaságirányitási rendszerünk fejládésének történeti utja' (The History of the Hungarian Central Economic Management System), in *Crisis and Renaissance*, Budapest, Kossuth

Balázs, K. (1984) 'Innovation without Adaptation', case study, Budapest (unpublished)

Frey, M. (ed.) (1985) 'Employment - Employment Policy', Budapest (unpublished)

Galasi, P. (1982) 'Bevezetö' (Introduction), in *A munkaeröpiac szerkezete és müködése Magyarországon* (The Structure and Functioning of the Labour Market in Hungary), Budapest, Közgazdasági és Jogi Könyvkiadó

Greskovits, B. (1986) 'Gondolatok a magyar fejlesztési politik áról' (Reflections on Hungarian Investment Policy), Tervgazdasági Figyelö, no. 1

Grootings, P., J. Bogdán, and M. Ladó, (1986) 'New Forms of Work Organisation: European Developments in a Comparative Perspective' in P. Grootings, B. Gustavsen and L. Héthy (eds.) *New Forms of Work Organisation and their Social and Economic Environment*, Budapest/Vienna, Vienna Centre and Institute of Labour Research

Grootings, P., B. Gustavsen and L. Héthy (eds.) (1986) *New Forms of Work Organisation and their Social and Economic Environment*, Budapest/Vienna, Vienna Centre and Institute of Labour Research

Héthy, L. and C. Makó (1981) 'A technika, a munkaszervezet és az ipari munka' (Technology, Work Organisation and Industrial Work), Budapest, Közgazdasági és Jogi Könyvkiadó

Héthy, L. (1984) 'A bér és az anyagi boldogulás perspektívája. A munka tartalma, a technika és a munkaszervezet' (Wage and Material Well-being. Work Content, Technology and Work Organisation), in *A munkásság helyzete az üzemben* (Workers' Lot in the Factory), Budapest, Kossuth

Kornai, J. (1980) *The Economics of Shortage*, Amsterdam, North Holland

Hungary

Köllö, J. (1981) *Taktikázás és alkudozás az ipari üzemben* (Bargaining in a Manufacturing Firm), Közgazdasági Szemle, no. 7-8

Laky, T. (1982) *Erdekviszonyok a vállalati döntésekben* (Interest Relations in the Decisions of the Enterprise), Budapest, Közgazdasági és Jogi Könyvkiadó

Makó, C. (1983) 'A megujulást akadályozó és ösztönzó társadalmi viszonyok a munkafolyamatban' (The Social Environment of the Work Process. Its Positive and Negative Impact on Innovation), Budapest (unpublished)

Nagy, K. (1982) 'Computerisation in a Changing Field of Force. The History of a Computer Centre in a Trust', case study, Budapest

Nagy, K. (1983) 'Limited Development - Limited Effects', case study, Budapest (unpublished)

Nagy, K. (1984) 'Compromise between the New Technology and the Traditional Work Organisation', case study, Budapest (unpublished)

Parányi, G. (1983) *A korszerüsitö fejlesztés* (The Innovative Investment), Budapest, Közgazdasági és Jogi Könyvkiadó

Szabó, I. and J. Szöllösi (1984) 'Az iparvállalati foglalkoztatás és a beruházások néhány összefüggése' (Employment Policy and Investment in Industrial Firms), *Munkaügyi Szemle*, no. 7

Tamás, P. (1983) 'A számitástechnika társadalmi környezetének jellemzöiröl' (On Social Environment of Computers), *Társadalomkutatás*, no. 1

Tardos, M. (1982) 'Program a gazdaságirányitás és a szervezeti rendszer fejlesztésére' (Programme of Development of the Central Management and Organisational System), *Közgazdasági Szemle*, no. 7-8

5
Technological Innovations and Work in the Soviet Union

Vitalina Koval and Michael Nochevnik

Introduction

Introduction of state-of-the-art microelectronics is one of the main manifestations of the current scientific and technological revolution at industrial enterprises. The novelty of the technology lies not so much in electronics being used in data processing but rather in a radical change in the very essence of production.

In big industrial enterprises microelectronic technology is used mainly in four areas: in small-batch production with numerically controlled (NC) machine tools; with robots, programmable automated devices and computers in large-scale production (automobile industry, machine building, electrical engineering, metallurgy); in automated continuous production and in computer-aided design (in electrical power engineering, electronics, automobile building, aeronautics, shipbuilding and others). We shall concentrate in our study on the first area.

Machine tools with microprocessors and computers have become known in the Soviet Union as Che-Peh-Ou machine tools, and abroad as NC/CNC machine tools. Equipping 1,000 numerically controlled machine tools with microcomputers makes it possible to make available for other tasks 2,500 workers. Microelectronic technology therefore is primarily labour-saving technology capable of savings in manpower and workplaces. In addition, the use of microcomputers in technological equipment will increase the reliability of that equipment by seven to ten times, decrease the manufacturing cost by five to seven times, and result in a significantly lower level of power consumption by control devices.[1] Due to inexpensive and prompt readjustment of machine tools the problem of organising the manufacture of new products using that equipment will be made much easier. Even partial use of microelectronics at enterprises leads to significant savings in manpower. For example, at one of the Soviet enterprises surveyed - the Vilnus 'Sigma' production association - the number of people in the section with microelectronics involved in production fell by 30 per cent, while the production output increased eight to ten times. At the 'Znamya Octyabrya' association in Leningrad at the section where microprocessor technology and flexible automation are used 12 people do the work done previously by 54. When the new section is compared with workshops in the same plant using traditional equipment 'there is at least a sevenfold difference between the two in the level of productivity' (Volostnikh 1985).

Modern NC machine tools have extensive technological capabilities and are highly automated. Nevertheless, there are a number of specific difficulties that stand in the way of their effective application. Among the problems of a technical order there are: the fact that the machine tools themselves are highly complicated and involve the interaction of mechanical, hydraulic, electrical and electronic systems and elements; the fact that they have a large variety of operating modes since machining is done on parts of vast nomenclature, and the parameters of a machine tool are controlled by automatic systems. There also appear a number of difficulties of a sociological and sociopsychological nature.

The introduction of NC machines in production processes has sharply reduced the amount of manual control over production. At the same time, however, we can observe in departments where production control has been largely automated that the remaining human control is being shared by workers of all professions and qualifications, that is to say, in such cases control functions are done by operators and adjusters, programmers and engineers, and specialists in microelectronics.

Significant changes are also observed in the character of the relationships among those who are working at sections with microprocessor technology. There is a more intensive contact between setters and operators and very often the former have contacts not only with operators, maintenance staff and other workers, but also with electronics engineers and managers. In some cases the frequency of contacts of adjusters with engineers and specialists is even higher than that with the workers. Engineer-programmers at sections with NC machine tools and robotics complexes spend between 40 and 80 per cent of their working time near the worker. Sometimes when there is a need from the point of view of the production, an engineer may substitute a worker at a machine tool, or he may be included in a team.

The composition of teams at sections with microelectronic equipment differs greatly from that of teams in traditional production processes as regards the numbers of participating engineers and technicians. While it was about 10 per cent in traditional sections, it has increased to 15 or 20 per cent in modern ones.

Such trends indicate the appearance of radically new tasks when studying forms and contents of social relations between people working with modern technology, given the fact that these are the basic factors that have a bearing on the efficiency of the technological and social development. There is evidence of man's being more and more alienated from the object of his work and also from the final result. It is as if the functions of the organisation of the work done by the individual worker, engineer, and technician have become interwoven, or 'merged', a process which has been strengthened also by the introduction of new forms of work organisation.

Our analysis is based on studies conducted in different enterprises.

- Enterprise No. 1 is among the oldest enterprises in the instrument-making branch of the economy (founded in 1886) where a large assortment of control and automatic control instruments is being produced for use mainly in the chemical, power engineering and metallurgical industries. The enterprise is situated in the largest industrial centre of Moscow. It fully satisfies the needs of Moscow's industrial enterprises and other installations in manometers and other instruments. The new production will involve investments in marketing, based on the experience that in 1983-84 the development of new types of instruments that can fully replace those currently produced was brought to a temporary halt due to the fact that it was not possible to market these products within a comparatively short period of time, making such production economically not profitable for the plant. On the whole the enterprise is characterised by a high degree of development of microelectronic technology.

- Enterprise No. 2 is involved in traditional production and is situated in Moscow. It specialises in products for electrical engineering (its output includes electrical machine parts for the underground railway, urban passenger transport, steamships, and for electrical units; shafts, flanges, frames, brackets). As we shall describe in detail below, at this enterprise microelectronic equipment is used in a radically different manner as compared with enterprise 1. The level of development and the prospects of technological innovations are rather high.

- Enterprise No. 3 is the oldest production association of Moscow specialising in products for the machine-tool industry. The main task of the plant is the production of metal-cutting machine tools of the latest design (primarily lathes and milling machines). The significance of introducing microprocessor technology is extremely high for the plant, because it produces numerically controlled machine tools. The production of these machine tools is done by active introduction of microprocessor technology into the traditional equipment already in place, as well as through including new modern NC machine tools into the existing stock of machines.

Decision-making and initiatives on new technology

The decision on the introduction of new technology in Soviet enterprises, including CNC machines, is usually taken by corresponding departments, i.e. ministries under which these enterprises function (for instance, the Ministry of Electro-technical Industry, in which one of the Moscow enterprises under study is included). Enterprises themselves can also display initiative in the introduction of new technology. For example, the enterprise can acquire, at its own initiative, a machine tool equipped with program control devices (CNC) or other equipment. But broad restructuring or the introduction of complex systems of machine tools are possible only upon approval at the ministerial level, or at the level of 'glavk' (special branch department working under the ministry).

Acquisition of new machines is performed on the basis of the financial funds of a ministry. A ministry buys and distributes new machines among enterprises. But enterprises also have their own 'fund for new technologies' and may acquire new machines of their own design. Certainly, financial opportunities of ministries are much greater than those of enterprises, and approximately 75 per cent of new equipment is therefore bought by a ministry.

Every ministry has a department (board) for the planning of scientific-technical progress. Every ministry has also centres for scientific information on work and management which keep permanent contacts with the enterprises. On the basis of recommendations by these organisations, the ministry distributes new technology to the enterprises. Enterprises are, however, not always prepared to receive new technology (they do not always possess the necessary personnel for new equipment, or have not prepared the necessary areas for new machines etc.). All these reasons are connected with the 'subjective factor', i.e. shortcomings in the organisation and management, or, to be more precise, with the insufficient level of personal and professional qualities of individual managers.

In case the initiative comes from the enterprises themselves, this is not only supported by the management, but also by trade unions and party organisations who are interested in making production more progressive, increasing its efficiency, making work less tedious and more intellectual, increasing the reliability of products, reducing in particular their weight (metal saving) and overall dimensions, as well as in increasing output and profits.

The common factor stimulating technological innovations is the need of the national economy, specific organisations, agencies and enterprises for new products which could be made more effectively by making use of microelectronics. And most often, therefore, the decision-making process is a combination of central and local initiatives in which the various levels of the Party organisation play a stimulating role.

For example, at the machine-tool enterprise that we studied, it was decided to introduce NC machine tools in accordance with the provisions of the socioeconomic development plan for 1981-85 (the plan is drawn up for a period of five years with yearly updating). The plant's trade union organisation favoured their early introduction, and problems connected with the introduction had been actively discussed already at workers' and trade union meetings organised at the plant from 1978 to 1980. The workers had put forward their own suggestions for improving working conditions as well as salaries in close connection with the introduction of new technology. Those suggestions were mainly of a sociopsychological nature, first of all for overcoming a certain mistrust towards new technology. The success of the introduction process to a significant degree depends not only on the trade unions' providing the workers with timely and complete information as to the forthcoming innovations, but also on their concrete actions to take into account the interests and value orientation of groups with different demographical and professional characteristics that are affected by technological change. Basic problems occur especially with regard to the organisation of work.

CNC and organisation of work

Different forms of implementation

In modern production, technology is not introduced 'in a pure form', exceptions being relatively autonomous shops and sections within the plant where microelectronic products are made on the basis of microelectronic technology, i.e. where microelectronics 'gives birth' to microelectronics. More often in numerous branches of industry, especially in machine building, microelectronics is integrated into traditional production, and becomes affected directly or indirectly by the latter. Sociological analysis makes it possible to identify not only the particular features of the content of work, the mixing of functions within 'mixed' production, but also new forms of interaction and contacts in the process of work.

In this connection let us consider two, significantly different, situations of production. First, we take the production where approximately half of the equipment is traditional, second, where NC machine tools and robots account for more than 90 per cent of the equipment.

The first type of production is characteristic of a so-called armature shop, with the NC machine tools accounting for 50 per cent of the machinery and the rest being traditional equipment with manual machining of parts. A major feature of the chosen production section is the fact that each worker services two machine tools at the same time: one being an NC machine tool, the other a common metal-cutting lathe (or a milling machine tool). Thus, at the machine tool with numerical control the worker monitors the program of making a part, the functioning of electronic equipment, and at the other, standing nearby, he machines the part manually in the traditional way.

What is the reason for such a workplace organisation and, accordingly, for the functions required from the workers? The reasons lie primarily in the demands of production. In this particular shop NC machine tools are not yet capable of machining all parts fully. The part is first machined at a common machine tool, and only after that this same part is machined at an NC machine tool.

The worker's functions make him spend 40 per cent of the time to attend to an NC machine tool, and 60 per cent to the manually controlled machine tool.

This section of production is of special interest, for it represents a kind of an intermediate link between a common universal machine tool and an NC machine tool. Here one can clearly see how different the functions of one and the same worker are when he is working on two radically different machine tools at the same time. In such 'mixed' sections the organisation of work is not different from that in traditional sections. There are no team forms of work. The worker is comparatively autonomous, and his wages are in direct proportion to his individual output. The differences exist primarily as far as control over electronic devices is concerned. A centralised service, as a rule, undertakes control and major repair functions. Minor repair work is done by the worker himself. Workers at a 'mixed' section often have contacts with specialists in electronics (engineers and technicians who are adjusters of electronic equipment).

The professional and qualification level of a worker at 'mixed' sections is significantly higher than at sections in traditional production processes. Here we have evidence of the effectiveness of the horizontal multi-valence of workers' activities making it possible for them to perform a broad range of professional operations.

The training of workers for this particular type of section is done directly at the plant. They are mainly cadre workers with large production experience (up to 20 years). There was a period when almost 90 per cent of such workers operated common universal machine tools. At present they have been working on new machinery for only two to three years. Not all of them to an equal degree have learnt how to operate NC machine tools right away. It took two to three months for 50-70 per cent of the workers to learn to do this, the rest needed up to six months. It should be underlined that not all the workers trained in traditional production managed to learn operating NC machine tools. These workers, due to their psycho-physiological qualities, had to leave for other sections and shops of the plant.

The level of physical work is very high. This is mainly due to the need to transport the parts manually from a universal machine tool to an NC machine tool. The level of mental strain is also high. The worker has to watch the functioning of two machine tools at the same time. In addition, various units of an NC machine tool require additional control. That is why the wages of workers dealing with 'mixed' types of technology are significantly higher (up to 400 rubles per month) than for workers at other sections of production.

The second major section of the production process is the shop for programmed machining of parts. Here 90 per cent of the machinery are automated machine tools that also use robot manipulators. The organisation of work, the machinery, the working conditions and the qualification of workers are all very different from those in the 'mixed' shop.

Each workplace is attended by an operator who monitors two to three NC machine tools and the robot manipulator that feeds and unloads parts to be machined. Each worker spends about 10-15 per cent of his time with physical work. The remaining time involves control over the production process. The work is organised in teams and is radically different from the organisation of work at the section with 'mixed' technology. The team includes not only workers, but also engineer-programmers, engineer-controllers, specialists in management and technicians. Work participation coefficient (WPC) indices are determined for workers, engineers and technicians on the basis of a single system. In accordance with the WPC the wages are determined depending not only on individual but also on collective contributions of workers and engineers to the overall technological cycle of production.

It is rather significant that the product of work made at the section undergoes one single technological cycle in which at one and the same time a number of NC machine tools, robot manipulators and various professional and qualification groups of workers are involved. For this section of the production the most characteristic feature is the multi-valence of engineers, technicians and workers both 'horizontally' and 'vertically'. Because of this the interrelationship of functions and that of the work of all the categories of the maintenance staff becomes most intensive.

With regard to wages, workers in type I sections are paid better (average between 300 and 400 rubles), type II workers receive between 250-350 and 200-300 rubles, depending on whether the teams include engineers and technicians (the first case) or not.

Multi-valent work

The achievement of a high level of multi-valence of work affecting the creative content and workers' interest in their job depends to a large extent on the initiative from 'below', i.e. on the part of foremen and head sections. As has been revealed by the survey done at type II sections, the variety of workers' functions both 'horizontally' and 'vertically' and the establishment of unified teams (including both workers and engineers) has not been the result of directives coming from 'above' (instructions of agencies, ministries). The initiative for creating new types of teams has come from engineers, workers, foremen and heads of section themselves with the due support from the top management echelons of the plant. This is another reflection of the increased role played by 'subjective factors' in modern production, that is to say of the initiative and creative activities of the members of work collectives in achieving optimum forms to combine the interests of the society, of the collective and of the individual in the continuous process of innovation in the production technology.

The method of 'multi-valence' of work makes it possible to significantly enrich the work of workers or make it less monotonous and consequently to broaden the traditional areas of training. In the Soviet Union the term 'multi-valence of work' is practically never used. Nor does the term 'multi-professional', which is similar in its meaning, in our opinion reflect the variety and complexity of the numerous functions of maintaining and controlling the process of production. May an NC operator, for example, who is capable of performing some simple functions of an engineer-programmer or an electronics specialist, be said to have a multiple profession, namely that of a worker-operator and an engineer-programmer? Certainly not. We are rather talking here about multi-valent training of a worker which makes it possible for him not only to match his function with the functions of the worker of another profession and qualification, but also to perform some engineer functions going well beyond the meaning of the term 'matching professions'.

At a modern enterprise there is both horizontal and vertical multi-valence. Horizontal multi-valence is characterised as the absence of precise functional responsibilities and an opportunity for the worker to quickly change his functions to fit several worker specialities. It is specially effective at sections having flexible automated production where there is a constant need for changing the type of products and correspondingly changing certain types of workers' activities. Horizontal multi-valence does not only greatly increase the flexibility of using manpower in production processes, but also stimulates the retaining of workers at an enterprise. The multi-valence effect becomes most vivid when in new technological processes use is made of mechanical and electronic devices and where repair work on the equipment is done by a comparatively small group of workers possessing a variety of skills. As a rule, in such groups (teams) absenteeism, lack of discipline and large labour turnover are all extremely rare.

Vertical multi-valence is characterised by greater responsibilities for workers (mainly operators) who perform simple functions, but who, on the other hand, have been trained to perform simple engineering as well as additional control functions. The strategy of vertical multi-valence allows the optimum mix of 'autonomous' individual responsibility and collective responsibility.

Thus, in modern production the trend towards multi-valence of work acts as a force against the de-qualifying of workers, on the one hand, and helps to increase their individual qualification and diversify their work, on the other. Multi-valence is a means of preventing insufficient workers' workload, and of making work teams respond quickly to changes in the type of products produced in small series. At the same time there is a process to remove the lines separating various professions, to expand responsibilities, to create favourable opportunities for the shifting and moving of workers within the enterprise, to consolidate non-formal production contacts, develop a positive attitude towards one's work, and increase the interest in work activities.

A generational problem?

Microelectronic technology may produce certain contradictions in work collectives. This is due to an inadequate perception of the new changes by various demographic groups of workers, especially to a 'psychological barrier' towards innovations (primarily among aged workers). Our research has demonstrated that people with insufficient educational background have an especially hard time when they are required to perform new functions. The overcoming of difficulties, therefore, depends on the careful preparation of activities preceded by economic and sociological analyses.

Our case studies do not support the conclusions of many authors that new technology like NC machine tools requires completely 'new' workers, asserting that workers who have been involved in traditional production for a long period of time would not be 'able to deal' with new requirements since they lack the needed professional skills and also bring into the work done with the use of complex-automated technology those orientations and habits that they have acquired before (Aitov 1981: 48).

There is no doubt that there exist certain obstacles and difficulties of a psychological nature when workers, especially those who have had long experience with traditional machine tools, begin to operate NC machine tools. These difficulties, though, should not be overestimated. At the sections we surveyed, 70 per cent of the workers had 5 to 20 years of experience operating the traditional equipment. Nevertheless, all of them have successfully become integrated in the production process with NC machine tools. It is obvious, though, that this has not been an automatic process. Measures had to be taken to retain and adapt the workers to radically new conditions of work, but in most cases simply new and young workers were and are employed.

New technology and qualifications

Most of the operators (up to 90 per cent) at the enterprises surveyed have general secondary education (ten grades). Up to 80 per cent of operators received vocational training directly at the enterprise, 20 per cent received training at vocational schools.

Few of the operators (approximately 15 per cent) previously worked at individual multi-purpose machines. The highly skilled workers operating multi-purpose machines are not attracted by the work of CNC operators, neither by its content, nor by its pay, since their own work is more interesting and the pay is higher. The 15 per cent of workers mentioned above who earlier worked at individual machines possess medium levels of qualification. Operators include males from 18 to 35 years of age.

The setters are specialists with secondary and higher technical education (about 30 per cent received specialised education). Their average age is higher than among operators (up to 55 years). Half of the setters formerly worked at traditional machines.

All programming engineers are specialists with high special education and, as a rule, receive additional training at remedial training courses and in special centres created to prepare specialists on new technology. The training is free with the complete preservation of wages. They are males, aged from 25 to 40.

Previous professional experience is of no importance for operators. The same may be said about programming engineers whose jobs have no equivalents in traditional production. It is different with the job experience of setters, which is retained in the new production conditions. Most of them (up to 70 per cent) worked in traditional production before, and the others are graduates of vocational schools and secondary technical schools.

The programs for CNC machines are made by engineers and programming technicians. A special group of programming engineers provide the whole enterprise with programs, including the shop surveyed. Along with it corrections and changes are introduced. Not all programs are, however, of a similar character; there are more complex and less complex ones. Operators are sometimes involved in making simple programs and correcting them. The management and trade unions stimulate operators for this work in order to increase the variety of their job and to increase their interest in the work.

The least skilled workers are the operators. Nevertheless, empirical research has demonstrated that the operator, notwithstanding the apparent simplicity of his work, may have a number of specific professional qualities. For example, a senior foreman in one of the CNC sections that we studied told us: 'A turner, being an operator, is partially a programmer and fully an adjuster. He is 100 per cent responsible for the quality of a part and its machining. He is a highly skilled worker, a graduate of a middle-level technical school. This worker is practically the only one who touches the machine tool, except when there is a serious breakdown, or when the machine tool is out of order'. This point of view reflects the situation as it exists at a given section of the plant. Circumstances in other sections and plants do not always make it possible to make use of an operator in such a way.

NC machine tools differ significantly from each other depending on the products that are made on them, and depending on the number of products in a series. In small-batch production the requirements for an operator, as to his qualification and skills, are relatively high. When NC machine tools are used in mass production the operator 'lacks' creative functions and carries out routine, monotonous operations. To this one should add prolonged periods of comparative 'idleness' when the machine is running, since interference takes place only in emergency cases. Before, the work process comprised continuous supervisory activities and interventions. After modern technology was introduced, these two became separated and supervision, or control, and the practical need for interference have become relatively independent. An engineer, or a technician who is carrying out the supervisory functions now also monitors the mode of operation of the equipment. But in contrast to the previous types of technology the machines are now controlled automatically without any assistance from man. What then about the human factor? An engineer-adjuster must interfere in the process in three cases: he must fix a broken-down machine tool; he switches the machinery on and off, and, when need arises, he changes the mode of operation of the machinery. An engineer-adjuster, who is at the same time a supervisor, must also be able to determine the symptoms of a breakdown, and what is even more important, to forecast possible deviations from the norm.

Given the fact that the majority of CNC operators actually perform rather monotonous routine work, in the Soviet Union conditions have been created to make the work of operators less monotonous, to fill the vacuum of 'comparative idleness' and, in the final analysis, to increase their interest in work. This takes the form of moving workers around the whole section, assigning them tasks beyond the immediate functions at their work place and making them perform operations that exceed their actual skills. The constantly changing production situation, the new requirements of professional training and use of workers have created an objective need to search for and develop new forms for the organisation of work.

In this connection special tasks have to be considered by trade unions and other organisations at the plant level. Such tasks have to do with the protective functions of these organisations in view of changes in the workplace, with their participation in the planning process of the introduction of modern machine tools and machinery, as well as with the timely taking into account of work-place requirements.

New forms of work organisation and the role of the trade unions

Development of team forms of work

During various periods of history technological progress has been accompanied by a search for new, improved forms of the organisation of work. The current scientific and technological revolution causes constant changes in this sphere, and the process of these changes is developing at a quicker pace than before.

132

As Soviet researchers point out (Weller and Domchello 1983: 64), for a team-type organisation of work to be established there need to be four groups of factors: technical and technological (the impossibility for a single worker to attend to the equipment and the technological process); organisational (the advisability of using the collective work of workers of one or several professions, united by common means of labour for the purpose of performing a single production task); social (the need to increase the content of work, one's satisfaction with work, the need to make work less monotonous, to increase the level of collective consciousness etc.); economical (the possibility of reducing the production cycle of the output, decreasing the labour intensiveness of the products produced by way of a more efficient use of workers' time, improved utilisation of workers, combining professions and functions etc.). We have to add to this a fifth group of factors as well, namely social and psychological (the necessity to maintain an optimum social and psychological climate within a work group, to have psychological compatibility among workers).

The practical experience of enterprises where new, progressive organisational forms of work are being introduced on a large scale demonstrates that such forms raise the productivity of labour by 5 to 10 per cent, while the losses from rejects are significantly reduced. For new team-type forms of work collective unity and collective work are significant and ever-increasing characteristic features. From the viewpoint of social psychology, an increased level of collective effort accompanied by greater co-operation within a group of workers (a team) acts as a stimulus building up a new force which is a result of many factors blending into one.

At the same time the significance of group thinking - the group's public opinion - becomes an important regulator in the assessment of the work done by each worker. It is of importance that the work, when done collectively, greatly affects production quality. Team-type forms produce additional possibilities for enriching the work with new functions, while the multi-valence of work grows and there is a sharp increase in possible interchangeability of workers with different professional skills. This in turn leads to a better relationship between independent and group activities or between individual and collective responsibility.

Remuneration on the basis of the final results of the work done (i.e. for the entire technologically complete work assigned to a team, and not for each interim operation) is a major principle of the team-type form of work. This means that incentives given to workers are aimed at having the plant produce the products it needs, rather than simply at increasing labour input measured in norms per hour. However, it is exactly here that one sees the difficulties in organising the wage scales that take into account the collective work of workers of different professions and different skills, and not only of workers, but also of engineers and technicians. This is particularly true as regards the sections equipped with modern technology where workers, technicians and engineers work in close contact and often make use of the principle of interchangeability. The problem is how to determine the personal contribution of each and every one in the common effort and how to determine the final result of people's work.

Team work in a machine-tool factory

By way of example we will summarise the formal practice for production teams and team leaders of the machine-tool factory as approved by the director after consultation with the chairman of the plant's trade union committee.

As an introduction to these rules it is pointed out that for a team to be formed it needs to be assigned a volume of work needed for the production of a finished product or a part of it (a machine unit, a complex of parts, a set for a team). The final product of the work of the team, and not the product of the individual work done by the worker, comes to be regarded as a unit for planning, assessing and for determining remuneration.

A team is established following an order by the plant's director after clearing the question with the trade unions and after the recommendation by a section chief. Workers' consent is necessary to combine them into collectives. The establishment of a new team is done on a voluntary basis.

Teams may be specialised and complex. As a rule, a specialised team comprises workers of a single profession, involved in similar technological processes. A complex team comprises workers of different professions involved in a complex of technologically different but interrelated activities covering the entire production cycle or part of it. To provide for interchangeability and broader combining of professions, workers in complex teams, in addition to the work done in performing their main profession (operation), have to master one or several other professions (or operations).

Specialised and complex teams can provide for work in one shift if all the workers within a team work in one shift, or can be of a mixed type, i.e. comprising those who work different shifts.

Piecework remuneration is used mainly, but accompanied by a system of bonuses for fulfilling and over-fulfilling quantitative and qualitative indices of the production plan (task), while taking into account the progressive character of the norms used.

In order to make the team members interested from the point of view of their wages in the common results of the work performed, remuneration is assessed on the basis of a single work order taking into account the final (collective) results of the work of the team. The distribution of the collectively-earned wages among the members of a team is done in accordance with job rating and the time that in fact was needed to perform a given task.

In the case of time wages, the distribution of the collective wages among the members of the team is done in accordance with the tariff categories assigned to the workers and the time that in fact was used to perform the work. To more fully take into account the individual contribution of every worker to the results of the collective work by the team, work participation coefficients (WPC) can be used following the decision by a team's general meeting. The minimum wages of the members of a team cannot be lower than the wages computed on the basis of their job rating index for the time needed to perform a certain task, except cases provided for by the labour legislation (non-fulfilment of the output norms, in cases of product reject, or idle time due to the fault of the worker himself).

The decision to distribute the collective wages on the basis of the work participation coefficient is taken at a general meeting of the team, and is made part of the minutes of the meeting signed by all members of the team. The general meeting also decides who is to determine the WPC - the team leader or the team's council.

Each month the acceptance by the members of the team of the actual WPC is recorded in a statement signed by each team member, by the foreman and by the trade union leader. In cases of differences of opinion concerning the application of the WPC, the question is settled at a general meeting of the members of the team, and when there is no agreement, in accordance with the labour legislation.

Special attention should be drawn to the piecework-bonus system of wages for young workers. Young workers who have been trained and have achieved a qualification category, who are graduates of vocational-technical schools, get wages on a piecework basis in accordance with the norms and tariffs that are currently in force at a plant. To contribute to a shorter period of adaptation to the conditions of the production, an additional bonus (reduced norms of the time) for a maximum of six months is established.

Each team has a leader who is an exemplary worker, a good organiser held in esteem by other members of the team. A team leader is not relieved of his functions as a worker. He has to have additional knowledge of the production technology, the organisation, norms and procedures for the remuneration of the work that are applied in the team, as well as of the product quality requirements. A team leader is appointed following the order of the plant's director and consultations with the trade unions, while the view of the team (the team's council) is also taken into account.

Additional payment to team leaders who are paid on a piecework basis and who are not relieved of their main functions is done on the following basis: for managing a team of five to ten people - they get ten per cent extra, and for managing more than ten people - 15 per cent of the wages determined on the basis of job rating and the category, while leaders working in a time payment system and managing more than five people receive ten per cent of the tariff wages.

A team leader is entitled to:

- participate in the elaboration of current and long-term plans of the team;
- give the workers of the team necessary instructions related to production which have to be carried out by them;
- submit to the management of the plant his proposals as to who should be made members of and who should be excluded from the team, taking into account also the view of the collective (the council) of the team;
- suspend work in cases when a breach of safety rules can result in a risk to workers' health or life; in such cases he has to report immediately to the foreman or to another superior;
- submit together with a trade union leader, after consultation with the collective (the council) of the team, proposals to the management of the plant concerning measures of public pressure or administrative action applied to some members of the team when they do not fulfil their responsibilities or violate the rules of internal work order.

136

When the team leader does not, or not properly, fulfil his duties, measures of public pressure and disciplinary action are taken against him in accordance with the legal norms, or he is removed from his post as the leader of the team. The latter action is done by an order issued by the plant's director with account taken of the view held by the members of the team (the team's council) and the trade union leader.

Positive and negative experiences

The experience with team forms of work organisation has so far shown a number of positive and negative features. In the machine-tool factory studied by us, participation of individual workers in management has increased and conditions have been created for job rotation (making work less monotonous) and for the necessary mutual teaching of and learning from other team members. Labour productivity and quality of work have therefore increased as well, for which especially the control of the group can be made responsible, given the fact that the team's income is largely dependent on its joint labour product.

Team members with longer work experience, and higher wages, are reluctant to include in their teams (or to join teams with) less experienced workers, because their training makes it difficult for them to achieve their normal wage levels. To cope with this problem, piecework norms for newcomers have been lowered for the first three to six months of their employment in order to compensate for the more experienced workers' loss of productive time in training the former.

Not always is the appointed team leader, or rather his behaviour and the way he assesses his team colleagues, accepted. Team members' opinions are therefore taken into account to a greater extent when nominating new team leaders. Some workers also refuse to become members of a team since they would lose by that the possibility to bargain individually with the foreman about profitable jobs and norms or about more favourable working conditions. In a team such strivings would always be at the expense of other team members and would not be possible without the interference of the team leader. Such workers and foremen undergo extensive education and the latter also receive training in social and psychological methods of leadership. There are also other reasons for workers not to be willing to enter a team, like lack of trust in a foreman or the team council and doubts with regard to the objectivity or fairness of their work assessment. Some workers also fear to go 'under' in a collective team and to be unnoticed as an individual.

The introduction of new forms of work organisation and of remuneration for work are an objective reflection of positive changes in the production as a result of scientific and technological changes. At the same time broad application of team-type forms has revealed a number of significant difficulties and contradictions in the work process, especially when modern technology is introduced. In this connection major qualitative changes in the functions of trade unions have been observed. These new functions include a greater control over the actions of the management, educational work and taking into account the organisational, social and psychological factors of the new production conditions.

About the role of trade unions

The level of activity of the trade unions was criticised considerably at the last congress of the USSR trade unions. This was connected mainly with the inability of many of them to use those substantial rights which are accorded to them by law, and also with their inability to make alternative proposals to management. Also their relation to the party has been subject to debate. The activities of the party organisation at the enterprise are determined by the role of the party in our society and are limited exclusively by moral impact. The rights of the trade union committees at the enterprises are provided by special legislative acts which regulate the legal framework of these committees in various spheres of economic law and social activity. Such rights have legal character and their implementation is provided not only by social but also by legislative methods.

The trade union organisation at the enterprise has a wide sphere of activities to cope with on the basis of legislation, like planning, the elaboration of legal acts on work and pay, implementation of these norms during employment, transfers and dismissals, organisation of socialist emulation etc. In practice, however, the party organisations deal with these problems. Intrusion of the party into the work of trade unions and other social organisations takes place, mixing up functions and leading to unnecessary repetitions, which is definitely beyond the normal practice of party work.

Under conditions of technological innovations the trade unions are therefore confronted with a number of problems:

- the renewal of traditional trade union functions in work collectives which reveal a weak organisation of the socialist emulation system;
- the strengthening of the trade union impact upon the economic activity of the enterprises through a reconstruction of their organisation, as well as of the forms and content of production;
- the development of new forms of work stimulation;
- the development of effective methods of trade union participation in designing new technology, taking into account not only technological, but also psycho-physiological conditions, connected with the optimisation of physical and mental loads for workers.

Note

1. Figures are taken from Economic Co-operation of CMEA Member States (1983), no. 6, pp. 27-28.

References

Aitov, N.A. (1981) *Sovetski rabotchii* (The Soviet Worker), Moscow

Economicheskoje sortudnitchestvo stran-chlenov SEV (Economic Co-operation of CMEA Member States) (1983), no. 6

Volostnikh, V. (1985) 'Skolko rabotchich mest nujno' (How Many Work Places are Needed), *Pravda*, 4 May 1985

Weller, M.V. and A.D. Domchello (1983) *Brigadnaja organizatzija raboti* (Team-type of Work), Moscow

6

The Taming of New Technology. A Polish Case Study on the Introduction of a Flexible Manufacturing System

Jolanta Kulpinska and Slawomir Skalmierski

Introduction

The research for this study was carried out in 1983, when in Poland the Martial Law that had been introduced in December 1981 was suspended. This had created a situation of general uncertainty, aggravated even more by a worsened economic situation. The Polish economy was in a deep crisis, which affected also the programme of economic modernisation that had been formulated in the 1970s. The Gross National Product, for example, had decreased in 1981 by 12 per cent as compared with the previous year, during which the level was already lower than in 1978. In 1985, not even the 1980 level was reached.[1]

Characteristic of the crisis was, however, that despite the obviously lowered tempo of production and the considerably decreased production output, enterprises still worked continuously and also employment was kept at the level it had reached before the crisis. There was only a slight decrease in overall employment of 2.5 per cent, which was basically due to the situation in the building industry and especially to the freezing of many capital investment projects. Investments in industry in 1982-83 were about 50 per cent lower than in 1978. As a result, industry was undergoing increasing decapitalisation.[2] The permanent deficit of resources, which is as such a structural characteristic of socialist economies, increased even more. In this situation, central government agencies obviously were able to strengthen their position through the distribution of scarce resources, despite the intentions of reform of economic management.

The economic crisis was accompanied by a crisis of many social institutions. Trade unions and workers' councils in the enterprises were suspended and were not able to exert any relevant influence. Their reconstruction only started in 1983 and this is one reason why we cannot say much about their role in the introduction of the new technology that we have studied.

At the same time the system of economic management underwent fundamental changes. Before 1982 it was based on central planning and administrative methods of central management. From 1983, an economic reform was launched, based on concepts elaborated already in 1981. The reform introduced three new principles for the functioning of enterprises: autonomy from central administration, self-financing and self-management. Unsatisfactory as it still may be, the reform has no doubt changed the conditions under which enterprises have to function.

Until 1983 the main goal and criterion of evaluation of enterprise management was maximisation of the production volume in accordance with a production plan negotiated with the Economic Centre (i.e. branch ministries, the Commission of Planning, the Central Committee of the Party etc.). Since 1983 production plans have been made at the enterprise level although there are persistent external pressures and there remains a need for material and financial support from the Centre.

Implementation of the production plan was previously a criterion for the evaluation of enterprise performance. It determined whether the enterprise could apply for a bigger wage fund (fixed centrally), obtain resources for investments from the state budget, and secure a positive appraisal of the management followed by appropriate premiums. Other items of enterprise performance, especially production quality and costs, were subordinated to such quantitative criteria. Quality of production was considered important only in those enterprises which produced for export markets, and thus, above all, in the capital goods sector.

Enterprises producing consumer goods, facing conditions of severe market disequilibrium (a seller's market) have never been interested in export, at least not in export on a large scale. The lack of price competition in the domestic market, and particularly the situation of unsatisfied demand, allows these enterprises to sell their entire output at home without paying attention to product quality. Moreover, export, which promotes higher quality, is only possible if one can ensure the import of indispensable components and tools.

The economic reform has changed the conditions in which enterprises are functioning in many respects. The two, frequently irreconcilable, goals which they face at present have also become the criteria for their evaluation:

- profit assessment, which includes the volume of financial resources for replacement, modernisation and development of capital assets;
- the value of net sold production (including the enterprise's own input of labour) which, in turn, determines the obtainable wage fund.[3]

As a result, the enterprise must choose between survival (replacement of capital assets), i.e. an orientation on profit, and day-to-day functioning, i.e. an orientation on production volume. With a low profit it is possible to achieve a high production value, and thereby an increase in the wage fund. The reverse situation is not possible. This situation has distorted considerably management's attitudes towards the use of technology. It should be emphasised that plan implementation is still the basic principle at the lower organisational levels of the enterprise (departments and sections) and still functions as a criterion for the evaluation of performance of both management and lower-level supervisors.

Clearly these methods of management do not promote technological progress. Before, enterprises were not interested in it, unless it was related to export. New machines could be acquired only for new investment projects, frequently through a licence purchase or through large-scale national projects into which the enterprise was incorporated. Sometimes also personal interests and ambitions of engineers and experts played a role.

The economic crisis and the economic mechanisms described above were especially effective in delaying the advancement of microelectronic technology. Specialists estimate the lag to be more than a dozen years. In 1983 the government made decisions aimed at improving this situation but their implementation has been obstructed by the general state of the economy and especially by problems of importing tools and other production components. Planning of technological advancement and modernisation was not a topic for enterprises in 1983. Nor was it discussed by the workers' councils. Attitudes of management towards technology are not only shaped by the macroeconomic conditions under which they have to run their enterprises. There are also more immediate factors, equally structural in character, that exert an influence. While the general conditions of the economy are not very supportive for technological innovation, these other factors explain why management is nevertheless in favour of introducing technology, if only in a very specific way. Two factors are of special importance here. First of all the situation on the labour market - which is characterised by a permanent labour deficit inducing enterprises to employ workers without applying any more demanding criteria of selection, and forcing enterprises to subordinate to individual strategies adopted by workers; and secondly the character of the organisation of work.

In the Polish industry, the Taylorist model of work organisation predominates, with numerous departures from it in the sphere of work discipline and the degree to which production behaviour is controlled. This situation is forced by the already mentioned characteristics of the labour market, the concentration of supervisors' attention on the solution of continuous production problems, and by the lack of awareness about organisational alternatives. It is typical of Polish enterprises not to employ specialists in business organisation and management and not to use their services either. Managerial cadres are dominated by engineers, who are oriented to technical problems of production and who do not possess any special qualifications in the area of production organisation and management. A basic element of their professional ideology is fascination with technology which they regard as the only remedy for production problems which are in reality mainly due to characteristics of the work system and, thus, the nature of work organisation (ways of task allocation, control and discipline of work). Another element of this ideology is a desire to promote technical progress by any means as an auto-telic value. In the past, this orientation was strengthened by investments being financed from the state budget, and thus by a smaller significance of the economic calculus of the enterprise.

The type of work organisation as well as attitudes and behaviour of management exert a major influence on workers' production behaviour. The fact that the evaluation of workers' behaviour is based on quantitative criteria and the application of piece-rate systems makes the workers strive for maximum production volumes at the cost of quality, the technical state of machines and tools etc.

All these factors in turn strengthen the orientation of management towards the promotion of new technology. A low level of mechanisation of production makes success of production dependent on workers' behaviour, while management is either unable or unwilling to channel this behaviour in a desirable direction by organisational means.

In management's opinion, the only way to eliminate production problems is to promote mechanisation and automation of production. It should be stressed here that in the Polish conditions automation is not a means of direct labour substitution (costs of direct labour are relatively low) but, first of all, an instrument allowing management to channel workers' behaviour to those areas which are strategically important for the success of the production process. New technology is seen first to reduce workers' influence on production volume and quality, and thereby to solve all problems.

This strategy resembles in its content the strategies applied by capitalist entrepreneurs although it derives from different prerequisites and determinants. The economic reform has not changed the orientation towards technology but has restricted only the material possibilities of its introduction. Difficulties encountered in obtaining resources for modernisation accompanied by the existing pressure to push up wages by any means have made enterprises face a production dilemma, while intensification of modernisation processes has declined (not to mention the obvious negative impact of the present economic crisis).

Description of the enterprise studied

The flexible manufacturing system that we have studied is located in an enterprise constituting the production centre of a large industrial combine producing heavy building machines.[4]

The enterprise, which employs about 20,000 workers today, was established in an agricultural region in the late 1930s. Industrialisation and urbanisation processes led to the formation of several urban centres there, where mainly heavy, engineering and chemical industries were located.

The co-existence of several major industrial centres meant that qualified labour resources were quickly exhausted on the local labour market. The present supply of labour on the local market accounts for 30 to 50 per cent of the existing demand, which for the most part is unqualified labour with a large share of women.

144

The main source of qualified labour supply for the enterprise is the system of factory schools training qualified workers (the so-called basic vocational schools) and secondary technical schools. Competitive wages offered by other enterprises are the reason why only some of the graduates undertake their work in the enterprise. Consequently, the deficit of workers employed directly in production amounts to about five per cent, which is accompanied by a declining level of employment in this category of workers. Constant shortage of labour also causes competition among particular organisational units within the enterprise striving to ensure better labour supply.

As regards its products, the enterprise is a monopolist in the domestic market, and it also has specialised production within the framework of the Council for Mutual Economic Assistance (CMEA). Most of its output is exported. Its main importers are the Soviet Union, followed by West European countries purchasing its products in smaller quantities, other socialist countries and the Third World.

The economic situation of the enterprise is quite complex. Long-term trade agreements with the Soviet Union guarantee regular sales of a big part of its production although the early 1980s witnessed mounting difficulties in the production and export of machines. The enterprise enjoyed its greatest economic prosperity in the second half of the 1970s, largely due to an agreement on co-operation and export concluded with a US concern, which paved the way for a considerable growth of its export to the USA and Canada and intensive modernisation of its capital stock.

The crisis of 1980 and thereafter created numerous difficulties in production, which were, to a large extent, the result of growing difficulties in securing the indispensable industrial supplies, as well as tensions in co-operative ties. The economic sanctions imposed by the US administration in 1982 blocked the enterprise's export to the USA and made it necessary to search for new outlets.

The enterprise consists of two main parts, i.e. a metallurgical factory dealing with steel-making and plastic working of high-grade steel, and an engineering factory, where metallurgical semi-finished products are processed into sub-assemblies of building and other types of machines.

The engineering factory is divided into smaller production units - plants - manufacturing a specific range of products and sub-assemblies. The FMS can be found in the gearbox plant, where gearboxes are made and assembled.

Introduction of the FMS as an element of the enterprise's production strategy

The analysis of innovation and modernisation processes in the enterprise indicates that most technological efforts are concentrated in the engineering factory, in which the final product is manufactured, while the production process in the metallurgical factory is based on obsolete technologies and worn-out machines and equipment which can hardly ensure an appropriate quality.

Investment outlays in the engineering factory were directed to the gearbox plant, with most of them being allocated to the modernisation of machining processes. Such a trend of modernisation adopted by the enterprise management was prompted by the establishment of close industrial co-operation with the Soviet Union - the plant became the main supplier of gearboxes for heavy building machines exported to the Soviet Union and other socialist countries.

The first sign of modernisation was the installation of NC machine tools in 1979, which were among the first installed in Poland. Their number rose so significantly in the following years that at present the plant can boast the highest concentration of such machines in Poland. At the same time, automated machining centres were installed.

The primary goal of the plant management in its investment policy was expanding the production potential. It should be noted here that automation as a costly substitute for direct labour is very seldom met in Poland due to relatively cheap labour. Secondly, a reorientation in the investment policy aimed at improving production quality was forced, above all, by the export to the USA, which is a market known for its high requirements and keen competition. New production techniques were expected to promote the achievement of these basic goals (improved quality and increased quantity of manufactured products) in two ways:

- by replacing morally and technically used-up machines and equipment which were of strategic significance for the success of the production process;
- by channelling workers' productive behaviour. New technologies (NC, CNC, DNC), characterised by a higher degree of steering autonomy, were providing management with the possibility of freeing themselves from the impact of insufficient workers' qualifications and from the lack of motivation for

146

good quality of work, and offered a chance to eliminate short-comings in the production process organisation through auto-mation.

The decision about purchasing and installing the FMS crowned the implemented strategy of modernisation. Enhanced production and export prospects revealed that the line producing gearwheels became a bottleneck in the production of gearboxes both quantita-tively and qualitatively. The heterogeneity of machines and equipment on this line, their poor technical state and simplified technologies made it impossible to attain the main production goals here. The situation could be improved by the introduction of a new production system based on utilisation of the FMS.

The designer and producer of the FMS was a machine tool combine in the German Democratic Republic. The decision about purchasing the FMS was taken by the Director of the Polish com-bine in 1975 and work on its designing lasted till 1979. The system was put on stream in 1982, and a year later, i.e. in 1983, the FMS was put into operation.[5]

The analysis of information collected mainly from experts and representatives of different levels of management indicates that the FMS was to play a very specific role in the process of production. It should be noted here that the basic aim and simultaneously a criterion of rationalisation in Polish enterprises (including the one under study) till the end of the 1970s was the implementation of production plans (in their quantitative dimension, and more sel-dom in their qualitative dimension). Due to the overpowering role played by the plan, all other values were subordinated to its im-plementation, including economic rationality at the enterprise and shopfloor level.

In addition, it is important to note that a characteristic feature of Polish management cadres in industry at all levels (including the enterprise under survey) is a vast predominance of engineers. Managers with a technical educational background, without any professional training in the field of production organisation and management, tend to treat technology as the only or perhaps the best means of achieving the enterprise's production goals. It could be generally said that the technical educational background of en-gineers accompanied by their managerial activity in the production sphere makes them overlook or fail to notice non-technical methods of achieving goals. The implementation of such a production strategy is also facilitated by the domination of the

147

earlier mentioned criterion of rationality. Economic calculus or costs of investments are a matter of secondary importance as long as resources are available for their realisation.

This way of thinking and the resulting mode of activity became very clear in the course of our talks and interviews. The managers - engineers of different levels - when speaking about the main advantages of the FMS would point, first of all, at the possibilities it created of excluding workers' influence on the quality of products during the performance of such actions as clamping and removing details from the machine (owing to the application of manipulators and a system of mechanised transport between work posts). In conventional production, after its removal from a machine tool, a gearwheel is dropped into a container by the worker. Carelessness with which this simple operation is performed quite often causes the teeth of gearwheels to be damaged, since they have not yet been submitted to the thermohardening procedure, which prevents further machining. Quite obviously, this problem could also be eliminated by the application of purely organisational measures (such as control of product quality between work posts, exacting higher discipline of behaviour etc.).

At this point, it is worth quoting arguments provided by those who opposed the introduction of the Flexible Manufacturing System. They claimed that a similar level of production quality and quantity could have been obtained through the installation of NC machine tools (FMS is an equivalent of about 150 machines of this type), strict observance of technological regime etc.

Technical-productive characteristics of the FMS

The FMS constitutes one of several production units, which jointly form the department of gearwheels (one out of many different departments in the gearbox plant).

The attitude of the department management to the system resembles its attitude to other units and reflects the role played by a given unit in the implementation of production plans.

The difficulties encountered in attaining the planned production capacity did not create a favourable atmosphere around the FMS, which, consequently, did not receive any broad support from management either. Its instrumental attitude towards the FMS was further strengthened by various problems faced by the plant and the enterprise at the time of the economic crisis. Production difficulties on conventional production lines diverted management's attention from internal problems of the system.

The FMS described by us does not differ from similar solutions in other countries as regards its functional technical parameters. It is composed of three main components:

1. Entrance and exit subsystem together with a high-capacity store.
2. Production line with a toolroom.
3. Computerised central steering system.

Entrance to the system and machine tools located along the production line is linked by an internal transport network (pallets steered by means of an induction loop). The system differs from other typical solutions by its lower level of mechanisation of machine tools. Turning is done on CNC machine tools, operations of milling, gear shaving and drawing are performed on automatic machine tools (steered by limit switches), which are specially designed for machining gearwheels with specific parameters. The type of machine does not create any impediment to obtaining the desirable production elasticity.

The major technical drawback of the system is the fact that it is not equipped with a heat treatment station - an indispensable element of production technology - which makes it necessary to use services provided by the heat treatment unit for the entire department. This undermines the autonomy of the system since its operations are dependent on the stage of production advancement in the entire department.

Each machine (apart from a few CNC lathes) is equipped with a hydraulic manipulator feeding and removing parts from the machine, and with a transport pallet. In the designed version, the role of each operator in the FMS is limited to preparing semi-finished manufactures (forgings), feeding them into the system by means of transport pallets, transmitting proper information and orders for computers, and controlling the work of machine tools.

Organisational structure and mode of the system's functioning

The organisational structure of the FMS as designed by the producer is a replica of a traditional production process organisation characterised by a strict hierarchical structure and a high division of labour. The line structure of the organisation consists of the manager, two senior foremen, each of whom co-ordinates the work of three production subsystems (distinguished with regard to the type of machines, for instance a subsystem of lathes, one of grinding machines etc.), six foremen supervising particular production subsystems, and machine-tool operators (in our description, we are omitting the entrance and toolroom workers).

Supervisors are for the most part mechanical engineers, graduates of extra-mural academic courses, with professional experience typical for conventional machining.

The headquarters of the organisation are staffed by dispatchers and process engineers (the latter delegated from the department or plant technological offices). The dispatchers are electronics engineers. Such an educational profile is a result of the conviction born in the course of designing and constructing the system that a high level of electronics incorporated into production processes calls for employment of exactly these specialists. As a result, dispatchers supervising and operating the computer steering system do not possess sufficient qualifications in the field of Electronic Data Processing and, moreover, they do not have sufficient knowledge about machining technology.

Consequently, this type of qualification hampers effective decision-making in unexpected situations (break-downs, necessity of changing a technology etc.), which makes it necessary to seek the assistance of process engineers, and eliminates any possibility of introducing major changes in the standard software of the system's steering processes.

The practical functioning of the FMS depends on the relationships between the type of applied technique and technology and non-technical determinants of work process realisation. Foremost among them are those between the system and its environment finding their expression in different logics of activity, specific characteristics of work within the system and levels of personnel qualification (both of supervisors and workers). Due to these factors deviations from the designed system functioning become necessary and moreover the achievement of planned production capacities is hampered. It should be noted here that the goal which has been unquestionably achieved (regardless of the production and social costs of the project discussed later) is an incomparably higher quality of production than in the case of conventional machining.

The primary goal and evaluation criterion of the FMS functioning is and remains the fulfilment of production plans. Their effective execution is hampered mainly by numerous shortcomings in the co-operation with the metallurgical factory (supplier of the semi-finished products - forgings). The production of the latter is characterised by irregularity of supplies, as well as negligence of assortment and qualitative plans of production. On the other hand, the most important advantage of the FMS is its ability to adjust its production profile promptly to changing requirements, with maximum utilisation of productive capacities (in the nominal work time). Both these goals can be achieved only provided the appropriate inflow of information to the steering-optimising system of the FMS is ensured. In the system under survey the storage capacity of the available computers restricts the planning-optimising horizon to two days of machine operation. Due to delays in deliveries of semi-finished products, accompanied by the pressure to execute plans, delayed deliveries are introduced to the system at once, irrespective of the system duty planned by the computer and its production profile (technology form) at a given moment. Any change in production assortment (even though it may concern only one item) calls for changes in the entire production process as it involves the role of machines and their tooling and, thus, the technological program. Time-consuming operations of withdrawing series under machining and retooling machines follow, which result in inevitable stoppages of some groups of machines or whole subsystems.

Shut-downs in the operation of the system are further prolonged by time-consuming operations of the computers. The optimising computer needs about two to three hours to analyse a situation, which causes delays in decisions about changes in the utilisation of particular machines. Another factor hampering production according to plans is the existence of so-called production priorities - a change in customers' orders creates a necessity of passing for machining other types of parts than those planned and gives rise to the technological and production problems already described. Thus, it should be underlined at this point that it is also the computer steering system which is responsible for difficulties in making adjustments to changing situations in production as it does not have sufficient decision flexibility (small operational memory).

In turn, helplessness of the automatic computerised system of work and production steering makes it necessary to involve line supervisors in the goal achievement process. Foremen and managers enter the decision process in the so-called 'manual' steering of the system. Such 'manual' steering of production consists in excluding the EPD system from its functions of steering the work of certain subsystems and in determining directly their production tasks. This is done either through direct management of production series by the dispatcher or through switching production from the conventional line onto idle machines, utilising manual transport and without making use of the manipulators (directly manual work). In the second case, it often happens that the dispatcher is not informed about a new load of machines, which causes further disturbances in the work of the central steering system. Exclusion of the dispatch centre and introduction of production from outside the FMS point also at the desire of attaining partial rationality and involving all the available machines. The foremen, who are responsible for keeping in constant operation all subsystems managed by them and are evaluated on this basis by the system's manager, often do not pay any attention to the future utilisation of machines as planned by the computer. Accordingly, it can be said that although goals of supervision and the central steering system are convergent, the ways in which they are being accomplished may be quite different.

The weak position of the computerised information system and of the dispatchers as its spokesmen is further undermined by unsatisfactory communication structures within and outside the system. Dispatchers are cut off from direct information coming from outside, and especially as regards information about production plans and envisaged changes. This is due to the fact that direct contact with planning units of the department and the plant is maintained by the manager and foremen, who pass on information already transformed into decisive decisions. The organisational structure of the FMS together with technical capacities of signalling-monitoring equipment account for the fact that dispatchers do not have at their disposal valuable information concerning the production process - information which is coming from the 'shopfloor'.

In unpredicted situations, workers do not contact dispatchers, because only foremen are allowed to evaluate the situation and take decisions. Simultaneously, due to the nature of their qualifications dispatchers are often unable to take appropriate decisions. In such a situation, all information and signals about the technical state of the system are sent to dispatchers by the foremen. At the same time, dispatchers are not valuable partners for the management of the system and department concerning basic information such as production volume, because they are cut off from the quality control section, which ultimately determines the volume of production. Hence, management do not maintain contacts with dispatchers either.

Another factor strengthening the position of line supervision and weakening the role of dispatchers is the specific nature of technological and co-operative ties with the environment, and especially the necessity of performing wheel-hardening operations outside the system in the thermal treatment unit working for the entire department.

Production priorities in the FMS and on conventional production lines inevitably lead to conflicts about priorities in thermal treatment operations. The department manager does not interfere in bargaining between the conventional machining and the FMS and, consequently, the result of negotiations depends on the position held by the system's representative, his personal characteristics, and primarily on his ability to enter into direct and personal interactions with representatives of the thermal treatment unit.

The dispatcher, placed within the headquarters of the system and spatially isolated from his environment, charged with the supervision of the steering system and deprived of good communication ties, is not the best partner for negotiations here. Hence, all such negotiations are conducted either by foremen or by the system manager.

The above examples indicate that full autonomy of the information system (independence of the line structure) and a high level of optimisation of the FMS work can be attained only with undisturbed and well-organised production. In unpredicted situations it becomes necessary to activate traditional organisational structures.

Any suggestion that dispatchers should be equipped with decision-making competences (which could be accompanied by liquidation of the foreman's role) can hardly be accepted due to the specific profile and level of professional qualifications of dispatchers and machine operators. The dispatcher should in that case be able to determine remotely and remove any work disturbances using the information system and verbal communication. This would only be possible if operators had comprehensive knowledge and appropriate skills and were able to define a changing situation precisely. With the dispatchers'

153

qualifications being inadequate for existing needs and the insufficient professional preparation of operators, a person equipped with proper technical knowledge, able to decide when it is necessary to switch off a machine and call in a repair unit, or able to decide about the substitution of machines and possible technological changes, is required for the shopfloor.

The line structure, for functional reasons, aids, replaces or doubles the computerised management system. Meanwhile, qualifications of representatives of this structure, i.e. foremen, are often insufficient, which frequently necessitates calling in process engineers and extends in this way the duration of shut-downs and delays in work. All this means that the production management system is surrounded by a network of various feedbacks and reinforcements, which are functional in relation to the goals of the system but disfunctional as regards the utilisation of its potential productive capacities. The existence of the line structure, taking into account the present technique and technology, the extent to which it has been mastered (at the time of our studies the system was in the first months of its planned exploitation), and its incorporation into the wider organisational framework, is an inseparable element of the system's functioning. The line structure, due to its different ways of attaining identical goals to those of the computerised information structure, is an impediment to the achievement of a high level of system utilisation. Thus, we have here an example of a case in which the traditional structure of labour division and management has been combined to make one whole with the organisational structure which is required by the technical system based on management without human participation (computerised information system).

The functional significance of the line structure, due to the existing and invariable characteristics of the environment, may be weakened only by the development of the dispatchers' and operators' qualifications and by improved organisational knowledge of the system's management.

Professional characteristics of FMS machine operators

The machine-tool operators in the FMS are young persons, which is a characteristic feature also of other categories of operators. Their average age is 27.1 years (NC-machine operators: 27.6, operators of conventional machine tools: 28.9 years); 77 per cent of all operators are under 29 years of age.

The analysis of their level and structure of education reveals several interesting facts. Taking into account the formal school background, the operators in the FMS are characterised by the highest level of education, and one can in fact generally observe a linear correlation between the level of mechanisation and the level of qualifications. This is illustrated by Table 6.1.

Table 6.1: Educational Level and Level of Mechanisation (in per cent) N = 216

Operators	Education completed		
	Elementary	Basic vocational	Secondary
Conventional	33	53	1
NC	13	59	28
FMS	7	34	59
Total	21	51	28

The basic factor determining this trend is a phenomenon commonly observed in the socialist countries of 'automatically' attributing qualification requirements to the level of automation, which is being done on the basis of the conviction (not based on empirical proofs) that a higher technical complexity of machines and equipment, irrespective of how complex their operation is, calls for higher school qualifications of workers. Participation of persons with a differentiated level of education in production based on the same level of technology shows that in practice there is no explicit criterion according to which complexity of tasks is evaluated. In fact, the search for principles underlying the employment policy pursued by the plant has provided information which largely undermines the cognitive value of the data presented in Table 6.1.

According to the original assumptions, the operators of machine tools employed within the FMS should have a secondary-school background and an appropriate length of work experience as operators of machine tools. The analysis of qualification requirements of the machines under study (excluding here the freely programmed NC machine tools) shows that the degree of complexity in operating them is similar to, or lower than, that of NC machine tools. The only more difficult element of work is the tooling and setting of machines (the machine setter's function has been eliminated in the system). As a result, the respondents have 'an excess' of school knowledge (formal qualifications). The analysis of professional experience of the operators and of the plant's selection policy performed at the same time indicates that the workers recruited for the FMS did not possess any adequate professional experience (length of service) and the only criterion taken into consideration was the level of school education.

Equally inconsistent proved to be the system of training operators for their work in the FMS. Only a part of all operators - the so-called pilot group (i.e. workers who began their work in the system at the time when it was being built or put on stream) - obtained thorough training including on-the-job training. Those employed later, who were recruited through negotiations between the system management and other units, were getting acquainted with their new tasks guided by their more experienced colleagues. Due to the labour turnover among the well-trained operators they accounted for barely 11 per cent of all FMS personnel at the moment normal production was commenced.

A more general conclusion which could be made here is that in the course of time, with a relatively stable structure of employees' formal qualifications, the level of actual skills required for operating the machines in the FMS tended to decline, while the number of those who were learning their new tasks was growing. This is well illustrated by the fact that 42 per cent of the respondents had no more than seven months' service and 74 per cent did not work longer than one year. It could be added that the profile and level of employees' qualifications were influenced by the employment policy and by external determinants (fluctuations). The mechanism and consequences of such a policy are shown in Table 6.2.

Thus, we can observe a paradoxical phenomenon: workers not possessing appropriate qualifications for existing needs contribute significantly to improving the general educational level and structure of the labour force.

This example may be a warning against uncritical definition of trends of changes in education accompanying changes in levels of automation. A similar phenomenon was also observed at lower levels of automation in the case of machining treatment.

The above observations allow us to state that in this enterprise a higher level of automation is accompanied by a greater diversification of qualification structures expressed by a diversification of qualification potentials of individual workers with relatively high formal qualifications. The absence of or deficiencies in a purposeful strategy of direct labour utilisation in the enterprise is caused by the occurrence of phenomena typical of Polish enterprises, i.e. a low share of human labour costs in total costs of production together with the concentration of management's attention on the execution of current production plans.

Table 6.2: Recruitment of FMS Operators and Level of Formal Qualifications (in per cent) N = 44

Character of professional experience	Educational background		
	Elementary	Basic vocational	Secondary
first job in life	0	11	89
shift from operating conventional and NC machines	12	46	42
shift from manual and clerical work	0	27	73
Total	7	34	59

If the structure of the personnel's qualifications does not affect the level of labour costs and if, simultaneously, priority in the production process is given to quantitative rather than qualitative criteria (plan execution), then the enterprise can hardly be interested in pursuing a rational labour utilisation policy based on an employment policy which is responding to clearly specified needs and requirements. This would call for the existence of a labour market to strengthen the operation of the mechanisms described above. However, due to a continuous labour deficit, generating competition for labour among the management of particular units and departments, qualitative characteristics of labour and its proper utilisation are no longer major considerations when production plans must be implemented.

The actual shortage of knowledge and qualifications of the FMS operators was also confirmed by interviews with the system management and by the results of a questionnaire distributed among the operators. It is interesting to note that, according to the interviews, the degree of difficulties encountered in the course of carrying out production tasks was strongly and positively correlated with the employees' formal educational level: the higher the level of formal qualifications, the greater the incidence of difficulties in the execution of tasks. This testifies to the significance of empirical knowledge and practical professional experience also at higher levels of automation.

Factors determining the FMS operators' behaviour

The technical-organisational determinants of the system's functioning discussed earlier, the strategies of management and dispatchers on the one hand, the operators' interests and the character of their qualifications on the other hand, largely determine the directions and constraints in the machine operators' behaviour in the production process.

When analysing the impact of these factors on workers' behaviour, the main emphasis was laid on two categories of operators:

- operators of CNC machine tools installed within the system and interconnected by a network of manipulators and mechanised transport;
- operators of CNC machine tools installed on the area of the FMS and working for it but isolated from the central steering and transport system and not equipped with manipulators.

Thus, both types of machine tools differ in the way in which their work is connected with the work of the entire FMS (degree of autonomy), and in their technical characteristics. The former belong to an older generation of machine tools whose system of steering resembles that of DNC machine tools. A microcomputer which is spatially isolated from these machines (located in the dispatch office and operated by a programmer-dispatcher) steers here the work of four machines. Thus, there are no technical possibilities for shopfloor programming, which are in contrast available in the second type of CNC machine tools.

The analysis of main strategies and behaviour of the operators of both types of machines points to a number of differences.

In the case of the operators of CNC machines located directly in the system, the technical parameters of the machines make the work situation, especially the so-called 'decision-making space' of the workers, similar to the situation of NC or CNC operators who have no right to write or optimise programs. The fact that these machines are included in the central steering and transport system restricts further their autonomy depriving them of any possibility to decide the time of starting work, the pace of work etc.

Lack of any technical possibility to influence work in an active way and the applied wage system (daily task rate) place operators who are interested in modifying the work of their machines in a very specific position. It should be underlined here that any program modifications can be carried out only in co-operation with a process engineer or a programmer-dispatcher. Propositions of changes coming from the workers are, moreover, not oriented at increasing labour productivity (as would be, for example, the case with operators employed in a piece-work system) but at the reduction of work load, which may increase as a result of errors or drawbacks in machining programs prepared by programmers. A well-written program eliminates the necessity of introducing frequent adjustments to a machine, provides a guarantee of good quality and, consequently, reduces the concentration requirement, frequency of control etc., and generally diminishes mental and intellectual strain.

A factor which does shape the operators' possibilities in this field is the type and level of their qualifications. They must be able to make a diagnosis of a situation and, especially, present concrete propositions of change. The heterogeneity of the level of qualifications of the CNC operators (real and not formal) deprive some of them permanently of any chance to alter their work process (professional experience must correspond here with knowledge of the principles of programming and steering these machines). Clearly this refers mainly to those operators who did not get on-the-job training in operating the machines.

A different work situation and a different direction of activities can be observed in the case of the operators of CNC machine tools, which can be programmed on the spot. These machine tools were installed in the FMS at a later stage, and they are incorporated in the production process in a conventional way. Utilisation of technical possibilities of self-regulation in the work process is also here primarily a function of the operator's skills, his superiors' competences, and the degree to which they supervise and control the production process. A worker may program his machine on his own account to ensure an optimisation of the program which would minimise his interventions in the passive part of the work process (machining of details). The task and time content of the program are not so important for him, because by programming by himself he also determines the technological time for himself and, thus, the volume of his daily tasks.

An even more interesting situation occurs when a process engineer deals with the programming of a machine. While getting a finished program, a worker is interested in how many interventions will be necessary in the course of machining details and, above all, in how much time machining takes.

Accordingly, when optimising the program and having in view his own interest, he often introduces major changes to the program, which may very well be detrimental to tools or to the machine itself. A program adjusted in this way or written by a worker is called by workers 'a private' program. Such possibilities of modification ensue from the insufficient knowledge and skills of process engineers in the field of writing programs (they are only acquiring this knowledge and skills), and from an equal lack of familiarity with the machines typical for 'non-workers'.

The present state of knowledge and qualifications of process engineers (programmers) and operators justifies the postulate that they should be co-operating in creating and optimising programs, but this solution at present seems to be irreconcilable with the rationality of the operators. For the latter the main aim for program modifications is a desire to 'save' working time. The shortening of machining time does not lead to production growth - all time reserves are hidden by the worker from his superiors and used for rest, talks with colleagues, abandoning the machine and so on. This allows him to regulate and reduce the work load. As one of the CNC operators put it, 'We do not want to heave up labour productivity, all we want is less strain and less running'.

The above remark explains why co-operation between the operator and the process engineer in the process of programming is not advantageous for the former. It would force him to reveal the real capacities of his machine and his own stock of knowledge, reducing, consequently, the range of freedom for his own autonomous activities. A paradoxical phenomenon can be observed here, namely that it is more advantageous for the worker when the programming function is taken over by the process engineer than if he were to program the machine himself. This is so because the process engineer signs with his name the technological time encoded in the program, while the same done by the worker might arouse the suspicions or distrust of his superiors. Hence, no wonder that one of the operators had to say about CNC machine tools, 'I have been dreaming about such a machine all my life'.

Meanwhile, the present system of wages does not provide an inducement for workers to increase production. Their wages and premiums are dependent on the production performance of the entire system. One of the operators put it in the following way, 'If I were to increase production by 100 per cent every day, all I could expect was a pat on the shoulder from my manager or foreman'.

This relatively big freedom in the way in which tasks are being accomplished is largely due both to the incompetence of the supervisory staff, who do not know much about production capacities of the machines, and to a more general situation in the sphere of production and organisation. The fact that managers and foremen must concentrate their attention on problems connected with current production brings about the situation that the group of CNC machine tools only receives marginal interest from the supervisors. It is, however, planned that the organisational situation of CNC machine tools will be an object of proper decisions and more stable solutions in the future. This refers also to such questions as productivity norms for these machines. For the time being, an ambivalent attitude of management to these problems is still favourable for the workers. The persons who are competent in terms of control of production behaviour of the CNC operators, i.e. the process engineers, are not interested in such activities, because the range of their duties does not include their aid and co-operation in programming these machines.

The supervisors who are certainly aware that machining programs are modified by the operators are at the same time unable (being unfamiliar with the machines) and also unwilling to make use of this knowledge. The system management - in their continuous struggle to win workers - are forced to maintain a good atmosphere in the workplace and see to it that the workers are well paid (even though that may be at the cost of labour productivity). We can observe here the phenomenon of a subordinate's discretionary power, because at any moment he may find another similar or better paid job with another employer. The workers, however, are also interested in preserving a consensus with management, which is mainly reflected in a very high quality of production. The CNC operators conceal their real skills and capacities, they do their best to prevent the training of new persons, trying not to expand the circle of those 'initiated'. And since newly recruited operators do not complete machine programming courses, they can only perform machine supervision and correction tasks, which puts them in a worse work situation.

The example of the autonomy and strategy of CNC operators discussed here points at the inter-crossing of technical factors (imposing some general constraints on workers' behaviour) and organisational factors with the level and type of workers' qualifications, which is quite significant in the case of new technologies. The real possibilities for taking decisions created by new techniques and reinforced by work organisation, as can be observed among the CNC operators, act against the achievement of such a goal as a desirable volume of production by the FMS.

Conclusions

The FMS case presented by us is an 'island' phenomenon since it does not alter the production process or the organisation of work and management in the overall context of the enterprise/plant. Its 'island' character is also manifest in the fact that it has been carried out as a special project, part of a Polish-East German joint venture, and has been kept, therefore, outside the 'normal' organisation of work in the enterprise.

We have suggested that the main strategic aim for the implementation of the FMS was the achievement of a higher quality of products through the elimination of scrap. We have, therefore, concentrated on the application of this new technology 'at the cost' of human labour which can be perceived as a strategy of 'dispossessing' the workers. According to the labour process theory this strategy is accompanied by a disqualification of workers, a separation of 'conception' from 'production' and a transfer of 'conception' to the centre of co-ordination and programming. We have found considerable distortions of this classical description that made it impossible for us to treat the workers as being de-skilled. Let us think only of the typical character of the relations between workers, and line and staff managers. The inefficiency of auxiliary services and the chronic shortage of materials necessitate frequent interventions and mediations. This illustrates disfunctions and deficiencies of management but also points to problems in the training of technical specialists resulting from the traditional division of educational programmes into engineering lines without any reference to modifications following the introduction of high technology. The engineers who are supervising the FMS have learned to handle this technology on a par with the operators, which seems to contradict the opinion that high technology contributes to the alienation of the shopfloor level from the 'conception' of production.

The situation found by us may, of course, be a temporary one resulting from the early adaptation period as well as from the experimental 'island' character of the technology. On the other hand, material shortages are built into the overall system, as is the employment policy. The mode of action observed in this particular plant resembles in many respects the attitudes recorded in studies of other enterprises.

We have mentioned in the introduction a number of factors that condition the functioning of the enterprise, such as the general shortage of labour, the availability of relatively highly educated workers and the 'inverse subordination' of workers. In such a situation the strategy of management is to use technology to control the production process and to tolerate the occupational autonomy of the relatively well educated technicians and supervisors. Although there is a detailed scheme of job assignments, the control of the process of work does not comply with this formal scenario. It is reformulated under the influence of strategies employed by workers to acquire the necessary experience and skills to master the new technology through formal and informal means (observing more experienced fellow workers, taking part in shop programming etc.). For this reason, we speak of a 'taming' of the new technology. This process of taming can be observed among operators, lower-level supervisors and all other groups that have to deal with the technology.

One of the major factors that affect the introduction of new technology is the typical education and training of qualified personnel. The formal education is predominantly technical with many narrow specialisations. Such a system of occupational education gives technical personnel a dominant position among the managerial and supervising staff but also supplies a relatively large number of workers with secondary technical education (in all technical lines) who are qualified and interested to deal with new technology. The existence of this type of qualification is an important reason for the successful implementation of new technology in enterprises.

Another factor is the organisational culture of workers and enterprises. It is made up of a certain collective technological and occupational knowledge as well as attitudes towards new technology and curiosity for new situations. The disposition to informal behaviour at work, which is typical of Polish workers, is an important feature of this culture.

Despite the exceptional character of the case studied by us, we believe that the mechanisms and strategies that we have found to play a role in implementing and working with new technology are not atypical and can equally be found in many other Polish enterprises. They point to the high social costs of technological innovation in the Polish situation.

Notes

1. See *Statistical Yearbook* (1985).

2. The value of capital assets acquired in 1981/82 was less than 50 per cent of the value (in fixed prices) of yearly acquisition in the period between 1976-80.

3. Under the conditions of inflation and major labour turnover the relative level of wages (in relation to wages in other enterprises within the same industrial branch or region) is of great significance for the motivation of employees; it influences their production behaviour, the will to stay with the company etc.

4. The study of Flexible Manufacturing Systems (FMS) is one part of wider empirical studies carried out in the summer of 1983 and encompassing also production based on conventional and numerically controlled machine tools. The basic information was obtained by means of interviews and questionnaire surveys conducted among operators, talks with experts and representatives of management, and observation of work processes.

5. Thus, the empirical studies which are discussed in this chapter were carried out at the time when various elements of the system were gradually moulding into an effectively functioning whole. As a result, the content of our observations and conclusions is determined by this.

Reference

Statistical Yearbook (1985), Warsaw, Centralny Urząd Statystyczny

7

Introduction of Computerised Numerical Control and the Rationalisation of Production: the Belgian Case

Roger Kesteloot

Introduction[1]

For Belgian industry in general and for its metal-working branch in particular, the years since the first oil crisis of 1973 have been marked by widespread rationalisation. Relative social harmony and economic indolence have been replaced by resharpened conflicts of interests and more or less harsh competition.

A period of 'monopolisation of economic structures, the completion of the monopolistic wage-labour relation through neo-Keynesian national consensus, the regulatory interventions of national states and the opening-up of world markets under U.S. pressure' has been ended by force of weakened cost structures of firms, retarded investment, worldwide inflation, monetary uncertainties and growing 'big spender' characteristics of Belgian government activities (Polekar 1985: 32-34). All this, moreover, has been combined with - and even those involved acknowledge this - a serious lack of entrepreneurial zeal and market awareness by firms' managers.[2]

During the second half of the 1970s it became clear that these processes had led to a weakened competitiveness of Belgian firms on the international markets, consecutive loss of market shares, mass unemployment and ever growing public budget deficits.

After an initial period of hesitation and relative immobility - which, perhaps, can be accounted for by the inertia of those social and economic institutions which had been created under conditions of growing wealth - the shock of de-structuring/re-structuring became visible in a neo-liberal governmental policy and intensified rush towards rationalisation at all levels of the economy. Both these facts can be seen as shedding an unmistakable light on the direction in which the previous 'balance of power' in the capital-labour antinomy has actually swung, once the wealth and harmony model had been left.

The rationalisation of the Belgian economy thus has had many appearances. On a macro-level, one could say that a high number of bankruptcies and the closing down (from 1980 on, in the metal industry alone, yearly 150 factories involving some 35,000 workers) or drastic slimming of divisions of multinational corporations are the main indicators. In the field of labour relations, the costly trade-off between a guarantee of social peace and real-wage increases has been replaced by the take-it-or-leave-it trade-off between giving in on wages, on trade union influence and on labour regulation in general[3] on the one hand, and maintenance of employment efforts and rather qualitative concessions[4] on the other.

Effects and indications of these tendencies can certainly be seen on the firm level, too. Here, however, some more specific strategies of rationalisation can be discerned, which are of special interest to us in as far as they are related to the use of labour in combination with the introduction of new technologies.

One of the aspects of the erosion of regulation mechanisms governing capitalist European social and economic systems in the post-war period can be described as the apparent failure of the Fordist/Taylorist principle of regulation in some sectors of economic activity. The tandem of mass production (based on parcelled labour and the separation of conception and execution) and mass consumption (based on the continuous increase of real wages, as a result of the trade-off mentioned earlier) has obviously reached its limits. This, at least, can be considered to be the case in those sectors of activity in which developments in the international division of labour, relative saturation of markets, consumers' preferences etc. have led to a combination of requirements on price competitiveness giving rise to production cost minimisation (thus undermining the basis for further real-wage increases) as well as to a set of new 'efficiency requirements' like:

- product quality;
- short throughput time;
- ability to avoid/deal with disruption and production break-

down;
- ability to handle different product versions and to change the structure of production;
- minimising the time required for re-balancing and running in when production volume or models are changed;
- ability to deal with variations in manning due to absences, holidays etc. without replacements (Grootings *et al.* 1986: 277).

The introduction of computerised numerical control machines, as has happened in the cases we have studied, and the way this has been combined with work organisation, job design and modelling of qualification structures can be analysed as a process of rationalisation by which management tries to meet those new requirements (Kern and Schumann 1985: 23-26).[5]

New technologies in metal-working: towards automation, flexibilisation and integration

When looking at recent trends in technological innovation in Belgian metal-working industries, one can discern some sort of 'ideal-typical' path which we would like to illustrate with the course of innovation in the use of machine tools.

In a first move, which for Belgium can be placed in the late 1960s and early 1970s - i.e. at the culmination point of mass production and full employment - conventional machine tools were gradually replaced by numerically controlled (NC) ones, in which NC stands for 'a form of programmable automation in which a programme of instructions, designed for a particular part, controls the sequences of operations to machine the parts. New parts designs are accommodated by means of new part programmes' (Herroelen 1982: 6).

This type of system, which constitutes a form of rather rigid automation, the main advantages of which are consistency in performing repetitive jobs and increased labour productivity, can have a high level of efficiency in the production of large series of very restricted numbers of relatively simple product types (Herroelen and Lambrecht 1985). In general, the work organisation combined with it (making abstraction of all gradations which are characteristic of real shopfloor life) was marked by a rather strict separation into a work preparation department, which included NC programmers, and execution on the shopfloor, where machine operators only had to keep an eye on the machine and the way it worked (possibly combined with minor maintenance and quality control tasks). Shopfloor practice, as was indicated by one of the case studies, could, however, show clear deviations from this ideal type. Frequent occurrence of hardly foreseeable programming shortcomings, for instance by not sufficiently taking into account the variation in quality of raw materials - especially in the case of cast iron - or the on-going wear and tear of the cutting tools, could cause serious breakdowns, unless in an informal and sometimes even clandestine way the operators were able and willing to 'mess' with the machine or the programming tape.[6] It is quite clear that the rigidity of this kind of system created some major efficiency problems in the flow of production when trying to meet the 'new requirements' of more complex products in a variety of types, produced in smaller batches. If production problems (such as frequent stoppages, qualitative inaccuracy, long running-in and re-balancing times) were to be solved and if the advantages of automation were also to be applied to the still more or less handicraft sector of existing small-batch production, greater flexibility was required.

During the second half of the 1970s and the early 1980s a solution to these problems was sought in the application of micro-electronics in machine-tool construction. This has led to the introduction of the computerised numerical control (CNC) machine, whose technical system remains basically the same as with NC, but now a mini- or microcomputer forms a substantial part of the control unit of each separate machine tool. By this the possibility of direct intervention in the program, of the workplace itself, is created. In general, also, the 'operational memory' per machine tool is larger than with plain NC. Still another difference is the possibility of avoiding punched tape data transmission.

All in all this means that, at least in theory, to the NC advantages of speed (productivity) and accuracy of repetition (with microelectronic control standing for still higher reliability and sharper margins of noticing faults), that of flexibility is added. CNC machines, indeed, are far more easily and directly re-programmable than their NC ancestors, i.e. when appropriate software is provided. The combination of this characteristic with the memory capacity of the microcomputer and with developments in the field of the mechanical parts of machinery (for example multi-axial operation, improvement in quality of cutting tools etc.) created the possibility of producing parts, the complexity of which formerly would have been technically - if not economically - prohibitive.

It should be quite clear, however, that with CNC innovation in machine tools has not come to an end. Alongside a development towards the introduction of CNC in measurement and quality control as well as in production, and a shift from the use of single-operation machine tools to multi-purpose machining centres, there is a general tendency towards further integration of management, design and manufacturing, to which microelectronics applications are considered to be of major help (Demeester 1981). A cornerstone of this management quest for integration (resulting in the magic of computer integrated manufacturing or management, CIM) could be found in the introduction of flexible manufacturing systems (FMS), which consist of 'a group of processing stations - numerically controlled machine tools with automatic tool interchange capabilities - linked together with an automatic material (parts) handling system, that operates as an integrated system under computer control' (Herroelen 1982: 8). In such a system, besides tool/parts contacts, also the choice, supply and positioning of tool and parts are determined in a computer-objective manner, for several processing stations at a time.

In theory, 'these flexible manufacturing systems could bring about an optimal combination of, on the one hand: efficiency of automated large batch and mass production and, on the other hand: flexibility of piece-by-piece oriented production. In this way, the previously existing efficiency and productivity gap in small-batch production is filled in:

- efficiency is reached by total integration of production units, which is realised by means of a central computer, starting from which the whole process of production can be changed and controlled;
- flexibility is realised by making use of Computerised Numerical Control machines and robots, which allow for on-the-spot changeability and adaptability of programs' (Raeymaekers *et al.* 1985: 23).

According to Herroelen and Lambrecht (1985), in its flexible form, automation can be applied to a range of activities which until now have been characterised by relatively low productivity and/or major production flow problems, and which - bearing in mind the global trend in Belgian metal-working towards more complex products, higher quality standards and smaller batch size - are becoming more and more important to our economy.

Finally, a point with flexible manufacturing systems which is of particular interest to labour researchers concerns the question whether the general introduction of FMS with its central computation and global integration possibilities would or would not be used in a move towards a (re-)Taylorisation of metal-working, even in those types of production where rigid forms of automation could not succeed in doing this. One of the main questions concerning the technology-labour combination in metal-working for the near future (at least in Belgium, but perhaps in western European capitalist economies in general) could be the degree to which the 'new paradigm of work organisation policy' proclaimed by Kern and Schumann (1985) - and which can also be found in the partial 'return of craftsmanship' and the increased use of workers' qualifications which has been claimed by Sorge *et al.* (1982) - is or is not of a very temporary nature. It could well be that the new concept of production, oriented towards (partial) reassembly of conception and execution, even in those sectors of activity which Kern and Schumann find to be in the centre of neo-industrialisation, only holds 'as long as necessary', i.e. as long as management has not been able to meet the new requirements using means which - in their logic of action - sufficiently combine efficiency with control.[7]

Decision-making on technological innovation

The decision-making context

We will analyse the introduction of CNC technology in the Belgian metal-working firms studied by us - and which from now on will be called VM firm and TW firm - in the context of rationalisation of production.

In our interpretation, technological innovation is seen as a result of the 'dialectical tension' between the individual (logics of) action of decision-makers and the structural - or societal - context within which they operate. In as far as innovation inevitably is a result of some kind of decision, these structural context features cannot have a direct impact on the innovation process: it is the perception of these features by decision-makers which brings the structural factor into action.

170

Therefore, we will give here an account of these perceptions as emanating from interviews with those people who proved to be the main actors in relation to technological innovation, combined with some specific data on the firms in which they work.

The major decision-makers define the structural setting of their field of action (and of responsibility) to be determined, first and for all, by the sellers' market character of the technology market, the sharp competition on the sales market and the cost of money. Labour market characteristics do not seem to be considered as important in connection with process technology investments. For the VM firm, one has to take into account that in the mid-1970s the US-based VM Multinational Corporation restructured its activities, which for the Belgian firm induced a reduction in the number of (types of) products, an initial decline in overall activity and a serious reduction in the workforce. Therefore, no new people have been hired for the last few years.[8]

Figure 7.1: Value Added (million Belgian francs) in the Two Firms 1977-82

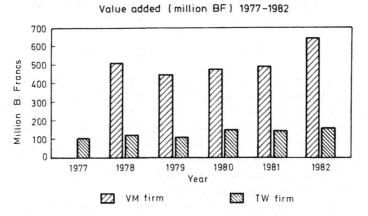

Before 1980, the VM firm encountered some problems in recruiting skilled workers with a three- to five-year experience on machine tools. These problems were tackled by introducing internal training schemes for those few school leavers who had to be recruited. One should note, moreover, that the demand for workers with useful and extensive experience fits into a context of rising standards applied in recruiting workers, which can be related to the large general surplus on the supply side of the labour market.

For TW, the situation on the labour market is likewise said not to have had any significant impact on technological innovation.

The firm has intensive (even kinship) bonds with local technical schools, and pupils who are 'destined for the firm' are trained according to a programme more or less adapted to this. Thus one of the schools disposes of second-hand machinery coming from the TW firm. In general, a non-specialised mechanics training on a medium secondary education level is required, although recently some higher secondary education graduates have been hired.

Figure 7.2: Employment Figures in the Two Firms 1975-83

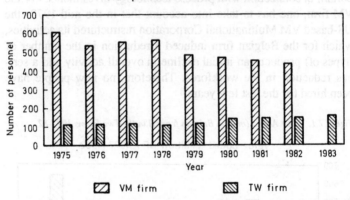

Total personnel number 1975-1983

Our case study firms seem, however, not to be fully representative of the Belgian metal-working situation. Employers' federations of all kinds of industries, but especially those of metal-working, raise quite a lot of questions of the educational system as to its quality (concerning the lack of useful qualifications pupils can acquire) as well as quantity (concerning the strong need to direct pupils into orientations for which there still exists a strong demand - of which mechanics is one).[9]

Regarding competition on the sales market, price marketing has shown to be more important for VM than for TW, where 'technical marketing' tended to be emphasised. VW produces special machines for food processing and equipment for the conditioning, packing and distribution of foodstuffs and other goods. Before the restructuring of the 1970s, it also produced (parts for) harvest machinery. It has been VM Multinational Corporation's leading European firm for special food processing machines for some years now.

TW, on the other hand, is a mainly subcontracting firm, specialising in machine-part construction. Specific products which are made by TW include gears (spur gears, helical gears etc.), speed reducers and accelerators and transmission elements. In recent years, the market of speed reducers - especially for the agricultural sector - has been lost to (Italian) competitors. A new market has, however, been found in the sector of high-quality, sophisticated military equipment (for example helicopter parts).

In both firms, a shift towards a demand for more complex and sophisticated products has been observed, but the market on which TW is operating proves to be a relatively protected one - as far as prices are concerned - compared to the more open and mature market of food-processing machinery. All this has led us to the expectation that for VM managers the logic of action in decisions on innovation would be more of an 'economic' rationalisation type, whereas we expected the TW management to follow a more 'technical' rationalisation logic with the first logic being concentrated on time and price calculations, and the second logic on technological production possibilities.

The organisational context within which the firms' decision-makers on technological innovation have operated has only loosely been connected with process technology decisions. Two aspects can help to explain this. First, in neither of the firms did there seem to be any major discussion on who should take those decisions: the positions of the different actors in connection with these matters appeared to be very clear. Second, the process innovations which have taken place during recent years have almost exclusively been 'replacement investments' and have happened very gradually on a machine-to-machine basis, thus already minimising the probability of seriously upsetting the organisation. The organisational context, and especially - from the innovators' point of view - the inherent inertia against changes, is more likely to be manifest when whole production systems are being changed in a concentrated period of time. Also, as can be concluded from interviews in other firms, the structure of the organisation tends to be more important for decisions on the introduction of new technology and its possible success, if local Belgian firms are mere subsidiaries of centralised foreign multinationals (thus sometimes being 'forced' to buy specific types of machinery or to function as a 'pilot' centre for the whole corporation).

VM as well as TW in this context showed (relative) organisational independence. VM's increased autonomy (and responsibility) after becoming a 'profit' centre seems to have led to increased activity of local management in the field of process technology. A very important constraint, however, still resides in the corporation's 'philosophy' (read: requirement) that its firms throughout the world should be best or - at the worst - second best on their sales market.

Finally, it is interesting to note that in neither of the firms is any significant practical impact attributed to government policies on technological innovation. National and regional governments can have an influence on the public's attitude towards new technologies by means of sensibilisation campaigns (for example the 'Flanders Technology' fairs), and can give incentives for managers to come together and confer on specific topics (for example the 'T-days' on robotics, CAD/CAM etc.), but have no influence on actual investment policies (although firms do have the possibility to apply for investment subventions).

The actors in decision-making

In Figures 7.3 and 7.4 the flowcharts of decision-making on the investment in CNC in the two firms studied are represented. Bearing in mind that these flows of decision-making processes hold for planning and implementation of replacement investments, one can see that:

- for VW, the core actors prove to be the Manufacturing Manager and the Chief Industrial Engineer;
- for TW, the impact of the Technical Director is predominant (however, the Director General is the one who formally takes the final decision and negotiates purchase conditions with suppliers).

It may be deduced from this that these core actors are 'technicians' rather than 'economists' (whose impact would certainly be greater if decisions were to be taken on extension investments or/and on the replacement of whole systems). This is also supported by considering their education and training backgrounds (all of them are engineers) as well as by their attitude to attach higher value to the formal organisational goal of 'organising production as efficiently as possible' rather than to that of 'developing market shares of the company'.

A difference between the two firms is to be found in the degree of formalisation and planning of decision-making processes. Thus, at VM investment decisions usually are made within the frame-work of the annual check-up on the five-year rotating planning of capital expenditure. This procedure is used in many large firms, especially in subsidiaries of foreign multinationals. With TW, 'ini-tiative' for new investments proves to be more diffuse and proce-dures in general seem to be more informal. This probably can be seen as a characteristic of 'typical' Belgian medium-sized or small family business.

Figure 7.3: Flow Chart of Decision-making on Replacement Investment at VM Firm

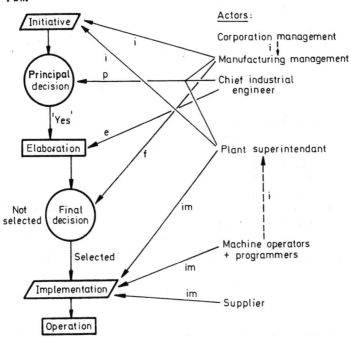

i = possible initiator(s) of new investment

e = actor(s) responsible for the elaboration of the file of information, on which the final decision will be based

f = actor(s) responsible for the final decision

im = actor(s) responsible for the implementation of the new investment on the shopfloor level

p = actor(s) responsible for the decision on the principle of making a new invest-ment

Figure 7.4: Flow Chart of Decision-making on Replacement Investment at TW Firm

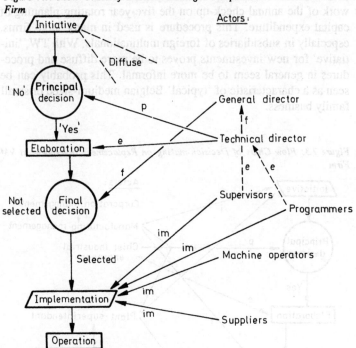

i = possible initiator(s) of new investment

e = actor(s) responsible for the elaboration of the file of information, on which the final decision will be based

f = actor(s) responsible for the final decision

im = actor(s) responsible for the implementation of the new investment on the shopfloor level

p = actor(s) responsible for the decision on the principle of making a new investment

Finally, a feature we can find in both firms is the 'line of demarcation' which separates the fields of action where one can see workers' participation and those which are considered to be part of the management. This is a characteristic of Belgian industrial relations in general. As Bundervoet (1974: 312) states '... all problems which appear to be unfit for negotiations in terms of wages, are - under the label of "economic problems" - considered to fall within the exclusive authority of the employer'. At least still in the period during which our research took place, investment in new technologies was defined as such an economic problem, and participation of the lower organisational levels as well as that of trade unions was poor to non-existing. As has been mentioned earlier, in the meantime a Collective Labour Agreement has been reached on the national level, which - under certain conditions - obliges management to give information to and to start negotiations with the workers' representatives on the enterprise level, prior to the actual introduction of the technology. The negotiations should include the eventual social consequences of the introduction. This agreement, however, only forms the framework for actual practice on the enterprise level, which has only begun to be evaluated by the 'social partners' themselves as well as by researchers.[10]

If, in relation to the processes of decision-making studied, there has been any form of involvement of the machine operators, it has taken place in an informal way and by an appeal to the individual's 'importance as an individual co-operator of the firm'. In our case studies, the traditional and formal structures for negotiation (such as the Works Council or the Safety Committee, in which both management and workers are represented at the enterprise level) have not been involved in decision-making, not even on questions of implementation.

To the general explanation presented earlier it can be added that recently in Belgian industrial relations a tendency towards 'individualisation' has emerged. On the enterprise level, this means that managers - certainly for shopfloor matters, but also for matters which traditionally were formally and collectively negotiated - now try to bypass the unions and to directly negotiate with individual (or small groups of) workers. According to Wijgaerts (1985: 51), this '(re)discovery of the individual in the labour system' is part of the general trend of flexibilisation and deregulation that can be explained as being a 'logical, further step in cost saving rationalisation of work organisation, which has been made possible by technological progress'. However, as to the specific point of deregulation of industrial relations, perhaps more important than technology could be the general economic and labour market situation, which puts trade unions on the defensive, and which offers managers far more room to manoeuvre than they had a decade ago.

Introduction of CNC and logic of rationalisation

Taking into account what has been said so far it should not be surprising that the logic in which the introduction of CNC machinery in the case study firms can be placed is basically that of tackling specific production flow and product standard problems as defined by the technical management.

To the dominant actors in the VM firm one of the main inducements to adopt CNC technology has been related to the complexity of operations and the quality of their execution, economic performance appearing to be considered as a rather fortunate result of CNC use. Nevertheless, the factor of productivity gain has been important especially in legitimising the introduction in the eyes of the European financial department of the corporation. The reduction of labour cost per unit of product has indeed been one of the other overall rationalisation objectives of the firm. At TW, the time-related aspects of production, also connected to the transparency of it, seem to be attributed a very important value. Thus, the reduction of throughput time has been one of the major objectives when introducing CNC. This mixture of technical/economic arguments can undoubtedly be connected to the fact that TW is a subcontracting firm where terms of delivery constitute one of the major factors of failure or success, and where a considerably diversified assortment of products are made (mostly in small batches). Another point in the technical translation of the decision's logic, namely the accuracy of reproduction that CNC technology offers, can be related to the relatively high quality standards which are set by the firm's newest clients (the military market).

Alongside these predominant factors in decision-making, some other - perhaps secondary - logic could also be discerned. Thus, there was a tendency with both firms' managers to favour the introduction of new technology, simply because it was new and 'Hi-Tech'. Some sort of 'adaptive modernism' logic, characterised by faith in modernism on the one hand, while on the other hand not wanting to play an avant-garde role, which was reflected in following rather conservative purchasing policies (sticking with suppliers already known), certainly played a part in the final decisions. Similarly, the fact that not using the operators' craftsmanship with existing NC machinery had in some cases led to a kind of passive resistance by some of the operators ('if they do not allow me to intervene in programming under normal conditions, they shouldn't expect me to do so if something goes wrong') has been an inducement - especially for VM's technical management - to favour the introduction of CNC technology. Operators doing nothing more than what was expected of them sometimes led to considerable stoppage times in case of disruptions, and to large workloads for the (expensive and mostly only daytime) work preparation staff.

In general, we can say that the introduction of CNC technology in the firms we have studied can be analysed in terms of a multiple logic of action complex, in which the perception of (new) structural requirements by management and, accordingly, the technical and economic rationalisation efforts with which they want to meet them, are intertwined with mainstream 'pro Hi-Tech' attitudes, with power relations - and thus with control - and with the technical orientations of the major decision-makers themselves.

The introduction of CNC and work organisation

Concerning work organisation, one can say that prime structuring of the production process is very much in the hands of the work preparation departments and programming offices. It is there, and this is largely similar to what was the case with simple NC, that the basic programs are created from which the parts will be machined. Thus, in principle, workers themselves do not decide on the selection of tools, the sequences of operations, basic machine pace etc.

On a conventional machine tool, autonomy of the operator certainly was larger: he could regulate his interventions in production more on his own, be it on the basis of a formalised blueprint of the parts and the operations to be performed. Control certainly was not built into the machine: control of the worker's performances - quantitatively as well as qualitatively - had to be done by supervisors and quality controllers.

With the NC system, work had been made rather clear-cut and interventions of the operator either had to get the approval (or required direct co-intervention) of the programmer or the supervisor, or had to be clandestine (for example reduction of the pace of the machine). Here, at least in theory, but certainly also as far as 'official' division of labour was concerned, a rather strict separation of conception and execution could be found.

With the introduction of CNC technology, the field of autonomous action of the operator again seems to have slightly increased: interactivity, i.e. the possibility to adapt and correct programs on the individual machines, is being used to the extent that only fundamental changes in the programs are prohibited to the operator or have to receive the preceding approval of superiors. The frequency with which this possibility of intervention is made use of in the actual process of production varies with the complexity of products and batch sizes. It is quite clear that, except for adjusting to the wear and tear of tools, the main occasions on which programs do not run as they should is at the beginning of the production of new (batches of) sophisticated, non-standard type products.

Another feature of change in work organisation is the weakened position of the supervisor as far as technical supervision is concerned. Much of his former function now resides with the programmers. So, if production flow problems occur, in many cases either the operator solves them himself, or they tend to directly get to the programmer, hereby by-passing the supervisor. The supervisors' job has actually become more one of co-ordination, distribution of tasks, administration, control and motivation. Moreover, this development has been taken into account less than that of the operators' job in the phase of planning the introduction of the new technology/work organisation, and has certainly not been consciously aimed at.

Two remarks can be made with respect to this development. First, it is not clear yet whether this change will prove to be long-lasting or not. One could hypothesise that this technical 'degradation' of the supervisor's place in work organisation could be based upon 'generation problems'. In many cases, supervisors are promoted from the shopfloor, thus generally have accumulated a lot of experience with the older technologies while not being the youngest any more. This can, in some cases, give rise to problems of flexibility in acquiring the skills and knowledge which are required for pursuing the traditional supervisor's role once the new technology has been introduced. Also the fact of not having had day-to-day practical working experience with the technology (unlike the operator and the programmer) can gradually undermine the supervisor's technical authority. If this hypothesis holds, however, with the career cycle going on, the technical role of the supervisor could be restored once some of the operators become supervisors themselves. In fact, in some firms management is speeding up this process of supervision-oriented accumulation of experience with selected operators, who are designated in advance to be promoted to a supervisor's position.

The second remark concerns the fact that one of the tasks of the supervisor, which now seems to become increasingly emphasised, namely motivation of the workforce, is becoming rather important in terms of production efficiency. When the quality of products and the matching of high product standards, on the one hand, and the minimisation of disruptions, on the other, become major topics in rationalisation strategies, it is quite obvious that (at least as long as these requirements cannot be met in an automated way) the production concept demands not only qualified, but also motivated workers. Therefore, if the supervisor's role in the firms we have studied has shown itself less central in a technical way, it certainly is not becoming totally peripheral to the production process as a whole.

Quality of work

With the transition to CNC equipment, the work content has changed in the direction of increasing correction and process control tasks, which presumes a degree of interactivity between man and machine that could not be realised on an NC machine. At VM, where the NC separation of conception and execution in the past had .led to more serious disruptions of the production flow, this change was emphasised more than at TW, and was more clearly defined - by managers as well as by workers - as a form of job enrichment.

The duration of jobs on CNC machines is extremely variable: it normally ranges from half a minute to fifteen minutes but, according to the degree of complexity of the product, durations of up to 32 hours may occur. Furthermore, transition to CNC has been experienced by the workers as being combined with increasing variation in production as well as in work, and also with a light tendency towards a decreasing batch size (batches now ranging from 1 to 500 pieces in the VM firm and from 1 to 300 pieces in the TW firm).

In terms of qualifications, most operators experience a large gap between the qualifications acquired in the educational system and those which are required to perform efficiently on the shop-floor. A minority is believed to have too low a level of school education, but compensation of this can be reached through on-the-job training and learning by doing. Most of the operators find their jobs provide opportunities for development of skills, which in the majority of cases consist of general professional skills. In a minority of cases, the qualifications which can be developed are said to be machine-specific. Most CNC operators, moreover, mention their jobs to require knowledge of the 'tricks of the trade'.

Figure 7.5: Change in Importance of Task Elements

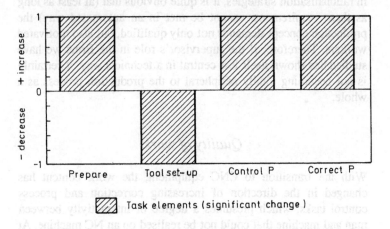

As far as 'general technical qualifications' and 'socio-normative' ones are concerned[11] CNC work stands for high mental concentration when starting up new batches or products, an average team spirit (especially with operators who take over the machine in the next work shift) and a fairly important degree of responsibility on the part of the operator. This is partly due to the possible impact of decisions to be taken in case of (impending) stops or breakdowns, partly also to the ever increasing value of the products which are machined. This picture, however, is not overwhelmingly different from shopfloor practice with NC machines - which tends to deviate from 'official' or theoretical organisation of work - only the specific features certainly have become more clear and outspoken.

Finally, before coming to a general conclusion, it has to be mentioned that for CNC operators' jobs recruitment has above all taken place on the firms' internal labour markets - a phenomenon which proves to be quite typical for the recruitment of operators with computerised machinery all over Belgian industry. Managers, in this respect, attach rather high importance to professional experience, the ability to adapt oneself to the firm as well as reliability. These are in fact the qualities which managers tend to look for before giving someone a 'fairly responsible' job and/or before investing in some additional training.

Conclusion

Considering the research results in the two case-study firms, one could say that in neither case has the quality of work-related impact of the introduction of CNC technology (which, it has to be repeated, happened rather gradually) been really spectacular.

In general, one could say that there are some signs of a 'return to craftsmanship' starting - although in practice it has never been really and totally far away - at least, as far as management considers it to be functional in the light of production efficiency. From the managers' point of view, indeed, it seems that NC equipment and the Taylorist principles of organisation combined with it, have proved to be too rigid, the total separation of work preparation and execution being too strict to remain practicable (i.e. without creating losses in production efficiency). Certainly with some managers the consciousness has arisen that with actual production requirements in their trade, craftsmanship is not (yet?) fully replaceable (although with increasing control and correction tasks, characteristics of this craftsmanship have changed). Thus the introduction of CNC technology and the combination of it with a concept of organising work in a way which again - or more openly - relies on the responsible intervention of the worker in the optimisation of production as well as on a more extensive use of his qualifications, can be seen as one effort by the management to rationalise production.

Finally, two open questions still remain. First, if this trend proves to be persistent, it will be interesting to see whether or not in practice a sort of new 'locus of integration' will be created within the firm for the elite of workers who have proved to be faithful to the firm, motivated, responsible and 'knowing their trade'. Apart from the relatively high pay level they would be rewarded with more interesting work, the possibility of coping with (relative) technical challenges themselves, the feeling of getting a better labour market position by working on modern, sophisticated machines, and possibly being listened to - on a man-to-man basis - when they think to know a better solution than the one presented by work preparers. Of course, integration of an elite could go hand in hand with segmentation, excluding those who do not meet the 'new machine operator criteria', either within the firm or on the labour market in general.

Second, it still is not clear to what degree this relative de-Taylorisation in the eyes of management is not a provisional 'least of two evils', involving giving in on control in order to preserve or increase efficiency. Kern and Schumann's new paradigm of work organisation will indeed have to prove its value, from the moment that management of the type of production we have described here has at its disposal other (technical and organisational) means to overcome the production problems encountered recently.

Notes

1. This chapter is largely based on case studies, including management interviews and workers' questionnaires in two Belgian machine construction firms, performed in 1983, and on additional management, trade union and workers' interviews held between 1983 and 1985.

2. See Verbond van Belgische Ondernemingen (1985).

3. Examples of this are the recent evolutions in flexibilisation/deregulation of working hours (the so-called Hansenne experiments), the factual and relative weakening of positions of workers' representatives, and employers' efforts to attack the rigidities of labour as a factor of production in general.

4. See, for example, the Collective Labour Agreement No. 39 on workers' involvement in decision-making on technological innovation (a discussion of which can be found in Van der Hallen, 1985).

5. Kern and Schumann (1985: 24) mention a change in paradigms of work organisation policy (*arbeitspolitischer Paradigmenwechsel*) which goes hand in hand with actual technological innovation, being together at the core of what they call 'neo-industrialisation' (*Neo-industrialisierung*).

6. This is, in fact, quite similar to some of the shopfloor practices described by Burawoy (1979) and to those which led Noble (1979) to proclaim the supremacy of shopfloor practice over planning of production, even under numerical control rule. Kern and Schumann (1985: 141) also confirm this in their case studies in machine construction firms, claiming that even for the pioneer plants it seems to have been characteristic that at that stage of development the shopfloor dominance was not at all eliminated. It continued to be a factor significantly influencing output quantity and quality.

7. See, for example Pot (1985).

8. Moreover, the firm has known increasing temporary unemployment, rising from ca. six days per worker per year in 1980 to ca. twenty days per worker per year in 1982.

9. See, for example, Verbond van Belgische Ondernemingen (1985); Fabrimetal (1986).

10. For a first evaluation, see, for example, Huys and Van der Hallen (1986). In this study, an analysis is made of those agreements which, on the sectoral level as well as on that of individual firms, have resulted from negotiations between

employers and trade unions. It shows that the most elaborate agreements on the handling of the introduction of new technologies are to be found in the press sector; industry is very poorly represented. Where the agreements are more or less detailed, topics on (re)training schemes and job and/or wage security for the existing work-force seem to prevail.

11. For definition, see, for example, Hancke *et al.* (1986), where an attempt is made to operationalise the concepts, first used for research on the qualifications required for operators' jobs in processes involving computer control in different sectors. Research is done on an 'intersubjective' basis, i.e. confronting the perceptions of operators themselves, foremen and production engineers and comparing them with the qualifications which are demanded by the firm's personnel officers.

References

Burawoy, M. (1979) *Manufacturing Consent*, Chicago/London, University of Chicago Press

Bundervoet, J. (1974) 'Vakbeweging in heroriëtering - aspecten van openheid en geslotenheid in de besluitvorming van de Belgische vakbonden' (Changes in Trade Unions. Openness and Closeness in Belgian Trade Unions), *De gids op maatschappelijk gebied*, pp. 303-320

Demeester, R. (ed.) (1981) 'Hoe zal een metaalverwerkend bedrijf er uitzien in 1985 en 1990 - Fabrimetal maakt een toekomstvoorspelling voor België' (What Will a Metal Firm Look Like in 1985 and 1990 - Fabrimetal Makes a Prediction for Belgium), Brussels, Fabrimetal

Fabrimetal, V.G. (1986) *Onderzoek naar de aanwerving van jongeren* (Research on Recruitment of Youth), Brussels

Grootings, P., J. Bogdan and M. Ladó (1986) 'New Forms of Work Organisation: European Developments in Comparative Perspective; Report of the Discussions', in P. Grootings, B. Gustavsen and L. Héthy (eds.) *New Forms of Work Organisation and their Social and Economic Environment*, Budapest, Institute of Labour Research/Vienna Centre

Grootings, P., B. Gustavsen and L. Héthy (eds.) (1986) *New Forms of Work Organisation and their Social and Economic Environment*, Budapest, Institute of Labour Research/Vienna Centre

Hancke, C., R. Kesteloot and M. Kooyman (1986) 'Project Onderwijs - Arbeidsmarkt, Analyse-instrument Vereiste Kwalificaties' (Research Project Education - Labour Market, Research Instrument Required Qualifications), RUCA working paper 1986/12, Antwerp

Herroelen, W.S. (1982) 'Automation of Small Batch Production - from Numerical Control to Flexible Manufacturing Systems', *Bedrijfseconomische Verhandeling*, no. 8204, Leuven

Herroelen, W. and M. Lambrecht (1985) 'Innovatie op het gebied van produktie- en voorraadbeleid' (Innovation in Production and Storing Policy) in *Innoveren en Ondernemen*, Antwerp, Vereniging voor Economie

Huys, J. and P. Van der Hallen (1986) 'Les accords de technologie en Belgique', Commission des Communautés Européennes, Doc. CB-46-86-703 FC, Brussels

Kern, H. and M. Schumann (1985) *Das Ende der Arbeitsteilung? Rationalisierung in der industriellen Produktion* (The End of the Division of Labour? Rationalisation in Industrial Production), Munich, Beck Verlag

Noble, D.F. (1979) 'Social Choice in Machine Design: The Case of Automatically Controlled Machine Tools', in A. Zimbalist (ed.) *Case Studies on the Labour Process*, New York, Monthly Review Press

Polekar (1985) *Het laboratorium van de crisis - debat over een nieuwe maatschappelijke ordening* (The Laboratory of the Crisis - Debate about a New Social Order), Leuven

Pot, F. (1985) 'Het einde van de arbeidsdeling? Kern en Schumann over technologie en rationalisatie in de jaren tachtig en negentig' (The End of the Division of Labour? Kern and Schumann about Technology and Rationalisation in the 1980s and 1990s), *Tijdschrift voor Arbeidsvraagstukken*, no. 2, pp. 79-91

Raeymaekers, A.M., E. Henderickx and R. Kesteloot (1985) 'Flexibele productieautomatisering in de metaalverwerkende nijverheid - onderzoeksmodel m.b.t. productie-en arbeidsorganisatorische aspecten' (Flexible Automation of Production in Metal Firms - Research Model for Production and Work Organisation), RUCA working paper, Antwerp

Sorge, A., G. Hartmann, M. Warner and I. Nicholas (1982) *Mikroelektronik und Arbeit in der Industrie* (Microelectronics and Work in Industry), Frankfurt/M., Campus Verlag

Van der Hallen, P. (1985) 'De vakbeweging als actors bij automatisering' (The Trade Union as an Actor in Automation), *Tijdschrift voor Sociologie*, no. 1/2, pp. 159-205

Verbond van Belgische Ondernemingen (1985) *Ondernemen in 1985* (Enterprising in 1985), Brussels

Wijgaerts, D. (1985) 'Flexibilisering en deregulering: naar individualisering van arbeidsverhoudingen' (Flexibilisation and Deregulation: Towards Individualisation in Industrial Relations), *Tijdschrift voor Arbeidsvraagstukken*, no. 4, pp. 41-56

Zimbalist A. (ed.) (1979) *Case Studies on the Labour Process*, New York, Monthly Review Press

8

The Introduction and Use of CNC in the Federal Republic of Germany

Otfried Mickler

Socioeconomic developments since 1945

The socioeconomic development of the Federal Republic of Germany can be described roughly in three phases: The reconstruction of the economy in the immediate postwar period was followed by an intensive economic expansion, which passed into a more crisis-prone development from the mid-1970s onwards.

The period of reconstruction (1948-55)

After the main deficiencies of the industrial structure consequent upon war destruction, loss of territory and dismantling, had been made good, at the beginning of the 1950s there was a very favourable production situation. This was so because prior to World War II industry had been effectively modernised for arms production, so that at the end of the war there was available a production apparatus of a considerable technical level whose capacity was being minimally exploited. The situation on the labour market was also advantageous for industrial companies. With the great influx of refugees and displaced persons from the East a surplus, relatively well-trained, labour potential existed, which was obliged and prepared to work under almost any conditions (Baethge *et al.* 1974: 24).

The firms utilised the favourable labour supply on the basis of the available technology. The great need of West German postwar society to make up leeway in consumer and capital goods brought about an enormous expansion in production during these years, which almost fully utilised existing production capacity until the mid-1950s. The extremely steep increase in labour productivity during these years (approximately 37.5 per cent between 1950 and 1955) was mainly due to the growing exploitation of production capacity.

Economic expansion in the period of technological renewal of the production apparatus (1955-70)

Towards the end of the 1950s the influx of labour gradually dried up; the labour reserves had been largely exhausted by the growing economy. In addition, during this period the agreed number of working hours was considerably reduced. This caused pressure on labour productivity which could be countered only by technological innovation in the production apparatus. The integration of the West German economy into the international market was also taking place at that time, and this, together with a still strongly growing domestic market, made necessary an extension of the industrial production potential, which under the special labour market and competition conditions could be accomplished only by increased product innovations and the introduction of new and more efficient production and organisation methods.

The difference between this and the reconstruction period becomes clear if one looks at the changes in the number of workers and in work productivity. Whereas between 1950 and 1960 a productivity growth of 75 per cent in the overall economy was attained with a 23 per cent increase in employment, between 1960 and 1970 a considerable growth in productivity of 55 per cent was achieved with the only slight increase of four per cent in employment.

During this phase the industrial branches of mass production in particular, for example the electrical industry, the chemical industry and the automobile industry, were modernised and brought to a high technological level. The latter in particular experienced an enormous expansion in consequence of the mass motorisation from the early 1960s on. It advanced with partial automation in mechanical production and conveyer belt assembly to become the 'pioneer industry' of industrial modernisation. Major firms in other branches for a long time oriented themselves on its production model.

The dependently employed profited during this phase from the country's fast expanding economy. Against the background of decreasing labour reserves - the unemployment figures in the Federal Republic of Germany sank from 10.4 per cent in 1950 to 5.2 per cent in 1955 and to less than 1 per cent in 1961 and remained at this level until the early 1970s - and the continuing economic expansion, the unions were able to achieve a considerable rise in real wages, a clear decrease in weekly working hours from 45 to 40, and an improvement in social security (Osterland *et al.* 1973).

The real wages of industrial workers almost trebled between 1950 and 1970, the largest rise taking place during the early 1960s. In no comparable period of social development in the Federal Republic of Germany during the past century have there been similarly high increases in real wages.

Economic stagnation and rationalisation through new technologies (from the mid-1970s)

The country's economic development from the mid-1970s on was marked by a weakly growing, in fact almost stagnating, industrial production on a high level, whereas labour productivity showed a considerable rise during the enforced introduction of new technologies and work organisational rationalisation measures.

Thus between the years 1973 and 1980 (both were 'peaks' of the economic cycle) industrial production rose by only a total of 7.4 per cent, whereas labour productivity rose during the same period by 33.4 per cent. Because of this, the number of workplaces in industry decreased greatly during the period, by 8.4 per cent, i.e. by an absolute 679,000 jobs.

The causes of this irregular development of the Federal German economy compared with the postwar boom are manifold and are both domestic and external, arising from the close involvement of the national economy with the international market.

From the middle of the 1970s the number of unemployed rose fast, especially because the reduction in workplaces went hand in hand with an increase in the number of workers resulting from peculiarities in the demographic development in the Federal Republic of Germany (those born in years of high birthrates entered working life). Due to this the average unemployment rate grew from 1.2 per cent in 1973 to 5.5 per cent in 1981 and 7.2 per cent in 1982. In this deteriorated economic situation it was difficult for the unions to maintain the high real wage level which had been attained and protect the safety-net of social security from incursions. Thus between 1976 and 1981 the rise in the cost of living of around 24 per cent was only barely balanced by the rise in gross weekly earnings of industrial workers (33 per cent).[1]

Changes in the structure of the labour force

In the course of the economic development since the postwar period, considerable shifts have occurred in the structure of the labour force. It is sure that these do not show any radical 'revolutionary' character, for after all the country in 1948 was already highly industrialised. They are the continuation of a long-term trend which began in the 19th century.

Thus the share of the self-employed decreased from about 32 per cent in 1950 to about 13 per cent in 1981, so that today the working population consists almost entirely of dependent employees (87 per cent). As in other industrial societies, a further shift of emphasis has taken place from the primary sector to the secondary and tertiary sectors (see Table 8.1). During the last decade the number of workplaces in the service sector exceeded the traditionally major manufacturing sector.

Accordingly the structure of occupations and professions has also greatly changed in the past decades. Conspicuous is first the greatly increased proportion of salaried employees and public servants among the dependently employed. Whereas in 1960 still about two-thirds of the dependently employed were engaged as workers, the number of salaried employees and public servants since the end of the 1970s has reached and surpassed that of the workers.

The sectoral shift in employment structure points to a considerable change in qualifications in workers' and salaried employees' jobs through the technical-economic changes in the Federal Republic of Germany. When the shifts in the occupational structure (measured according to occupational preponderance) are considered, the following striking phenomena appear between 1950 and 1970 (Baethge *et al.* 1974: 44) (see Table 8.1):

- a drastic reduction in the primary sector occupations, i.e. of farmers, farm labourers, domestic occupations etc.;
- a continual increase in the proportion of commercial occupations (trade, office, administration); with this the volume of professionally qualified occupations *in toto* increased greatly,

190

even if a number of the office workers do comparatively simple jobs;
- a major growth in technical occupations (technicians, engineers, scientists), directly due to the increased technological complexity of production and the intensified innovation activity of the economy. This too should be evaluated as a tendency towards higher qualification;
- on the other hand the group of 'anybody's jobs', i.e. the unspecified unskilled jobs, has grown, a fact which is to be interpreted as an expression of de-qualifying processes in partial areas of industry.

If, however, the structure of vocational occupations in industry itself is considered, no particularly momentous shifts in qualification can be statistically established in the period under consideration (Mickler *et al.* 1978).

Table 8.1: Labour Force Structure of the Total Economy (gainfully employed in per cent of the overall economy)

	1950	1960	1970	1980
Primary sector (agriculture, forestry)	24.8	13.8	8.8	5.9
Secondary sector (industry and processing, manual trades, energy supplies)	42.6	47.7	48.7	44.8
Tertiary sector (trade, state employees, transport, private service industry)	32.6	38.5	42.5	49.3
Overall economy	100.0	100.0	100.0	100.0

Source: Statistical Yearbooks of the Federal Republic of Germany, author's calculations.

Between 1962 and 1974 the proportion of skilled workers' occupations compared with all vocational occupations in industry remained astonishingly constant at about 40 per cent. If employees' occupations are added, during this time the proportion of vocationally qualified occupations of all technical industrial occupations increased slightly from 46.9 per cent to 48.5 per cent: accordingly the proportion of trainee occupations and unskilled jobs decreased slightly from 53.1 per cent to 51.5 per cent. The relative constancy of the industrial occupational structure on the level of employment statistics conceals, however, some rather momentous qualitative shifts in the vocational demands on industrial workers, which have resulted in a devaluation of many traditional skills and the emergence of new skilled jobs and technical occupations (Mickler 1981).

Under the educational reform introduced in the mid-1960s, which led to a quantitative expansion of courses in higher and further education, the structure of school leavers has changed considerably (see Table 8.2). In particular it has shifted to a great extent towards intermediate and higher educational qualifications. This has meant that the proportion of only basically educated school leavers (*Hauptschule* with and without graduation certificates) has almost halved, from some 80 per cent in 1965 to approximately 43.6 per cent in 1980, while the share of intermediate school graduates, at 37.1 per cent, has already surpassed the share of *Hauptschule* graduates (34.1 per cent), and the group of school leavers with matriculation has risen from about 7 per cent to about 19 per cent.[2]

Table 8.2: Pupils Completing General Education, According to Educational Qualifications (in thousands and in per cent)

Year	Total school leavers	Hauptschule pupils without graduation, special school pupils		Hauptschule graduation		Intermediate graduation		University entrance	
			%		%		%		%
1965	701.7	134.6	19.2	422.8	60.3	93.8	13.4	50.5	7.2
1970	780.7	140.3	18.0	348.8	44.7	200.1	25.6	91.5	11.7
1975	954.9	114.6	12.0	347.1	36.3	320.0	33.5	173.2	18.1
1980	1,147.8	109.4	9.5	390.9	34.1	426.7	37.1	220.8	19.2
Difference 1965 to 1980 in %	+ 63.6	- 18.7		- 7.5		+ 355		+ 337	

Source: Federal Minister for Education and Science, basic and structural data 1981/82, p. 60.

Vocational training following general education takes place partly - as in other countries - in specialised vocational schools and colleges, though most young people (about two-thirds) undergo a training under the 'dual vocational training system' which lasts two to three years. This 'dual' vocational training takes place mostly in manual trades and industrial or service firms. In most cases it is complemented by one or two days' attendance each week at the state vocational school. Training is permitted only in occupations recognised by the state according to appropriately established occupational models and training regulations. After completion of the vocational training the skilled worker or skilled employee with his certificate in a state-recognised occupation represents a definite type of qualification on the labour market - *Facharbeiter* - towards which specific employment strategies are oriented.

In 1978, 36 per cent of the newly created vocational training places were in manual crafts (Baethge *et al.* 1980). This structure was retained at the beginning of the 1980s. The far above average increase in training places in manual crafts as compared to the few apprenticeships in previous years may perhaps alleviate the problems of youth unemployment and lack of training, but contains the danger of a deficiency in those qualifications required by industry. Only a small part of those who complete their training in a manual craft are employed as skilled workers in manual trades; the greater number must later undertake jobs in industry alien to their expertise, For this group the employment risk has greatly increased in the recent years of the economic crisis. The number of training openings offering qualifications in industry has in contrast risen below average in recent years.

Technological development and policy

Financing of research and development

The economic development and ability to compete on the international market of major branches of industry in the Federal Republic of Germany is crucially dependent on the ability of enterprises to introduce innovation in products and processes. This tendency has steadily increased in importance since the beginning of the 1960s. It is particularly true for the electrical engineering industry, the chemical industry, mechanical engineering and automobile industry. Financial expenditure by private firms for research and development usable in practice in the companies therefore greatly increased in the past 20 years from around 2,150 million DM in 1962 to 13,200 million DM in 1977.

An exclusively privately organised programme of research and development, however, runs the danger of omitting unprofitable economic research areas and in particular of neglecting basic research. Since the beginning of the 20th century therefore, a tradition of state promotion of research and development has existed, which finances research projects via independently administered scientific institutes (Max Planck Society, German Research Society - DFG), university institutions, and non-university research institutes (Frauenhofer Society), as well as via subsidies and increasingly via direct aid to firms. State expenditures amounted to 13,250 million DM in 1977.

In the past decade the development of new technologies was also to an increasing extent promoted by the Federal government. Thus for instance the promotion of data processing, information technology and electronics increased fivefold between 1969 and 1977, while research and development expenditure only slightly more than doubled during this period. The main emphasis of state promotion of innovation in recent years has been on the development and utilisation of industrial robots. For this the Federal government alone paid out 76 million DM up to 1980.

Dissemination of new technologies

The use of new technologies based on microelectronics has particularly strongly increased especially since the end of the 1970s. As important examples of microelectronic production techniques, the spread of programmable industrial robots and CNC machine tools in the Federal Republic of Germany is given in Table 8.3.

Industrial robots were first tested in firms in the 1970s, but only since the beginning of the 1980s can one speak of a breakthrough in production use. Measured against the numerous possibilities of use of industrial robots, the Federal Republic of Germany is, however, only at the beginning of a wide dissemination. In 1981 there were a total of 6,000 programmable industrial robots in use in Western Europe, 2,300 of them in the Federal Republic of Germany. The point of concentration here as elsewhere was in the automobile industry, in which above all spot-welding was favoured for robotisation. Whereas the first industrial robots at the beginning of the 1970s were imported from the USA, today most of the robots in use in mechanical engineering, and to a certain extent also in the automobile industry, are produced by the industries themselves.

Table 8.3: Use of Industrial Robots and NC/CNC Machine Tools in the Federal Republic of Germany

Year	Industrial robots	NC/CNC machine tools
1971	ca. 30	2,630
1974	130	4,400
1980	1,300	25,000
1981	2,300	30,000

Source: IPA Stuttgart, ISI Karlsruhe.

NC machine tools began to be used in the Federal Republic of Germany as early as the beginning of the 1960s. Until the mid-1970s, however, NC machines were only very hesitatingly introduced by firms, because compared to their performance they were too expensive and not flexible enough in use. Only with the introduction of computer-controlled machine tools (CNC), which was fully effective from 1975, was there a breakthrough in company usage. Since 1979 some 90 per cent of numerically controlled machine tools produced in the Federal Republic of Germany have been equipped with CNC. Through the widespread use of CNC machines the share of all numerically controlled machine tools by 1980 had increased to about 50 per cent (Rempp *et al.* 1981). Of an estimated total of 1.2 million machine tools in the Federal Republic of Germany in 1981, around 2.5 per cent were numerically controlled. These figures do not, however, demonstrate the real significance of numerically controlled machine tools, being two to three times as productive as their manually controlled counterparts, for production and personnel employment.

Technology policies of the unions

The socially explosive potential of the enforced introduction of new technologies in a situation of continuing mass unemployment in the Federal Republic of Germany becomes clear if one realises the average loss of workplaces per newly introduced machine. Empirical surveys have shown that per industrial robot four to five workers and per CNC machine two workers are replaced. This means that at the beginning of the 1980s each year some 8,000 to 9,000 workers were being replaced by industrial robots, and 10,000 workers by CNC machine tools.

In view of this high loss of employment, which is increasingly affecting the skilled industrial worker who is the basic figure of union interest representation, the attitude of the unions towards technological development and its social consequences has changed in recent years. The German industrial unions in particular have always been proud of being no Luddites, antagonistic to machines. As early as in the 1920s especially the metalworkers' union (today the IG Metall) was of the opinion that the perfecting of technology and the mechanisation of the work process were a decisive step on the road towards economic and cultural emancipation of the working classes. In the 1950s and 1960s too, IG Metall, as the central union interest representation of the widespread and strongly expanding metal industries, supported the enforced modernisation of production in order to push through rises in real wages, shortening of working hours and better social security for the dependently employed.

The union and the Works Council were able, in the phase of economic expansion, to react to the rationalisation process in firms with a policy of securing active property and individual adjustment. In this way social consequences for those affected could be mitigated, even if working conditions in parts of the firm were made worse. For the skilled workers affected there were, at that time of continuing growth of employment, possibilities of avoiding disadvantages through promotion within the firm or by changing firms. The deterioration through rationalisation thus primarily affected newly arriving workers (unskilled women and foreign workers). With diminished economic growth and decreased employment with mass dismissals in industry today, even the skilled worker is no longer safe from workplace loss. The consequences of rationalisation in firms today also lead in different ways to the devaluation of acquired qualifications, a loss of status, and a lower categorisation with reductions in wages.

The introduction of new technologies has thus negative significance today for those affected and for the unions, characterised by a loss of workplaces and deterioration in working conditions. There are therefore signs in Works Councils and unions of a stronger politicising of the social consequences of new technologies. In this context the strike in the Baden-Württenberg metal industry of 1978 can be mentioned, as a result of which the union was able to achieve better protection against lower wage categorisation due to rationalisation measures.

Mechanical engineering in the Federal Republic of Germany

Structural characteristics

As part of the machine and machine-tool manufacturing industry, mechanical engineering in 1980 was responsible for almost one-tenth of the production volume with some one-seventh of the labour force of the total industry, and hence according to the number of employed (1.09 million) was the largest branch not only of the capital goods industry but of industry on the whole. Within mechanical engineering, the manufacture of machine tools, accounting for 9 per cent of the production and 9 per cent of the labour force (99,000 employed in 1980), was the largest of a total of 24 specialised branches. Machine tool manufacture includes the CNC plant under study here, described later in more detail.

Mechanical engineering, through the provision of the means of production, is responsible for the rationalisation of the whole industry. It is therefore obliged to carry out constant product innovation, which, however, conflicts with the standardisation and rationalisation of its own production. Typical therefore is the small-batch but high-precision character of the complex, technically highly developed product, which represents more a 'materialised' problem-solving than a standardised product. The complexity and high degree of technical know-how of the product is reflected in the far above-average proportion of technicians and engineers among those employed in mechanical engineering.

The small-batch specialised character of the products explains to a large extent the stable continuation of the medium-size structure of companies. Even in 1979, in the category of firms with 500 employees and more - i.e. rather large firms - there worked only slightly more than half (54.6 per cent) of all mechanical engineering employees, whereas, with a rising tendency, about 14 per cent of employees were distributed among the roughly 3,200 small firms employing 10 to 100 workers (see Table 8.4).

Economic development

Mechanical engineering firms were destroyed in the Second World War and, as former arms producers, were limited after 1945 in their production through the Allies' embargoes on production and

197

dismantling. With the currency reform of 1948 and against the background of changed political conditions, the embargoes which up to then had applied to production were raised, and at the same time the nascent reconstruction of the West German economy triggered off an expanding demand for mechanical engineering products, which meant that in the 1950s this industry grew more strongly than industry in general.

Table 8.4: Development of Labour Force Proportions According to Size Categories of Industrial Mechanical Engineering Firms (in per cent)

	Firms with				
	10-99	100-199	200-499 employees	500-999	1,000-
1962	11.5	10.1	19.6	14.5	44.3
1966	12.4	10.4	19.6	16.3	41.4
1970	12.5	10.6	19.8	16.4	40.8
1979	14.2	11.2	20.0	16.6	38.0

Source: Federal Office of Statistics.

The below-average increase in labour productivity from the mid-1950s onwards (24.6 per cent in mechanical engineering against about 38 per cent in industry in general between 1955 and 1960), however, hints at the dilemma of the industry which, in the transition from extensive to intensive growth of the economy, is providing the specialised technical solutions for mechanisation and automation of production, but at the same time is increasingly limited to conditions of single and small-batch runs. Mechanical engineering delivered in the early 1950s a large volume of standard machines in medium-batch runs for the basic equipment of the metal-processing firms. With however the concentration on clients' wishes and the construction of special machines for the planned rationalisation of the user firms, the batch size in component production decreased, manufacturing costs increased and the manufacturing process became more complicated.

The slower growth in demand for capital goods in the Federal Republic of Germany, which had set in at the end of the economic reconstruction period from the early 1960s on, limited the expansion of mechanical engineering. In spite of an increase in exports (from 36 per cent to 52 per cent in 1972), this meant that production between 1960 and 1970, at around 51 per cent, grew less than the industrial average of about 72 per cent. The tendency observable from the mid-1950s towards the construction of specialised and specific machines was strengthened under these conditions in the 1960s. This, it is true, permitted mechanical engineering firms, through emphasis on the special character of problem-solving and the high precision and quality of their products, to withdraw to a certain extent from direct price competition on the national and international markets, but on the other hand made them more dependent on the wage- and qualification-intensive work processes of single and small-batch production. This dependency was particularly perceived from the early 1960s when, following the numerous decreases in working hours and major rises in wages, personnel costs rose considerably and consequently the comparatively work-intensive firms of mechanical engineering became greatly pressurised by costs,[3] which could only partly be passed on in prices. The resulting deterioration in production profitability may therefore have been the cause of the increased rationalisation measures in mechanical engineering firms which set in after the market crisis of 1966/67 and were indeed specifically tailored to the particular production conditions of this branch.

The diverse, reciprocally inter-meshed technical-organisational changes during this time were rarely of a spectacular nature in their attempts to tighten up the production process through the improving of machine tools on a conventional basis or by purposive product design and work-organisation measures. They were nevertheless finally of great consequence in the long-term 'creeping' reorganisation of the work process. Even the introduction of numerically controlled machine tools, which at first sight might seem the most spectacular technological innovation of the 1960s, is in this typically 'sluggish' process of change in production structure, considering the complex character of mechanical engineering, to be seen as one important measure amongst others rather than as the one bringing about a sudden reorganisation.

The economic situation in the 1970s became more difficult for mechanical engineering in the Federal Republic of Germany, especially for the machine-tool manufacture. In this period it moved into a longish phase of stagnation, which originated in particular from the great decrease in domestic demand for mechanical engineering products as a consequence of the generally falling investment activity. Even a great expansion of exports could not completely compensate for this drop in demand. Particularly in machine-tool manufacturing, increased international competition became noticeable in the 1970s on the domestic market, caused on the one hand by the growing supply of cheap standard machines from industrial countries with low wage levels, and on the other by typified, mass-produced NC machine tools from Japan. Thus from 1974 to 1980 the proportion of import compared with export values of machine tools rose from about 13 per cent to 29 per cent. The trend towards complex, customer-oriented individual production was greatly strengthened by this development. As a consequence of the unfavourable economic situation, employment in machine-tool manufacture between 1970 and 1980 decreased considerably, by 21 per cent (the decrease of employment in mechanical engineering between 1970 and 1980 was about 11 per cent, in industry as a whole 8 per cent).

Among the enforced rationalisation measures in mechanical engineering from the mid-1970s the introduction of CNC machine tools plays a special role. From the beginning mechanical engineering, and here especially machine-tool manufacture, used the majority of numerical machine tools in its own production. Thus in 1973, of all NC machines utilised in the Federal Republic of Germany, 65.4 per cent were used in mechanical engineering, and of these 25.6 per cent solely in machine-tool manufacture.

Employment structure

A glance at employment statistics makes clear the high demand for vocationally qualified employees in mechanical engineering, and even more in machine-tool manufacturing (see Table 8.5).

The proportion of technical employees among all those productively employed in mechanical engineering as early as 1962 was about one-and-a-half times as high as the industrial average and grew until 1972 noticeably faster than in industry as a whole. In machine-tool manufacture there were as early as 1972 more technical employees than 'other' workers, i.e. workers trained on the job and unskilled workers. The proportion of skilled workers among those productively employed in mechanical engineering both in 1962 and in 1972 surpassed the industrial average by almost 10 per cent. Even higher is the proportion of skilled workers in machine-tool manufacture, where about half of all productive activities are classed as vocationally skilled work and some 70 per cent of workers' activities are graded as requiring skilled qualifications. In contrast to industrial development, where the skilled-worker share in work activities declined slightly between 1962 and 1972, namely from 41.3 per cent to 39.7 per cent, in mechanical engineering it remained almost constant, and in machine-tool manufacture it even rose slightly.

Remarkable in mechanical engineering is the above-average share of the vocationally trained, from whom firms traditionally meet their high demand for skilled workers and technicians, a large proportion of whom have attended further-education technical colleges only after completing training as a skilled worker. Compared with all the productively employed, in mechanical engineering between 1962 and 1972 the number of apprentices trained as skilled workers was more than double, and in machine-tool manufacture even triple the industrial average (see Table 8.5).

Table 8.5: Structure of Gainful Employment in the Federal Republic of Germany in 1962 and 1972 (proportion of gainfully employed in per cent)

	Year	Total industry	Mechanical engineering	Machine-tool manufacture
Skilled	1962	36.1	45.1	51.8
workers[1])	1972	33.3	42.5	48.0
Other	1962	51.4	33.2	24.0
workers	1972	50.4	31.8	21.3
Technical	1962	9.1	13.6	14.0
employees[1])	1972	13.2	19.5	21.7
Vocational	1962	3.4	8.1	10.2
trainees[1])	1972	3.1	6.2	9.0
Skilled	1962	41.3	57.6	68.6
workers[2])	1972	39.7	57.2	69.3
Women workers[3])	1972	28.8	9.8	

1) In all cases as percentage of all productively employed, i.e. without proprietors, office workers and non-trade trainees.
2) Skilled workers as a percentage of all workers.
3) Percentage of all workers.

Source: Federal Office of Statistics, Fachserie D, Reihe 4, 1974.

Introduction of CNC in a machine-tool enterprise

Plant characteristics, product structure, labour market

The firm under study in 1982 had ca. 800 employees. It is an independent family firm, which for 100 years has been producing machines - at first textile machines, later machine tools.

The firm, which had employed about 150 employees before the Second World War, began again after the war with some 100 employees to repair and overhaul machine tools. At the beginning of the 1950s it developed, with a horizontal boring machine, its own product, which formed the basis for the great expansion of the enterprise in the 1950s and 1960s. At the beginning of the 1970s it belonged, with some 1,000 employees and a turnover of around 60 million DM, to the 12 major machine-tool producers in the Federal Republic of Germany.

During the recession at the beginning of the 1970s, the firm experienced a serious crisis. This was made worse by the fact that the firm had failed to keep up with the development of machine tools at that time. Only with the successful development of a new generation of products in 1976/77 did the firm overcome its economic crisis, and at the beginning of the 1980s it reached its old volume of production. The years 1972-76, during which turnover sank drastically, marked a phase of extensive restructuring and rationalisation in practically all departments, including management. During this time the number of employees was drastically reduced by some 25 per cent, through normal labour turnover but also through mass dismissals. Although turnover has grown considerably since the end of the 1970s (between 1979 and 1982 by almost 50 per cent) the increased production is achieved with a barely increased labour capacity (plus 8 per cent between 1979 and 1982). The greatly increased labour productivity shown here can be partly explained by the increased utilisation of new technologies - in particular through computer use in commercial administration and through CNC machines in mechanical production - and partly also by a considerable increase in efficiency (particularly in assembly).

The firm specialises in horizontal boring machines and processing centres in three sizes, each with several equipment variants, for the processing of small, medium and large workpieces (from 160 mm shaft diameter, 50 t weight). These are all highly technical precision machines, each of which can, in spite of a

202

system of standardised units, be constructed according to the particular processing requirements of the customers. All machine tools are offered today with CNC control, palette system and automatic tool changer. Recently a small machining centre has been produced which is more strongly typified than the other machines and is intended to contribute to the full basic utilisation of the firm's facilities.

The firm is in worldwide competition with five or six enterprises, and within the Federal Republic of Germany has a market share of about 50 per cent. The export share is on average 50 per cent. The firm delivers machines to the whole metal industry, though mechanical engineering, and in particular machine-tool manufacture, forms the major emphasis.

The plant lies in an area of industrial concentration (city of around 260,000 inhabitants) which has an above-average regional unemployment level (in April 1983, 11 per cent), due to the decline of the traditionally dominant textile industry. The firm has a strong position in the specialised market for skilled metal workers since it offers more than other firms in the region in terms of payment and social benefits. In spite of this at the end of the 1960s it had difficulties in recruiting skilled workers and also trainees for work in the mechanical workshop, in particular turners and boring machine turners. However, from the mid-1970s the situation has changed. Today, for each training place for turners or boring machine turners there are up to six applicants, and the external recruitment of experienced skilled workers is again possible.

Production organisation

Organisational scheme and management structure

The firm is headed by a managing director and a deputy manager, under whom are the main departments of: development/design, production planning, production, personnel, material administration, financing, and sales. The quality control department is directly under management control. The seven main departments are in turn divided hierarchically into numerous sections, headed by department heads at a sub-level of management. Only in production departments with a large number of staff is there a further hierarchical division with foremen (*Meister*) who are responsible for individual phases of production, such as boring-machine processing. It is, however, characteristic of the decision-taking attitude of the management that important decisions are not taken hierarchically by the firm management alone, but are prepared and voted on in a co-operative fashion on the upper level of management, that is by the managing directors and all the heads of departments. This co-operative principle of decision-making is called the 'workshop' procedure. True, the hierarchical structure of the actual work is not affected by this. The interests of workers and employees in the lower echelons are represented according to the Works Constitution Act by an elected Works Council, whose members are released from work duties for their (legally defined) activities.

To give a general idea, Table 8.6 presents the numbers of staff in a few of the important departments (as of December 1982).

Table 8.6: Employment Structure of Plant

Design/development		77
Production planning		84
of this:	Work preparation	42
	Production control	14
	Tool manufacture	15
	Maintenance	13
Production		315
of this:	Mechanical production	124
	Paint shop	6
	Mechanical assembly	126
	Electronic assembly	59
Administration		121
General services (including trainees)		178
		775

Work flow, organisational structure of mechanical production unit

The work flow begins with the conclusion of a contract for a new machine tool. With the help of a construction design diagram it is first established how many components for the new item are already known and how many components must be designed afresh. Usually some 20 per cent of machine components have to be newly designed. At the same time the production planning department decides which components must be bought, which are in stock and which have to be produced in mechanical fabrication.

For those parts which have to be mechanically produced, work plans are prepared as soon as the construction diagrams are available and - if an NC machine is to be used - NC programs are drawn up. Following a weekly time plan calculated by computer, the individual jobs are distributed in detail to the machine tools of the mechanical fabrication. The completed workpieces are then checked by the quality inspectors and temporarily stored until assembly.

Before assembly begins, the purchased components and those specially produced in the plant are checked to see that they are all complete. Large assemblies (for instance gear cases) are assembled according to a division into workshops and groups of workers, the mechanical assemblies are put together, the electrical control units, motors and electrical connections installed and the whole machine tool put into operation.

The use of CNC machines especially affects the mechanical fabrication and the process preparations, in which one group produces the NC programs. The mechanical fabrication of the firm can be divided according to the size and complexity of the workpieces into the 'heavy parts' and the 'light parts' spheres. In the heavy part workshop there are the large milling and grinding machines, which are worked in three shifts (one foreman, nine workers), and several numerically controlled and conventional horizontal boring machines as well as one machining centre (one foreman, 21 workers) working in two shifts. The light machine workshop includes first the turning shop (including a sawing shop: one foreman, 18 workers) and second a milling shop, gear-wheel production and grinding shop (one foreman, 25 workers). These mainly work a single shift.

In contrast to the heavy part shop the machine tools of the light part shop are rather out of date. Apart from two ten-year-old NC machines there are only two NC vertical boring machines. The heavy part shop, on the other hand, has nine modern CNC machine tools. The cases described below are chosen both from the heavy and the light part production.

Introduction of new technologies

The firm was one of the early users of NC machines in the Federal Republic of Germany. As early as 1962 an NC vertical boring machine with straight cut-control system was introduced for experimental purposes in the firm's own production. From 1964 horizontal boring machines with NC control began to be produced in larger numbers, but the firm did not yet at that time use the NC horizontal boring machines in its own production, as they did not seem reliable enough for this purpose. In the period 1969-72 a wider introduction of NC machines can be observed, during the course of which, besides simple NC vertical boring machines, several NC lathes and also the firm's own NC horizontal boring machines were put into use. These are NC continuous path-control machines on the basis of an integrated circuits (IC) technique which are controlled by perforated tape.

The storage and correction of fed-in data are not possible at the machine. The NC programs are centrally prepared by a programming group in work preparation and corrected by the same team after running-in. The programming team also produces NC programs ordered by customers who have bought the NC horizontal boring machine from the firm.

The implementation of NC machines was not the only technological innovation in the firm's mechanical fabrication in the 1960s. Thus the cutting speed of machine tools was greatly improved by new cutting materials (hard alloy turnover board, ceramics). Considerable repercussions were caused, in particular for the number of machines in the mechanical fabrication, by the use of continuous-control direct-current motors in the machine tools produced by the firm: a major proportion of the moving parts in the hitherto complicated mechanical gearings (cogwheels, shafts, gears) became unnecessary, so that considerably fewer turret lathes were needed for their production.

With the overcoming of the economic crisis a second wave of introduction of numerically controlled machine tools took place from the mid-1970s and continued into 1982. These were all modern storage-programmable CNC machines for which the NC programs are centrally produced but which can be optimised and corrected at the machines. It is noticeable that these CNC machines are intended exclusively for the heavy mechanical production, i.e. for the processing of complicated prismatic workpieces: three CNC horizontal boring machines, one CNC milling machine, one CNC processing centre with automatic machine-tool changing and palette system and two large CNC milling machines, of which one is integrated with a grinding machine and the other replaces several parallel planing machines (see Table 8.7).

There were also changes in NC programming. Early on, only the lathes were semi-automatically, and all other NC machines manually programmed. In the meantime a computer-aided programming process has been introduced with the help of which the programmer can program prismatic workpieces in dialogue with the computer at the terminal. Programming time has thus been considerably reduced.

Table 8.7: Number of NC/CNC Machine Tools in Operation

	Lathes	Vertical boring machines	Horizontal boring machines, milling machines	Processing centre	Heavy milling machines	Total no. of machines
As of end 1974						
No. of machines	2	2	2	-	-	6
Number of shifts worked	1-2	2	1	-	-	-
As of Jan. 1983						
No. of machines	2	2	6	1	2	13
Number of shifts worked	1-2	1	2	3	3	3

Decision-making process

It is not possible to identify exactly who was responsible for the initiative to introduce NC machines. The production management in particular played an important role as an initiator, although the decision was made by the firm management. This division between initiative and decision has continued right up to the present. However, the highly important investment decisions for the large waves of NC introduction at the beginning of the 1970s and 1980s were made within the senior management after a long period of preparation and discussion (on the workshop principle).

To prepare the decision on the choice of appropriate numerically controlled machines as well as on their technical and organisational integration into the plant, a committee was formed with representatives of production planning and all production departments right down to the foremen. This committee visited trade fairs and professional conferences and made contacts with NC-producing firms. It also began to plan NC introduction a year in advance. The questions of tooling system, programming and machine operation were also dealt with.

Whereas in the 1960s the first NC machines were chosen primarily on technical testing aspects and not so much on economic criteria, all further NC/CNC machines were subjected to a systematic computation of profitability. The essential criteria of profitability - assuming a two-shift utilisation on the expensive machines for economic reasons - were, on the one hand, the shortened processing time per workpiece (lowering of piece costs) and, on the other, the faster movement of the workpiece through the whole production process in order to decrease the high storage costs. There was in addition a saving in space, an NC machine usually replacing two to three conventional machine tools, and with the prismatic workpieces there were savings in appliances and clamping tools which until then had been fabricated by qualified toolmakers.

In addition to these quantifiable savings in cost, the management quotes further important reasons for the introduction of NC/CNC machines. In particular there was expected a high constant precision of all pieces in a series of complicated workpieces as well as a high repetition accuracy in workpieces which were produced only from time to time. The numerical machine tools, in so far as they were products of the firm, also served display and demonstration purposes. For potential buyers the practical usefulness and profitability of the introduction of NC machines could be demonstrated.

The management, however, also mentions uncertainties and wrong estimates concerning the profitability of the first NC machines in the early 1970s. In view of the expected great reduction in piece costs, the reorganisation difficulties connected with NC implementation were greatly underestimated. Based on experience gained up to then with conventional machine tools, there was too much concentration on the technical conditions of the innovation and a neglect of the integration of high-performance machines into the more 'handicraft'-improvising organisation of mechanical fabrication. Frequent hitches and underuse of the NC machines were the first consequences of these omissions.

Under the economic necessity of utilising these expensive high-performance NC machines more effectively, the firm perfected the preparatory and planning characteristics of work organisation. The central programming office was just as much involved in these measures as, for instance, a special work team for the pre-adjustment of tools. Even though some organisational measures for the tightening-up of the production process were made independently of NC introduction, this implementation, however, formed the decisive stimulus for a radical reorganisation of the mechanical fabrication. An important step along this path was the introduction of computer-aided production planning and control at the beginning of the 1970s, in order to systematise and stabilise the hitherto often chaotic work flow which had been mainly controlled by the foremen.

With the new batch of CNC machine tools at the end of the 1970s, the problem of keeping the machines fully occupied became more serious, since on the one hand the implemented CNC horizontal boring machines, processing centres and milling machines were extremely expensive, and on the other hand the complicated workpieces, which in spite of large dimensions had to be processed extremely precisely, represented a special source of adjustment difficulties and processing upsets in the co-operation between programmer and machine operator.

For the CNC machines two shifts were introduced, for the large milling machines and the processing centre three shifts. Furthermore, the firm moved partially away from the principle of increasing centralisation and separation of work preparation functions, by using the new technical possibilities of a simpler machine programming by CNC, leaving the adjustment and optimisation of the centrally prepared CNC programs to the skilled worker at the CNC machine. In this way an attempt was made to reduce the common difficulties in the co-operation between programmers who were preparing 'practice-alien' NC programs and machine operators who had to work with faulty programs - difficulties which lowered the full utilisation of the machines. The machine operators' professional competence and responsibility for programming and processing was thus furthered and an attempt was made to replace the confrontation with programmers by comradely co-operation.

This concept of a comprehensive usage of the workers' skills and motivation is not uncontested. It is principally the production management which supports it, because they see in it the possibility of coping with the daily pressure of production with a too small but professionally qualified group of machine operators. Against this, some of the firm management and the work preparation management fear a resulting, too great autonomy of the workers, which in the long run could lead to a non-transparency in the production process. The difference of opinions between the two factions is not yet settled, even though at present the comprehensive concept of the production management is being practised.

It is reported from within the firm that the firm management a year ago wanted to return to a stricter division of work, by forbidding the machine operators to undertake the correction of NC programs. Upon this, the workshop, with the consent of the production management, practised a work-to-rule, causing the use of the CNC machines in the heavy part shop to drop drastically. A return to the original practice, i.e. letting the workers undertake the correction of NC programs, was therefore considered unavoidable.

Organisation of work

Change of work organisation through NC innovation

In the mechanical fabrication at the enterprise the new NC machines were distributed according to their processing types among the technologically homogeneous groups of conventional machine tools (vertical boring machines, lathes, horizontal boring machines, milling machines) which were organised into individual domains under foremen. Because of this, there gradually arose a mixture of numerically controlled and conventional machines, although the latter were in the majority.

The traditional mechanical fabrication was also divided into preparatory and direct production functions. There were work preparation, tooling, the tool-grinding shop and maintenance. With the introduction of NC technology these functions were, however, partly enriched in content, partly supplemented by new tasks.

A new functional sphere was formed by the NC programming office as a sub-department of work preparation. It fulfils at the same time a service function without authority to give instructions to production workers.

With tool setting also a new step has been taken in the plant's work division. The group of tool regulators works on all NC machines in spatial concentration and functional specialisation.

In maintenance the demands on skills and the pressures for a swift and reliable sorting-out of hitches increase with more complicated techniques, in particular with the increase in electronic and hydraulic machine components. However, repairs to electronic controls are carried out by the service personnel of the manufacturing firm.

Through the withdrawal of work preparation and planning, being the core of traditional skilled machine work, the work on numerical machine tools is reduced to a simple attendance on the machine. Apart from loading and unloading the NC machine, observation and control of the automated manufacturing process become the main content of the job. However, at the firm under investigation it remained the duty of the machine operator, also in the first NC implementation with tested NC programs, to set up the workpieces in the machine. In many other firms this task is undertaken by a special skilled worker or the foreman.

With the increased use of CNC machines from the end of the 1970s the work division between programming and machine operation in the heavy part shop was modified (with the NC machines of the light part mechanical fabrication, however, the old form of strict division of work remained). The new division of work can be described as a mixed form between the production of programs in the central NC programming and their testing and optimising by the skilled worker directly at the CNC machine. It is based on co-operation between programmers and machine operators, in which, on the one hand the programmers before programming discuss difficult workpieces with the machine operator or foreman concerning the best method of procedure, and, on the other hand the machine operator informs the programmer of his correction and optimising moves.

The production management regards this form of work division as the most economical solution at the moment, since it avoids both bureaucratic opposition of programming and workshop in the case of a pure 'office programming', and also cuts out long breaks through pure programming directly at the machine in the case of the so-called 'workshop programming'. It is, however, expected that in future, with further advances in computer-aided NC programming (geometric processors, clear presentation of the programmed metal-cutting machining) small, uncomplicated workpieces will be programmed economically directly on the CNC machines. At the firm, however, no decision in this direction has been taken yet.

Task structure

As new activities in the environment of the NC system, programming, tool regulation and machine operation have emerged.

The programmer produces the NC perforated strip, the clamping plan and the tooling plan in the programming office according to information from the workpiece blueprint and the work plan. He works at a computer terminal upon which he can very simply carry out geometric calculations and call up stored cutting values. For NC turned parts and vertical boring programs he runs in the new programs together with the machine operator and in case of need also corrects them, though with prismatic parts this is not necessary for him.

The tool installer fits the tools according to the NC tooling plan onto the appropriate tool holder and adjusts it with the help of an optical adjusting apparatus to the prescribed length. The tools can thus be fitted in the clamps of the NC machine by the machine operator without any delay.

The CNC machine operator first fixes the workpiece according to the clamping plan and adjusts the prescribed tool according to the tooling plan. Then he feeds in the NC perforated strip and in the case of a new program tests this phase by phase for any faults, and also attempts to optimise the processing parameter according to his own experience. The corrected program is stored in the CNC control and finally fed out as a perforated strip. With a program which has already been tested the operator concentrates primarily on any irregularities in the automatic processing (material faults, tool breaks). Especially at the end of the processing he checks with measuring instruments the observance of the prescribed measurement tolerances. The workers are so-called 'self-checkers', i.e. an external control of quality takes place only after completion of the whole workpiece.

At the end of 1982 about 25 per cent of the workers in mechanical fabrication at the enterprise were CNC/NC operators (27 in all) and tool adjusters (three). If considering only those employed in the CNC/NC system, there were 17 per cent programmers, 8 per cent tool adjusters, 58 per cent CNC machine operators (with program adjustment) and 17 per cent NC machine operators (without program adjustment). Since the mid-1970s the proportion of programmers to those employed in the NC system has sunk by almost half from 30 per cent to a current 17 per cent.

Changes in manning and qualification structure

Regarding the changes in manning in the NC system, the number of NC/CNC machine operators almost trebled (from 10 to 27) between 1974 and 1982, whereas the number of programmers and

212

tool adjusters remained practically constant.[4] The personnel management therefore during the past few years has basically only had to concern itself with the recruitment and vocational training of CNC machine operators.

Looking back, it is clear that the recruitment and training of suitable workers for the new work-places in the NC system did not present any serious problem for the firm. Only the programming jobs presented new and higher qualification demands. All programmers are skilled metal workers (centre lathe operators and drilling machine turners) from the plant who first successfully completed a REFA course and following that a programming course (half a month to one month with the manufacturers).[5] With their promotion to the programming office the skilled workers were classed as salaried employees and their financial standing improved. There were therefore no problems in finding enough skilled workers who were willing to move up to this activity. Tooling adjustment was a favourite task for older skilled machine operators who did not want to do piece-work any more.

At the beginning the manning of the NC machines was more difficult. Skilled workers were used for the running-in phase, but they remained after that only on the NC horizontal boring machines. For the NC lathes the firm would also have liked to keep skilled workers as machine operators, especially since the wage difference between skilled workers and experienced workers trained on the job was negligible. The centre lathe operators, however, all went back to their conventional lathes over time, since to them the work conditions there seemed to be relatively more favourable: varied work, greater margin of independence in arranging work, no shift work. The firm therefore put onto the NC lathes turret lathe operators trained on the job, and also on the NC vertical boring machines workers trained on the job were employed - which had been planned from the beginning.

Since the end of the 1970s the importance of numerical machine tools has changed. It is true that on the NC vertical boring machines there are still workers trained on the job, but in the meantime all the other NC/CNC machines have been manned with skilled workers (turners or boring machine turners). In particular in the heavy part shop, training as a skilled worker was considered an absolute necessity to guarantee frictionless co-operation between programming and machine operating on the complex CNC machines, and to ensure the work quality on complicated workpieces. A large proportion of the CNC workers has already attended programming courses (primarily intended for customers) organised by the firm, can correct NC programs and produce smaller NC programs themselves.

The fact that in the meantime the two NC lathes are also operated by skilled workers is explained primarily by the worsened labour market of the past few years for trained turners.

Let us briefly glance back at personnel policy in the firm from the mid-1970s on. In the course of the economic crisis of the mid-1970s the staff of mechanical fabrication was reduced in the same proportion as the total staff (by about 19 per cent), but the reduction in personnel hit the different groups of employees to very different extents. Thus the on-the-job learners, who in the mid-1970s were the largest group of employees in mechanical fabrication (48 per cent) were reduced in number by natural wastage and dismissals by about two-thirds, while in contrast at the same time the skilled work staff was increased by about one-third. As a consequence of this intentional concentration of personnel policy on skilled workers, which was based in particular on the increased training by the firm of turners and boring machine turners, the skilled worker share of mechanical fabrication rose from 47 per cent to 77 per cent between 1974 and 1982.

This greatly increased potential of skilled workers formed the basis for the closer skilled co-operation between programmers and CNC machine operators. In a time of mass unemployment it also allowed the firm to employ qualified skilled workers at comparatively restricted workplaces, as is the case in NC turning machine operation, which they could have successfully refused in times of better labour market conditions.

The skilled workers, in the majority fully trained boring-machine turners with long work experience, were not really systematically introduced to CNC programming. They only took part in the one-week programming course also offered to customers. Thus there are considerable differences in professional competence in handling NC programs among the CNC machine operators, according to individual abilities and learning motivation. At present therefore there is a situation from which a 'natural' polarisation with long-term consequences for the internal workshop division of work can develop between those skilled workers who through their own efforts can check and correct even difficult programs on the CNC machines and those who more or less never get beyond the point of simply 'muddling through'. This obvious lack of training in programming of the CNC machine operators is an expression of the unsureness of the management over the future conception of work division between programming office and machine operation. The middle path pursued today of co-operation between programmers and skilled workers is for the management not yet a securely based conception, and it has therefore so far had only half-hearted consequences on the firm's policy of further training. It is possible that the management will return the sole competency for CNC programming to the programming office, in which case the skilled workers at the CNC machines would be limited entirely to simple machine operating.

Quality of work

Through the introduction of numerically controlled machine tools and the division of work into planning-preparatory tasks, on the one side, and processing tasks, on the other, the hitherto traditional unity of practice and brainwork has been dissolved. In the environment of the NC system at least four new activities have arisen which differ concerning the qualification demands but also concerning other central conditions of work. These are programming, tooling adjustment, NC machine operation (without programming) and CNC machine operation (with programming).

With the programming job a technical activity has arisen in which abstract systematic thinking - for instance planning work sequence or putting blue-print geometry into mathematical program sentences - is interlocked with the practical experience of metal-cutting manufacturing technology. The possibilities of influencing programming to an optimal and precise processing of the workpiece are great, but at the same time more difficult to grasp than with traditional skilled machine work. They mean not only a great responsibility for machine and workpiece but also cause specific stresses which are increased by the daily 'frictions' with skilled workers and foremen. On the other hand, the programmer has an important position in the firm as the main contact partner of the workshop in programming problems.

For the tooling adjuster there remains only a small scope for independent work action, since the work plan prescribes all steps right down to small details. Above all great care in the adjustment of tools and a wide knowledge of functions and quality of different types of tools are demanded of him. Since the work is carried out as time-work and usually not under pressure, the worker can easily regulate his amount of work. The noise-reducing separation of the adjusting room from the workshop also contributes to this job's appearing comparatively pleasant from the point of view of stress.

For the NC machine operator (on the NC vertical boring machine and the NC lathes) technical knowledge and technical sensitivity are demanded, above all during the setting-up of a new series. Since, however, he works only with tested NC programs and may not alter these, he possesses only a comparatively narrow margin of disposition in the shaping of the work process. Technical intelligence is hardly needed in this work, for this is taken over by the programmer. His responsibility for the product quality and processing time also decreases; on the other hand, the conservation of the expensive and productive NC machines gains in importance.

For the NC machine operator the structure of dynamic muscle stress is different from that in conventional machine work. He has, it is true, to load and unload more workpieces because of the now shorter processing time, but can get by without manual physical intervention during processing. Stress is increased by noise, since the NC machine runs at a higher rotation speed, greater cutting speed and with fewer breaks in production. This also demonstrates the characteristic psychological demands well known to controllers of automated machines. Particularly stressful is the strained readiness to step in in normal situations, since even in a smooth running of the machine, quality losses and machine breakdowns can arise at any time through material faults or tool breakages. Added to this are monotony and the feeling of unimportant dependence, since the qualified, varied parts of the work are carried out by the programming office. As in the NC system two shifts are worked, and there is in addition the well-known stress of shift work. The workers concerned feel this as additionally restrictive, since in general in conventional production only one shift is worked.

In contrast, the work situation of the CNC machine operator shows several significant differences. In comparison with the NC machines of the light part shop the workpieces processed here are incomparably more complex, so that each time complicated clamping and adjustment operations are necessary, and the processing time of a workpiece often surpasses tenfold that of the light part shop. In particular the skilled workers can intervene in the program sequence and themselves program minor sequence changes at the machine. During the running-in of new programs the skilled worker must be able to control the algorithms of the programs through his background of practical experience. He must possess certain programming talents in order to undertake program changes independently. The consequently necessary optimising procedure demands thinking of an abstract kind. Through his influence on programming, his responsibility for production achievement and product quality grows.

From the point of view of work content, the inclusion of programming enriches the variety of work and represents for the machine operator a challenge to his skill and an extension of his own qualifications. The programming work and the close co-operation with the programmers raise his social recognition, in particular also in reference to his superiors, some of whom cannot program, and make the position of the skilled worker stronger in the firm, since the firm is particularly dependent upon these skills.

The increased responsibility heightens the mental stress, since the possibilities of making mistakes have grown. On the other hand, the increased transparency of processes, which is a consequence of the greater knowledge of programs, decreases any uncertainty in the handling of the complex machines, and thereby contributes to mental stress relief. An important stress factor for the CNC machine operator is, however, undoubtedly the shift work, for on all CNC horizontal boring machines two shifts are worked, three on the CNC milling machines and in the machining centre.

Industrial relations

The firm is a member of the employers' association which represents all metal-working firms of the Federal Republic of Germany in the annual wage negotiations.

In 1982, 46 per cent of the employees were organised in unions (40 per cent in 1974). Of these, 62 per cent of the workers (60 per cent in 1974) and 25 per cent of the salaried employees (20 per cent in 1974) were organised. In the firm one union only is dominant, the industrial union of metalworkers, of which both the workers and the salaried employees are members.

The actual representative organ of the employees in the firm is the Works Council. It is composed of eleven Works Council members (seven workers, four salaried employees) elected by all employees, including non-union members. Of these, two members of the Works Council are released from their work for their Works Council activity. Remarkably, the majority of the workers' representatives on the Works Council come from mechanical fabrication (five out of seven), although these make up only about 24 per cent of all workers; the majority of the salaried employees' representatives on the Council are technicians (three out of four).

The Works Council members themselves are members of the IG Metall and some of them are also union officials in the local section of the union. The co-operation between Works Council and union in important problems of the plant is, however, very loose. The Works Council complains of lack of support and authority on the part of the local union officials. Recently it has, however, obtained support from an expert of the head office of IG Metall in negotiations concerning an agreement with the firm on data protection.

For the relationship between firm management and Works Council it can be said that their common concern is a search for compromises rather than an escalation of problems into conflicts. The Works Council, however, reports that it can only intervene in problems which fall under worker co-determination according to the Works Constitution Act. To these belong in particular wage categories, hiring and firing of staff, overtime agreements and the way staff data are handled. Through its participation in important committees of the firm, such as the economics committee, the personnel committee and the wage and piecework committee, the Works Council obtains information about planned measures of the firm management and can to a certain extent influence them.

Thus the Works Council was informed early via the economics committee about the impending introduction of NC/CNC machines. It was, however, not able to influence the form of this innovation, though at that time it did not even have the intention of doing so. It first intervened when a deterioration in the financial situation of the NC machine operators became noticeable.

During the NC changeover at the beginning of the 1970s the machine operators at first worked for about a year on time-work according to the average of their previous piecework wage. With the changeover to piecework rates at the end of the running-in period it became obvious that the NC machine operators' scope of arranging work had decreased so greatly that they were totally unable to reach anything like their previous level of income. The Works Council therefore, in negotiations with the management, achieved an addition of 35 per cent to the piecework rate and later, as this was insufficient, the upgrading by one wage group.

At that time, in a period of prosperity at the beginning of the 1970s, the workers did not need to worry about their workplaces in the firm. Today the Works Council reports that it is massively confronted with the problems of mass unemployment and the enforced introduction of new technologies into the firm. The Works Council in the past few years therefore worked towards a reduction in overtime so as to employ more workers instead. It has been partially successful in this, but has had to overcome resistance by some of the workers who did not want to give up overtime as an additional source of income.

The Works Council says that it was above all startled by the speed and massiveness of technological development in the plant during recent years. It complains that the existing skeleton wage agreements and the agreements concerning protection from rationalisation were no longer effective in this situation, but that possibilities of regulation under the Works Constitution Act were very limited. In order at least to account to itself for the consequences and regulation needs of the new technology, the Works Council in 1982 founded a 'rationalisation committee'. This is supposed to be concerned with all current and future rationalisation plans in the firm and to inform the Works Council in good time of all new problems arising for employees as well as to prepare methods of solution.

In general the representation of the employees' interests is undertaken by the Works Council in a way very typical of Federal German conditions. The Works Council is informed by the firm management of important measures. It can often, it is true, not directly exercise influence upon these, but it knows that the management cannot ignore its views in the regulation of many questions. From this a certain margin of negotiation emerges, which the Works Council in particular attempts to use for the conclusion of contracts between plant and management.

Changes in work culture

A characteristic of skilled mechanical engineering workers is their vocational continuity from training - often in the firm in which they later work - to their position as experienced skilled workers. They possess a remarkable self-confidence as practically indispensable experts who know their value to the firm and are used to defending their own interests and even sometimes to going it alone. They are the practical people without whom the designers and planners could not create any of their machines. This pride of the producer does not exclude their finding the work arduous, with high physical and psychical demands through piecework and time rating. But it contains, besides production stress, considerable potentiality for independent work activity, the invention and use of numerous tricks and stratagems which make up the essence of these 'vocational workers'.

> '"Autonomy" is the key category also for self-interpretation. It enables one to cope with the demands for performance, within this one finds oneself again as a practical expert, it bestows a certain exclusivity. Autonomy is too often lacking in "only semi-skilled" workers - both in their own self-image and in the way they are regarded by their skilled colleagues' (Kern and Schumann 1984: 203).

Rationalisation processes in firms due to the introduction of CNC machine tools affect, as we have seen, different groups of workers in different ways, according to whether they are granted participation in programming as CNC operators or are employed as traditional skilled machine operators in one of the professional 'reservations' still protected from the new technologies.

The CNC machine operators

In so far as skilled machine operators participate in programming and optimisation, they feel their new work to be a definite improvement and a re-evaluation of their professional competence. They have had to learn the logic of programming and generally adapt to a more abstract, systematically planned way of working. This has a fundamental significance for the way they regard their work.

> 'For them the change means progressing from being only empiricists to being theoreticians too. They see this exclusively as progress because this transformation does not endanger their position as practical men. For them, the basis of their new activity, although determined by theory, is still their original training as metalworkers and their long practical experience on the machine.
>
> Of course they see that a number of manual skills and sectors of knowledge belonging to the old professional image have today lost their value and are hardly required any more, but this is compensated for by increased demand

for qualification in other sectors. At least until now, therefore, the NC development has been seen not as an undermining of established positions and allotment of tasks, but as a rearrangement of the skilled worker profile which must be borne in the interest of the company. Once the fears and worries rooted in the usual conservatism in work policy have been overcome, the self-understanding of the skilled worker comes to the fore. Keeping up with the new technologies leads to more demanding and more interesting work and certainly means a new professional challenge - besides raising the market value of the worker's training' (Kern and Schumann 1984: 207).

This positive picture is not significantly clouded when work stresses in the new work situation are taken into consideration. It is true that workers report stress in the learning period, especially from high learning demands, and this is not mitigated by any systematic training by the company in programming on the CNC machines. However, after completing the training period, they recognise that in the stress balance there are also advantages, such as that a number of physically strenuous jobs (tool-changing, manual positioning) are now automated. The psychical demands are certainly still present, with heightened concentration and greater responsibility, but after some experience on the new machines a certain scope for manoeuvring is recognised, which can be exploited to reduce stress.

If the CNC operators have, as the survey shows, been mostly able up to now to cope with the changeover, they still experience considerable insecurity with regard to the future. It concerns less the fear of losing their jobs as a consequence of further rationalisation than that of losing their newly attained status as experts because of further steps in automation which they might not be able to accomplish.

From their entry into CNC technology they have had a glimpse of the potentialities in today's computer techniques, and have personally experienced how fast traditional jobs can change.

'They do not wish to exclude the possibility that full automation could within the foreseeable future overtake their work and that with completion of measuring and control techniques and perfecting of programming their newly attained field of activity could disappear. In the range between "button-pusher" and "electrical engineer" the question must be asked, say a number of the CNC machine operators, whether in future there will still be a place for the genuine skilled worker. The newly expanded expert status could prove to be merely a transitional phase which will not stand up to further technological complication of production.

It has by no means yet been decided where all this is leading for CNC machine operators. The prognosis of a total disappearance of the practice-oriented metal-cutting expert is not yet totally excluded, even if it is not any more inevitable. For most of them, the question which is still definitely open is: Can our skilled worker status be revoked? This glance towards the future therefore dims the otherwise intact self-confidence of the skilled worker group. And it is for this reason that they have set binding priorities concerning their attitude in further rationalisation processes. In any case, any production concept which serves to confirm their expert status finds their undivided support' (Kern and Schumann 1984: 210).

The traditional skilled machine operators

The traditional skilled machine operators have in the meantime realised that the trend of new technology is passing them and that they have been shunted into a siding. They are now convinced that it is only a matter of time before their field, too, is taken over by CNC techniques. They are right to be worried that they may thereby be destroyed.

There are many reservations about a changeover to CNC techniques. In a way CNC work is the negative equivalent of their own professional work. They are afraid of losing their skilled competence and their own style of work, and also of being subjected to higher achievement stress.

'That this concern is not really applicable to CNC changes is obviously very difficult to explain in words to the traditional machine operators. There is very little interchange of information concerning experience between the operators on the conventional machines and those on the CNC ones, which would help in forming judgments. The explanations of colleagues are apparently not trusted, and are often suspected of being due to the wish to gloss over a new work situation whose humiliation should not be publicly seen and thus expose a wrong choice made. The prestige of rank between conventional and CNC machine work has, it is true, already been decided in favour of the latter, but this provokes, among those "left behind" such styles as that real expert machining work is demanded only of the old machines' (Kern and Schumann 1984: 212).

The current wave of rationalisation is regarded as signifying the end to the old profession of metal-cutter who fear to be forced completely onto the losing side by further automation measures. Certainly the younger among the trained workers will sooner or later make the leap into the CNC camp in spite of previous reservations. Problems, however, appear concerning older and semi-skilled workers. Older workers can only hope for early retirement. Those only semi-skilled, however, who were already the first to be dismissed during rationalisation measures, must more than ever fear for their work-places. Their insufficient qualifications are regarded, from the point of view of the firm, as a hindrance to retraining for the new CNC jobs.

'In the current wave of modernisation they would prefer to retain the status quo, but for the propagation of this position they have neither the power to succeed nor can they find allies. Their thorough scepticism regarding all further rationalisation is more than justified; they not only see themselves completely shunted into a siding, but additionally as in danger of being uncoupled from the train. In such a situation, who wouldn't be afraid?' (Kern and Schumann 1984: 213).

Resistance or co-operation in further automation?

In general, collective resistance by skilled production workers in mechanical engineering is not to be expected so long as internal rationalisation of the firm's work is concerned and not the closure of the firm. To them, rationalisation of work appears to be just as much a necessary policy as it does to the management. They know, from other firms which have gone bankrupt, that whoever shows weakness is fired. From this the workers draw the same conclusions as the management:

'It is essential to be able to manufacture the most modern products by the most effective methods and to put them on the market. And precisely because these skilled workers regard their own contribution to the high-value product as being by no means a minor one, they are trapped by the firm's insistence that in this everyone is presented in the same way with a challenge, that they are all in the same boat rowing together with one another in a struggle with rough seas. It is of no consequence that the man at the helm has a different share from the one at the oar' (Kern and Schumann 1984: 215).

From this willingness to take on co-responsibility for a stabilising modernisation of the firm there arises, however, no right to co-determination of the form which rationalisation of the firm could take.

'It is true that there is no lack of criticism of the intact monopoly of decision-making enjoyed by a firm's management, but this is registered as a fact and adapted to. The shop stewards and the metalworkers' union are both seen as having no influence on decisions and concrete forms of the rationalisation process. Only in the subordinate questions of the execution of the measures or of their effects, possibilities of influence are seen. In how far they are realised, the estimates vary greatly, but the criticism of the lack of protection in rationalisation is consistently stronger than the conviction that there are at least feasible counter-positions in reserve to be opposed to the concepts of the management' (Kern and Schumann 1984: 216).

In the expected co-operative support of further automation by the skilled production workers, an important role is played by their traditionally individual pattern of the representation of their interests. Negotiation of working conditions is traditionally regarded by the skilled worker in mechanical engineering as his own responsibility, to be delegated only to a limited extent to the shop steward or the trade union.

'Resistance has been tried out as an individual, sometimes as a group attitude, but as a rule not as a collective one.

Estimates of the probability of success correspond to the amount one can expect to achieve oneself; partially collective agreements within the work group are, in spite of the extensive loss of a relationship secured privately, seen as still comprehensible and thus able to be estimated. In actions involving all employees there was extreme scepticism whether solidarity could be formed with others and common action thus made possible' (Kern and Schumann 1984: 216).

Since however, as we have seen, the introduction of CNC machines affects the interests of the individual groups of workers to very different extents, a common basis for collective resistance is rather hindered than promoted. CNC machine operators already occupy good positions in the trend of modernisation. They would only resist a management strategy which threatened to remove their newly-won expert status in production through a policy of strict division of labour and petty restrictions. On the other hand, the group of the traditional machine operators already feels itself too weak for a common resistance, especially as here too different interests are present and further splintering threatens to occur. Individual attempts to master the situation seem to be the most probable reaction.

Notes

1. Since in the same period the social dues (deductions for sickness, pension, and unemployment insurance) were rising considerably, the increase in net earnings barely kept pace with the rise in the cost of living.

2. The proportion of those who annually wish to go on to university has, however, fallen from 87.2 per cent in 1971 to 68.2 per cent in 1981.

3. The drastic increase in wage rates from 40.4 per cent in 1960 to 54 per cent in 1970 demonstrates the greatly increased proportion of labour costs in the production figures of mechanical engineering; by contrast, in industry as a whole the wage rate rose only from 34 per cent to around 41 per cent during this period.

4. During this period a second programming office was established which produces NC programs for customers of the firm's CNC machine tools. In work overload situations the programming offices help each other.

5. REFA is a large private institute of further education in the Federal Republic of Germany, with emphasis on the training of skilled workers and technicians for work preparation and timing calculators.

References

Baethge, M., F. Gerstenberger, H. Kern, M. Schumann, H.W. Stein and E. Wiene-mann (1974) 'Produktion und Qualifikation Vorstudie' (Production and Qualification) *Schriften zur Berufsbildungsforschung*, volume 14, Hanover, Jänecke Verlag

Baethge, M., W. Bauer, W. Mohr, J. Münch, I. Schöll-Schwinghammer and M. Schumann (1976) *Sozialpolitik und Arbeitsinteresse* (Social Policy and Labour Interest), Frankfurt/M., Campus Verlag

Baethge, M., E. Brumlop, H. Faulstich-Wieland and F. Gerlach (1980) 'Ausbil-dungs- und Berufsstartprobleme von Jugendlichen' (Youth Problems of Training and Starting Work), research report, Göttingen

Bergmann, J., O. Jacobi and W. Müller-Jentsch (1976) *Gewerkschaften in der Bundesrepublik* (Trade Unions in the Federal Republic of Germany), Frankfurt/M., EVA

Kern, H. and M. Schumann, (1984) *Das Ende der Arbeitsteilung? Rationalisierung in der industriellen Produktion* (The End of the Division of Labour? Rationalisation in Industrial Production), Munich, Beck Verlag

Mickler, O., W. Mohr and U. Kadritzke (1978) *Produktion und Qualifikation* (Production and Qualification), Berlin, Bundesinstitut für Berufsbildung

Mickler, O. (1981) *Facharbeiter im Wandel. Rationalisierung im Industriellem Produktionsprozess* (Skilled Workers in a State of Change. Rationalisation in Industrial Production), Frankfurt/M. and New York, Campus Verlag

Osterland, M., W. Deppe, F. Gerlach, U. Mergner, K. Pelte and M. Schlösser (1973) *Materialien zur Lebens- und Arbeitssituation der Industriearbeiter in der BRD* (Materials on the Living and Working Situation of Industrial Workers in the Federal Republic of Germany), Frankfurt/M., Campus Verlag

Remp, H., M. Boffo and G. Lay (1981) *Wirtschaftliche und soziale Auswirkungen des CNC Werkzeugmaschineneinsatzes* (Economic and Social Effects of Using CNC Machine Tools), Eschborn, Rationalisierungskuratorium der Deutschen Wirtschaft

9

Technological Change in Four British Factories: Some Lessons from the Introduction of CNC Machine Tools

Arthur Francis

Introduction[1]

In Great Britain in the late 1970s there was an extremely high level of public, governmental and academic awareness of microelectronics as a new technology with possibly profound social and economic consequences. One strong element of concern about this new technology, espoused by the government in particular, was the extent to which it represented industrial and commercial opportunities and threats for British industry. Would British companies manage to take up the new technology at a fast enough rate to maintain, or increase, their competitive position in international markets? Another, expressed most forcibly by Clive Jenkins, the General Secretary of Great Britain's largest white-collar union, in his book *The Collapse of Work* (1979), was the potential of the new technology as a job-killer. In addition, the small academic community of sociologists of work, alerted by Braverman (1974) about the extent to which technologies had in the past been developed and implemented by management in capitalist enterprises in ways which had divorced conception from execution, stripped control over work from the craft worker, and had broken the power of organised labour, were concerned to explore the extent to which this new technology would be subject to the same processes. This time round there was also considerable interest in the extent to which trade unions, now more aware of these potential conflicts of interest between capital and labour over work organisation and job design, would be able to oppose managerial attempts to de-skill and reduce union influence in the workplace.

As our concern at the outset was rather wider than just that of work organisation, our cases are set in the context of the broader industrial structure of British manufacturing industry, the national economic context of the time and the British industrial relations structures. Our own research developed in parallel with rather rapid developments in the theoretical debate surrounding Braverman and the de-skilling thesis. Similarly our own empirical findings, reported here, match the more recent theoretical critiques of the Braverman thesis[2] which emphasise the extent to which specific institutional and historical factors, including those relating to the individual national context, need to be taken into account for a full explanation of the labour process and work organisation.

Our description of the forms of work organisation resulting from the introduction of new technology is therefore preceded by a discussion of the general context of its introduction in terms of the economic situation facing British firms at that time, the industrial structure of the firms involved and the forms of trade union organisation. Our general conclusion is that while the de-skilling thesis points to a powerful tendency operating within firms, a full understanding of the effects of the introduction of new technology requires a more comprehensive economic and social analysis along the lines attempted here, and that the particular institutional and economic circumstances of any one country may have as powerful an explanatory value for forms of work organisation in a particular country as any general tendency within capitalism and amongst management.

The competitive position of British manufacturing industry

At the time of the study, manufacturing industry in Great Britain was under very significant competitive pressure from overseas manufacturers in both home and export markets. The performance of the manufacturing sector of British industry was very low by international standards, in terms of profitability, productivity and productivity growth. The manufacturing sector, and engineering in particular, was, and is, in the process of long-run adjustment. Until the early 1960s it had faced virtually a sellers' market, but the greatly increased internationalisation of trade, including loss of protected home and Commonwealth markets, threatened exports and increased imports. Competition became much tougher, but not just on the basis of price. Buyers were preferring non-Great Britain manufactured products for non-price reasons such as better quality and timely delivery (Pavitt 1980). This perception of British manufacturing industry being in a 'five-to-midnight' crisis was shared by many managements and trade unionists and reflected by the academic community at that time in, for example, the production of a number of analyses of the situation including Blackaby (1978), Beckerman (1979) and Carter (1981).

Additional to this long-run adjustment problem was the immediate crisis of 1979-81 brought about by a combination of one-off factors including the arrival of North Sea oil and high interest rates due to the government's monetary policy. This led to a massive revaluation of sterling which had an additional effect on the international price competitiveness of British products, a substantial proportion of which are traded internationally. In addition, the second oil-price shock at this time led to a further recession in world output and trade. As a result, manufacturing output in Great Britain fell by over 14 per cent in just two years, with consequential job losses of one and a half million.

It was against these three major economic factors of long-run British industrial adjustment, world recession and the rise in the value of sterling, that British firms were attempting to introduce the new microelectronics technology at the turn of the decade, a technology characterised by its productivity-enhancing/job-displacing potential.

The structure of manufacturing industry in Great Britain

As Prais (1976) points out, manufacturing firms in Great Britain are rather highly concentrated, and therefore large compared to other European enterprises, but comprise a large number of relatively small plants. This form of industrial structure results in large measure from the pattern of industrial development in Great Britain, whereby today's large firms came into being not through organic growth but by a series of mergers. In many cases these mergers were defensive, in the face of international competition (particularly from the 1960s onwards), and many of these merged companies were very slow to integrate their operations.[3] Some of these mergers were undertaken primarily to protect market share and to limit competition between rival British producers, and only later did it become apparent that there were substantial advantages to rationalising production and other operations. Even when such rationalisations occurred they were, inevitably and sensibly, adaptations to existing structures and thus often incorporated multi-site production facilities where a greenfield site start-up might have resulted in a single-site operation. In addition, even after rationalisation, corporate memories are long and new organisation structures are unlikely to erase long-held patterns of organisational power and influence. Each of the firms in our case studies showed strong evidence of the hand of history within its present organisational structures and processes.

The structure of industrial relations in Great Britain as related to the introduction of new technology

By far the most significant feature of the industrial relations system in Great Britain for the introduction of new technology is its strong craft traditions, many of which are rooted and grounded in the engineering industry. One of the earliest trade unions in Great Britain is that which organised skilled machinists and is now incorporated into the Amalgamated Union of Engineering Workers (AUEW). Though many non-manual workers in the engineering industry are also within this union they are represented by a separate section, the Technical and Supervisory Staff (TASS), which is organisationally distinct, even to the extent of having its own General Secretary and Executive Committee. TASS has traditionally had very solid representation in the drawing offices of engineering companies. Clerical workers are often represented by the Administrative, Professional and Executive Association (APEX) and technicians and some professional engineers are members of the Association of Scientific, Technical and Managerial Staffs (ASTMS). Most non-skilled manual workers in the industry are organised by the Transport and General Workers Union (TGWU), and there are a plethora of other unions for particular occupational groups.

An implication of this fragmented union structure is that there are a variety of different organised interests with regard to the division of labour associated with the introduction of new technology. While at first sight it may appear to be in the interests of the

AUEW to oppose any de-skilling of machinists' work, and therefore to be opposed, in principle, to programming of CNC machine tools being done by anyone other than the machinist, in fact the union's stance has usually been to accept programming off the shopfloor, and merely to argue that whoever does do the programming should be an AUEW member. They are opposed in this by their own white-collar section, TASS, and, where present, by ASTMS, and in many cases have had to accept NC programming being designated as TASS work.

From this it can be seen that labour opposition to management about changes in work organisation as a result of new technology has more usually been focused on sectional interests to do with union representation rather than the nature of the work being done. To this general point we shall return within the case studies, where evidence will be presented which supports this assertion in general, though with some particular complications.

The cases

Reported here are the experiences of two companies' attempts to introduce new technology into the workplace in the form of CNC machine tools. Each company comprised a number of operating divisions and separate plants and the research on which this account is based investigated the experience of two plants within each company.

Both companies were large British-owned multinational enterprises, each among the largest 100 British companies at the time of the study, with the bulk of their products being in mature markets and using well-established technologies. Both were multidivisional engineering enterprises and, like many large British companies, were the result of a series of mergers in the 1960s.

One of these, to which we have attached the pseudonym 'British Engineers', by the late 1970s had to some extent rationalised many of its activities. Each of the two subsidiary companies reported on here manufactured large precision-engineered machines to customer order. The CNC machine tools were used to produce some of the components, either singly or in small batches, for these machines. Though within the same corporation, and subject to the same Head Office constraints, the two subsidiary companies were quite different in their experiences of introducing new technology. Though both companies were facing severe competition, and struggling hard to meet it, subsidiary A appeared to be in a fundamentally stronger position than subsidiary B and this may have been a major source of the observed differences in their experiences. These differences are described in some detail below but in brief in subsidiary A the adoption of CNC control for machine tools appears to have been rather gradual and incremental, with decisions for adoption taking place within the normal capital equipment decision-making procedures. In subsidiary B, in contrast, the adoption of CNC appeared to be much more of a step-change, pushed through partly by the enthusiasm and drive of one particular technical manager, and with less satisfactory results.

British Metals (also a pseudonym) was more conglomerate, with a very small headquarters and an apparently highly decentralised organisation structure. Many of its operating companies had been acquired by the corporation within the decade prior to the study and retained much of their original identities. Both the subsidiary companies under investigation were typical 'metal bashers', many of the products being pressings or forgings for other companies to their designs. The CNC machine tools in these companies were usually located in the tool-rooms and used to make one-off or pairs of dies for the presses rather than end products. The scale of operations throughout British Metals was much smaller than with British Engineers. The corporation as a whole was about a tenth the size, and individual operating companies numbered their employees in tens and hundreds rather than, as in British Engineers' case, thousands. The introduction of CNC in British Metals was, partly for these size reasons, much more centrally directed. Much of the initiative for adopting CNC came from the Technical Director at Headquarters, and the process for introducing CNC into the organisation took the form of setting up a separate small company as a centre of CNC and computer-aided design (CAD) expertise within the corporation. This company, comprising about 30 employees, offered a variety of services to the operating companies. It was a CAD and CNC programming bureau; it gave advice and acted as a demonstration centre. The bureau service was also sold to third parties. The investigations reported here examined the roles of Head Office, this computer-aided engineering service company (which we will call Design Co Ltd.), and three of the operating companies which had bought CNC machine tools.

British engineers, subsidiary A

Company background

This subsidiary (which we will term British Engineers A), produced large, extremely expensive (multimillion pound sterling) precision-engineered machines to customer order. Though profitable, it was operating in an extremely competitive international market. Competition was on price, quality and lead time for delivery. In some sectors of the market this last factor was not very important; in others it was crucial. The company (and by 'company' is meant British Engineers A and not the entire enterprise) was thought to be very good in its technical performance but weaker with regard to price and delivery, with the result that manufacturing process innovations were directed towards these areas. The basis of the technical success was the modular design of the product which was developed in the early 1970s. This allowed tailoring of the product to individual customer requirements whilst cutting engineering costs.

With the product being of this high value it was not surprising that it was produced on a one-off basis. Thus batch size for most of the components was small, running from 100 to, at most, 200.

Though there had been a substantial amount of rationalisation since the 1960s' mergers, production still took place in four separate sites, each the location of a previously independent company. The CNC machine tools described in this case were all located in one plant, though. This plant employed nearly 2,000 people at the time of the study.

The introduction of CNC machine tools was in the context of a long-running programme of investment in the production facilities. Advanced computer techniques for production control had been in operation since the early 1970s, and since the mid-1970s there had been the development and implementation of a broad strategy to improve lead times and reduce production costs. In common with much British manufacturing industry, as outlined in the Introduction, the company was facing a loss of its domestic markets and therefore the need to sell in highly competitive world markets. For British Engineers A the reduction in domestic sales had been particularly sharp, due to a collapse in the Great Britain market quite outside the company's control. To compete successfully in world markets the company was aiming to halve its production lead time, and this seemed to be management's main concern in their capital

233

investment strategy. Though not unmindful of labour cost savings, they said that reducing labour costs was not a significant factor as they were a relatively low part of the costs compared to, for example, the cost of the materials and, therefore, work-in-progress.

The full package of new technology being introduced in the company included a computer-aided-draughting package, a production planning program, and several CNC machine tools but it is only the last of these that is described in detail in this case.

Company organisation

The company operated a form of matrix organisation. The main functional departments were design, manufacturing and sales, with a Project Management Department (PMD) to co-ordinate each specific contract.

This basic form of organisation was complicated by the multi-site operation of the company. Though engineering design was an integrated operation within the company and mainly took place at the location under study, manufacturing took place across all four sites under the control of one Manufacturing Director. Each site had its own General Works Manager, who reported directly to the Manufacturing Director, and each Works Manager had his own Works Engineering, Manufacturing, Personnel and Industrial Relations Managers. This structure meant that some of the corporate Directors with specific functional responsibilities had no effective power base beneath them. For example, the Personnel Director could advise site personnel departments, but could not enforce policies. This situation could create problems. There was, for example, no way of ensuring a pay structure would be enforced for all relevant workers. Even more importantly, each General Works Manager had his own Manufacturing Development Manager, one of whose responsibilities was the consideration of new production process equipment such as CNC machine tools. Though this may have been a strength in that there was a substantial amount of local knowledge about the particular requirements of each site, it meant also that there were difficulties in ensuring compatibility between systems between sites.

A detailed breakdown of the 2,000 employees of British Engineers A by function and skill level is given, in percentage terms, in Table 9.1. As can be seen, a high percentage of the employees were white-collar, and a high percentage of the manual workers were skilled. These figures reflect the complex nature of much of the work.

Table 9.1: Employment Structure British Engineers, Subsidiary A

Manual workers	
Skilled	24%
Semi-skilled	13%
Un-skilled	1%
Sub-total	38%
Staff employees	
Managerial	5%
Superintendants	1%
Foremen, technicians and technical graded staff	16%
Staff covered by Joint Manual Unions	
(inspectors, chauffeurs, canteen workers etc.)	3%
Professional engineers (including accountants)	13%
Clerical	13%
Apprentices	9%
Sub-total	62%
TOTAL	100%

Reasons for innovating

The primary reason for introducing the various microelectronics-based production process innovations, including CNC machine tools, into the company was, as has been stated, to reduce lead times. It had already been reduced by 30 per cent and the aim was to halve it, to the level which the Japanese competition promised they could achieve already. British Engineers A felt that new technology was an important factor in their competitors' ability to offer shorter and more secure cycle times.

Though cost was still a major competitive factor for the company, cost reduction (either of labour or of work-in-progress) was said not to be an objective in introducing CNC, though quality, in particular consistency of quality, was a factor where the new technology was believed to yield major benefits.

The decision to innovate

The CNC machine tool purchases were decided upon in the way capital expenditure decisions were normally taken. No special budget was set aside for new technology. No decision was taken to move into CNC in principle. The move was said to be a normal incremental one.

Although payback was important in theory, the company did not rely on sophisticated methods like discounted cash flow to assess capital investment proposals in production. Most decisions were apparently made on a 'common sense' basis. The policy was to proceed slowly, take the minimum risk and to spread the risk as far as possible with the equipment supplier in the way it negotiated its contracts.

Once a decision was made to purchase a new piece of equipment or a system, the handling of its introduction was determined by the managers involved. There was no central policy or strategy on how the change should be introduced. The four sites were independent in industrial relations terms and negotiations over the acceptance of new equipment were carried out at site or even departmental level. The Personnel Director, as mentioned earlier, had only a co-ordinating role.

CAD at British Engineers A

Although the main focus of this case study is on the introduction of CNC machine tools we describe briefly an associated investment decision at British Engineers A, that to buy a computer-aided-draughting (CAD) system. This is of relevance to the CNC machine tool question, first because part of the CAD system was to program these machine tools and secondly because the NC programmers were members of the same trade union as the drawing office staff and subject to the same procedures for negotiating the introduction of the new technology.

The company as a whole was investing over 1 million pounds in CAD at the time of the study. The company's first foray into CAD was in 1979 and after an experimental period a system was installed at one of the other sites in the company, eventually being used both for draughting and part programming the CNC machine tools at that site. In 1982 CAD was extended to the site under investigation, one terminal being dedicated to part programming.

236

Previously all part programming at this site had been done on a stand-alone computing installation without graphics. The CAD facility, by providing a visual display of the part and of the tool movement, and by giving the part programmers direct access to the database of drawings, was expected to increase part-programming productivity tenfold.

The introduction of CAD into the part-programming process was not without incident. There was a high level of unionisation within British Engineers A. Hourly paid workers had 100 per cent union membership, as did the Drawing Office. The latter were members of the Technical and Supervisory Staff Union (TASS), as were the NC programmers. Though industrial relations on the site were generally considered to be good, and there was a strong identification with the company's product, there was some feeling that the staff unions were learning to flex their muscles. There had been some conflict over the introduction of job evaluation and in the later 1970s, when CAD was first introduced, TASS complained that they had not been consulted early enough. When the next wave of CAD introduction was announced in 1981, union representatives were sent to the site that already had CAD; the union committee helped plan for the system, including where VDUs would be put; and there was consultation about health and safety aspects including visual strain and working time to be spent at terminals.

Though TASS nationally had a policy of accepting new technology and trying to gain tangible, although non-pay, benefits, at company level the union wanted payment for change. Management's response was that the new technology was being introduced to improve competitiveness and, furthermore, that the technology made jobs easier. Eventually a site agreement, called a 'Code of Practice for the Introduction of New Technology', was reached. A once-and-for-all payment was given to all on site for accepting new technology and further payment of 100 pounds sterling was to go to those using it once they were trained. The Code of Practice expressed the unions' willingness to use new technology to its best advantage. It specified the consultation procedure to be used and how staff reductions and redeployment would be dealt with, but committed management to no redundancies for two years after the introduction of new equipment. Salary adjustments would be treated separately, however, each case on its own merits.

The pay and position of the NC programmers was a matter of

dispute. There was disagreement about their pay relative to the draughtsmen and planning engineers (it was the same but the programmers wanted more). Moreover, some of the programmers had moved off the shopfloor into NC, resulting in a drop in pay, with most of them not regaining their former income until after months of training. In their view they have bettered themselves but this was not reflected in their pay.

Some of the men described the dispute as bitter, involving the company threatening to close down the programming section. Against this threat the NC programmers signed a new technology agreement and although this formally settled the dispute some dissatisfaction remained.

CNC at British Engineers A

The decision to innovate

Though NC machines were first introduced on-site in 1966, programmed from an NC office, the first CNC machine to be introduced to the site was fitted only with manual data input (MDI). The machine, a horizontal borer and believed to be the largest ever made up to that time (1977), was operated by skilled machinists for whom off-shopfloor programming was generally thought to be unacceptable. However, by the time of the study, five years later, the company was planning to install a second horizontal borer, fitted with tape input, and to retrofit tape control onto the older machine.

By 1982 the site had a number of CNC machines, many made to the company's specification. These included two small and a number of larger lathes, a milling machine, a vertical borer and a production line comprising three NC and three CNC machines. The purchase of further CNC machines was under consideration.

Reasons given by management for CNC purchase were its ability to deal with complex shapes and its improved speed and accuracy. Cost reduction was not an objective. Indeed, it was only possible to show a cost advantage to CNC when comparing the purchase of conventional versus CNC machines. Partly because of the age of the company's capital stock, and hence many machines being fully depreciated, it was usually not possible to show a cost-saving by replacing existing machines by CNC.

The case study within British Engineers A focused on two complexes of equipment - a CNC vertical borer and a small production line for one particular type of component. The borer had cost over half a million pounds sterling, twice the cost of the conventional machine, plus the cost of the software, and was expected to use initially more operators (see below), but the decision was felt to be justified by the increased quality and quantity of output. The production line had been built up over the previous three to four years and represented a switch from a production process based around particular machining operations (lathes, mills etc.) to one based on the particular component, the extra flexibility of CNC being a cause of the rearrangement. The replaced conventional machining arrangements were operated by semi-skilled operators with skilled setters travelling between machines. Because the CNC machines performed several operations in one set-up - in one case six operations had been reduced to one - the production line had become more viable.

The company did not see any benefit in replacing the three conventional machines on the production line with CNC, nor was it planning to introduce automated handling.

Management of the change and industrial relations
Industrial relations on the shopfloor were very stable. There had been no industrial action aimed at the company since 1962. Many manual workers had been employed at the factory all their lives and for them working at British Engineers A was a family tradition. The Amalgamated Union of Engineering Workers (AUEW) was the predominant union, but there was a joint manual works committee of seven unions. Hourly paid workers were 100 per cent unionised.

With regard to CNC, shopfloor unions have always been consulted and informed about impending purchases and representatives taken to machine demonstrations. When machines are installed they are termed 'under development' for a period to allow management and unions to assess each new machine's capabilities and decide which occupational group should operate it. There had been initial difficulties in establishing which trade should maintain CNC machines. These had been resolved by the AUEW convenor forming a unit and handpicking apprentices from different trades to be trained for it. This appeared to have worked well.

The shopfloor unions said they were generally satisfied with management's handling of the introduction of CNC, although they expressed some worries as to whether the company had been investing fast enough. They were worried about the long-term effect of new technology on jobs, but they felt that the company would lose out if they did not invest. The AUEW had not sought or got a new technology agreement, or, until just before the study, payment for change. For example, the first CNC machine was brought into the tool-room without any additional pay. The AUEW subsequently felt they had made a mistake in not asking for money given the extensive introduction of CNC, and at the time of the study had put in a claim for the whole shopfloor. Management was likely to reject this, arguing that only those who used CNC should get additional pay to ensure that there would be an incentive to go onto it.

Shopfloor workers were paid under a job evaluation scheme. When a new machine came in, the jobs would be re-evaluated by an independent assessor along with the supervisor and the convenor. Sections could go up or down a grade or stay the same. The workers on the CNC vertical borer went up a grade, benefiting all those in that section by three to four pounds sterling per week. Pay for those on the production line, in contrast, was unchanged.

The lack of automatic additional payment for working on CNC could have been a problem because at least initially some skilled men had been afraid to move onto CNC. For the vertical borer it had been difficult to get the right men to move over. The good older experienced men did not volunteer, so were told to move. However, some young men in particular had moved over because they believed CNC to be a way to get on.

Skilled men had been sent on the manufacturers' courses but most people felt there was a need for more hands-on training within the company. There was no CNC machine in the training school, because the company felt that it wanted its apprentices to learn conventional skills, but it seemed likely that they would get one soon. The setters and operators said that they learned most by doing and they felt that it would be months before they became really proficient. For example, a setter on the production line said that his five-day course only became really useful with experience, but he felt it would take six to twelve months to become fully effective. Quite a few machines were still under manufacturers' warranty but experienced men and apprentices were being sent on maintenance courses so that the company could take over when the warranty expired. The AUEW had expressed some dissatisfaction with the fact that the company tended to send only one or two men on courses for operators and then let them train the others.

Initially the men's attitude to the new machines had been

favourable. Those on the vertical borer were still learning, but they appear to have been excited by working on it. They reported that it involved less manual work but they had to think faster. The setters on the production line found it challenging, but they were not sure that it would remain so interesting when they had finished learning and there were more repeat pieces to make and fewer problems to sort out.

TASS had also accepted CNC when it came in. They felt they could not object to CNC programming because the NC office was already set up. Their own concern was to ensure that the programming was done by the part programmers rather than by the operators, and they had always been successful in that, except in the toolroom where CNC operators had negotiated the right to program their machines in return for accepting them.

Part programmers had been recruited from a variety of sources. The first had been brought in with experience of NC programming in another similar industry. Of the others who then joined over the years, the supervisor had been a jig and tool draughtsman, as had one of the other programmers. Others had shopfloor craft backgrounds, one having come from toolmaking, another from operating a horizontal borer. The company had looked for a cross-selection of machining and computer skills, with a general background in engineering and an ability to do sketches and calculations. Three positions were filled from within the company, the jobs having been advertised internally, and the selection procedure including an interview and, in some cases, a maths test.

The first programmers had learned largely from books. Then training became more systematic and took 18 months. The first step was a general introduction to programming and, for men from the shopfloor, getting used to working in an office. Next they would be sent on a machine tool manufacturer's course which would usually be one or two weeks long. They would be given a simple job and would start by learning by doing. Although a man would initially be assigned to one machine, the company hoped that he would eventually know them all. They wanted the men to be specialists but to have some idea about the other machines. Evidently in most other companies programmers specialised on one machine only. At this company when a machine arrived, one programmer would go on the course, but they would all read the manuals. For CAD all staff went on a basic draughting and mechanics course to learn how to create parts, and on the advanced 3D course.

The men seemed to have moved into part programming for two reasons; either because they felt there was more future in it than on the shopfloor or in the drawing office, or because they hoped to improve themselves. Some older men also wanted a regular day job. When they moved they had found they had an immediate drop in pay. They lost their shift pay during the training period and only caught up months later. This all caused a lot of resentment and contributed to the bitter feelings during the dispute over their pay for accepting CAD.

Despite the problems with money, the programmers appeared to enjoy their work. A common first reaction to the work was surprise that it was more tiring than physical work. One former draughtsman said that he liked seeing the outcome of this work. With NC and then CAD, he created a thing in his mind, programmed it and could then go down to the machine to see it machined. Those spoken to said they would not want to leave part programming. The only reason they would leave would be because of pay. The only other problems they faced came from outside the programming office. They felt a lack of co-operation and information from the shopfloor and from middle management. The former group did not understand how long programming took and the middle managers had not kept up with the technology.

Changes to jobs, skills and work organisation

The company's policy was to retain their labour. They felt they had a skilled and specialised workforce who would be needed and able to utilise best the new technology. There was also no shortage of work in the near future. It was felt that CNC was unlikely to reduce labour requirements. Though jobs might spend less time on the shopfloor there would be more development work done in the office. The view expressed by the work manager was that within a stable overall employment requirement there would be a shift away from shopfloor jobs to staff and technically more advanced jobs. The union implication of this was a growth for the white-collar union TASS and a decrease for the AUEW. The latter was resisting this both by opposing to release their members who wanted to move into white-collar jobs and, if they did move up, by insisting that they retained AUEW rather than TASS membership.

The increase in jobs on the vertical borer, referred to earlier, had been because its three operators (two during the day, one at night) were equivalent to the operators of the three conventional borers it replaced, but the CNC machine also required part programming. Moreover the maintenance requirements were greater. However, there was greater output and one operator was not likely to be replaced when he retired.

There had been a loss, estimated by the union, of four or five jobs when the production line was introduced. These were dealt with by natural wastage. The convenor refused on principle to discuss the idea of a redundancy agreement and anyway saw no problem at that time about job losses, though the AUEW was increasingly worried, as mentioned above, about the long-term effect of CNC on jobs.

There was some expectation that CNC programming jobs might decrease in the future. Investment in more post-processors and technological developments such as direct numerical control (DNC) were seen to have labour-reduction effects. Moreover, the company did have the policy of using CNC in order to bring in less skilled labour, though at the time of the study CNC usually required skilled operators. On some larger machines, particularly those cutting forgings, some manual input was still necessary in order to cope with variations in the amount of material to be machined. The AUEW thought that the effect of CNC on skills was variable. The calculations and programming involved in CNC were new abilities which might outweigh the loss of hand skills, particularly in the toolroom, but on the shopfloor operators may end up simply pushing buttons.

The CNC operators spoken to took the former of the above two views. Practical skills had diminished but new skills were being acquired. They also commented on the creation of new jobs such as planning and programming. Specific skill changes commented on by those working on the vertical borer were the loss of skills in grinding tooling (the CNC machine used disposable tungsten carbide tipped tools) but the gain through using tapes and working with programming.

On the production line the setter noted a reduction in the need for hand-eye co-ordination but a greater requirement for calculations and other skills and knowledge in setting up CNC machines.

The question of whether operators or programmers programmed the CNC machines was clearly an area of potential conflict as it affected both job numbers and skill levels for both groups of the workers. The men in the toolroom insisted on having the right to program the CNC gauge-maker when it came in and they retained the right despite objections from the NC programmers. Elsewhere, the part programmers did the tape preparation. But the system was fairly flexible and seemed to work. The operator edited an unproved tape if he felt it was similar to another job - he may have altered the speed and feed, for example. Once the edited tape was proved and the output passed inspection, they took a portable punch down to the machine and then took the program from the memory; this became the master for the job. If the operator felt he could not manage on his own he could call the programmer or the foreman. On most of the new machines, the operators could and did edit the tape, but the programmers often went down and watched. On the production line, for example, the setters knew the routine, so they usually did not have to involve the programmers.

This system meant that there was a certain loss of management control, but the NC supervisor and the production services manager both felt that the system worked well on the whole. In their experience an operator usually only modified a tape to improve it. In their view the extent of control needed depended on the jobs. For the production line and jobs done in batches, control had to be with tooling and planning. But for one-off jobs it was often better to give the skilled man his head and take advantage of his skills. For example, there were problems with the vertical borer in getting at part of a cylinder. The operators thought about it, made up the tooling and resolved the difficulty. Not everyone was so confident, however, and one reason for retro-fitting the old horizontal borer with tape input was to ensure that technically correct decisions were made. There were some fears that leaving too much control with the operators would lead to their setting speeds too low in order to spin a job out or too fast at night so they could have a sleep during the night shift. Tape input was also preferable for machining inside pieces.

The shopfloor unions raised with the works management the issue of operators doing their own programming. They clearly saw the potential impact on their jobs and skills. It would also have affected their grading in the job evaluation scheme. While operators could edit tapes, it was agreed with the AUEW that the programmers were not allowed to operate machines. They could issue instructions but could not push buttons. In any case, it was felt that it was safer to let the operator do it because with so many different systems, a programmer might have made a mistake.

It was not clear whether supervisors' jobs were changing significantly. It seemed likely that keeping the large machines busy would become an important part of supervisors' jobs (see below). The supervisor of the production line felt that his job was different, but he highlighted the fact that he spent less time ensuring that pieces move from one machine to another - he had more control with less supervision. Previously there had been 60 machines in the machine shop and it had been hard to know where things were.

One area which CNC would most certainly have affected was hours of work. Most machines were worked on two shifts, but both management and unions recognised that if demand for the product was to rise to a sufficient level, then 24-hour working was desirable to ensure a reasonable return on such expensive machines. Many men would not have wanted it, although the AUEW recognised that it would create jobs.

Benefits and problems

It was generally accepted that CNC had reduced lead times in manufacture and improved quality and accuracy. The evidence with regard to any cost saving was more equivocal and there was general recognition that the level of utilisation of the machines could be significantly improved.

On lead times, the conventional arguments in favour of CNC seemed to have been confirmed. Components were now on the shopfloor for days rather than months, principally because there were fewer operations and so components spent much less time on the floor queuing for the next machine, but also because of faster tooling. One particular machine had replaced 14 operations, more than ten machines previously used to machine one complex part of a component. The job time had gone down from 14 weeks to two or three days. This reduced the pressure of deliveries, the amount of work in progress, and the number of fixtures and amount of tooling required.

Quality and accuracy were improved on the vertical borer because, for example, big radii on the conventional machine were extremely hard to get right but were now 'superb'. (Some jobs were also done in half the time.) On the production line there were improvements because the workpieces were now handled less often. The introduction of throwaway carbide tooling also helped.

On costs, though the company could not provide detailed figures, it estimated that some CNC machines resulted in 50-70 per cent cost reduction but one or two others failed to cut any costs. One problem was the low utilisation of some machines. Opinions varied about the extent of this problem but one manager described the situation of some machines as varying from 'awful to appalling'. The horizontal borer was one problem example, which also had the problem of not being fully loaded, and it had been made a priority to put jobs onto it.

Three factors were identified with regard to low machine utilisation. One was their availability. Though the company had a tight system for dealing with breakdowns and warranties and tried hard to force its suppliers to guarantee up time, difficulties remained. A second was with getting the correct tapes and tooling to the machine. In some cases, for example the production line, the system was fairly new and people were still on a learning curve, but the company was looking at new ways of supplying tooling to minimise set-up times and of using more relevant datum points to speed up the machining.

The third factor seemed to be the difficulties the company was experiencing in the pre-production area. It was not clear how far these difficulties were the result of CNC machines generating a faster flow of work than previously, putting extra pressure on the production planning process and having shorter cycle times than the conventional machine tools to which they were linked in the production process, but the company was developing a new production planning process intended to sort out some of these problems.

The company at the time of the study was in the middle of assessing CNC utilisation rates, office procedures and machine performance, and had already tightened up production services. There were, however, some difficulties in assessing CNC performance. The traditional measure for conventional machine tools of productive hours was deemed inappropriate for CNC because of its much faster rate of working and the production control manager seemed to be adopting an experimental method of assessing scheduling, by feeding more of the production through the higher technology machine tools to see if the company met its schedules better and whether costs and lead times were reduced.

British engineers, subsidiary B

Company background

This subsidiary shared many of the features of its sister company within British Engineers, producing capital goods with a high engineering content to customer orders. Though the company operated on two sites, each was largely independent of the other and this study reports on just one site, employing a similar number of people as the site studied in British Engineers A.

Although, like British Engineers A, subsidiary B produced only one product type, its product range was much wider than that of subsidiary A and the average order value much lower, the cheapest product being priced in thousands rather than millions of pounds sterling. Batch sizes for machining operations were thus much larger.

The market for the product was highly competitive and fully international. The product was, in life cycle terms, mature and competition was more on the basis of price and quality rather than on innovative features. Lead time for delivery was a less crucial issue than for British Engineers A, and the pressure to reduce manufacturing costs was dominant. Moreover, the market had declined just prior to the study to such an extent that in early 1981 the first redundancies in the plant for 20 years had been declared, with nearly 100 people leaving. Further redundancies were in prospect at the time of the study as senior management had demanded a further round of 20 per cent cuts in all departments.

The introduction of CNC machines into this plant was in the context of a general programme for re-equipping the machine shops after many years of apparent neglect. It was alleged that until the most recent merger within British Engineers 15 years earlier there had been no new investment at that site for very many years. After the merger a number of senior people was transferred into this site and in the early 1970s British Engineers Head Office made a policy decision to make substantial capital investments there. Among the first of these were new facilities for assembly operations, developments in computer-aided design in the design offices and a computer-based system for production control and operations planning. Attention was then turned to machining operations, the new equipment for which is described below.

Company organisation

The organisation of British Engineers B was broadly functional, though with some product-based organisation at workshop level where there were two separate machine shops for particular product subgroups.

There had recently been a reorganisation within the design

247

function. Whereas previously design work had been done within individual engineers' departments and co-ordinated by a design committee, the most recent product development had been done by a multi-disciplinary group consisting of people with commercial, engineering, manufacturing and draughting backgrounds.

The adoption of CNC machine tools within British Engineers B had been largely the responsibility of one person, the chief manufacturing development engineer. Though his own view of the company organisation was that it was highly flexible and organic, our own impressions were of rather strong departmental boundaries in some cases, particularly between design and production. The organisation chart also showed a well-developed staff organisation to support the line functions, of the kind typical of small-batch production technologies.

Reasons for innovating

The decision to bring in CNC machine tools took place within the context of a general investment programme and from the need to replace worn-out machinery rather than from the specific advantages of the new technology. Additionally, it was steered through by an innovation champion, the chief manufacturing development engineer, who saw it as a step towards an unmanned, fully automated factory with a fully integrated computer-based information system linking all departments.

The decision to innovate

One of the earliest exercises to generate information and suggest a strategy for the new investment was contained in an internal document written by the product champion and sent in mid-1975 to the Managing Director of British Engineers B, all those reporting to the managing director (MD), and a number of more junior relevant managers. This was to be the first of 'periodic progress reports' to give interested parties the opportunity to assess, criticise and comment since 'the end result will almost certainly demand changes in attitudes and functions of all parts of the organisation'.

In this report the notion of 'family grouping' as opposed to 'jobbing' was introduced and this was used as the basis for arguing the usefulness of a CNC machining centre to do most, if not all, of the necessary machining operations for heavy workpieces at one location. The report argued that 'family grouping' and machining centres would impose a discipline on production and improve the pace of manufacture. It also laid out the argument for purchasing one specific machining centre.

By December of that year a further report detailed a long-term investment plan which would build up from the single machining centre already proposed to form what was termed a 'variable mission system'. This would include two lathes, two machining centres sharing one bed-plate, a pallet set-up station and an inspection machine, would contain the possibility of being driven by direct numerical control and would include the possibility of incorporating an automatic pallet handling system with a high degree of automation. This extended proposal, amounting to a fully-automated, unmanned flexible manufacturing system (FMS), was envisaged to take up to ten years to achieve, depending on the 'availability of capital and the *development of people*' (emphasis added).

However, it proved very difficult to justify this proposal on financial or any other particular criteria. The new cell would give a considerable increase in capacity (indeed it was impossible to specify a machining centre which, in order to be large enough to handle the physical size of the individual components to be machined and because of the inherent high speed of CNC operation, would not have a throughput capacity of about twice the current demand with two-shift working) but there was no suggestion that this extra capacity was needed to meet future market requirements. Despite the age of the existing machines there seemed to be no complaints about the quality of the work.

One attempt at financial justification for the project suggested that it might give a payback period of four to five years mainly from reduced labour and other operating costs and from the extra capacity generated, but this exercise gave no details of the bases on which these calculations were made nor of how such labour reductions might happen.

Other specific reasons given for buying the new technology varied from document to document and from person to person. The mid-1975 document first setting out the case stated that 'the fundamental reason for adopting this approach to layout and new plant (the change in manufacturing system philosophy from 'jobbing' to 'family grouping') is that it reduces opportunities to stock bank work in progress, thereby significantly reduces overheads in progress, paperwork and supervision. It simplifies incentives and cost systems, and improves the operator working environment'. In late 1978 a note providing justification for the project emphasised the reduction in manpower, use of buildings, levels of maintenance and lost time due to over-planned payments, waiting time etc. with the major financial justification being the first of these reasons.

Despite the apparent lack of clarity in the arguments for justification it was decided to order the first proposed machining centre, and to accept the principle of an FMS, in early 1976, the former decision being authorised through the usual channels whereby individual applications for specific items of equipment are judged on an item by item basis. Authorisation would not have been needed from British Engineers corporate headquarters. The purpose of the analysis within this part of the study is not to demonstrate the adequacy, much less the correctness, of the decision-taking process, but to illustrate the difficulty of rational decision-making in the face of the uncertainty surrounding step changes in technology. In these circumstances the close relationships between the senior management team at British Engineers B (they had all come from another site at the time of the merger) may have increased their ability to decide to go for the new technology in the absence of hard information upon which a decision could be based.

At the time our study ended (in 1982) the one machining centre and one of the two projected lathes had been bought and installed. It was too early to assess the likelihood that these would eventually be linked into the planned FMS. The division of labour between operators and programmers was very similar to that within British Engineers A and there had been no distinctive differences of which we were aware between the two subsidiaries in the way in which the industrial relations aspects of the introduction of the new technology had been handled.

British Metals

Company background

As already noted, the average size of British Metals plants was much smaller than that of British Engineers. Of the two British Metals subsidiary companies reported on here one employed under 1,000 people, the other less than 100. Moreover, the corporation was much more diversified and highly decentralised. At the time of the study group sales were continuing to rise, but sales from British subsidiaries were falling as a percentage of total sales, largely for the national economic reasons already discussed. Profitability of the group as a whole had also been reduced by over 30 per cent in the year prior to the study, and a reduction in people employed of 20 per cent in the same period was due both to the effects of the British recession and efforts to reduce costs and improve efficiency. One of the two subsidiaries we studied had nearly a third of its workforce made redundant in the previous year, but the other had got through without any redundancies by using short-time working.

Many of the company's various products resulted from metal-stamping operations and so a major machining requirement in the group was for tooling fordies. Thus, although most products were mass-produced, the requirement for CNC machines was for small-batch, and often one-off applications.

Not only were British Metals subsidiaries smaller and more decentralised than those in British Engineers, but the products were a great deal less sophisticated and required a much smaller amount of engineering input. There was therefore less capacity within each subsidiary to develop its own expertise in CNC. It is not surprising, therefore, that the initiative for the adoption of CNC came from corporate headquarters via the formation of the central facility we have called Design Co Ltd.

Company organisation

Although British Metals comprised over 100 subsidiary companies, it had a head office staff of under 50. The heavily decentralised control was backed up by rather tight financial control and an elaborate hierarchy of management boards. For example, any investment over 50,000 pounds sterling and below 100,000 pounds sterling had to be approved by the appropriate sub-divisional board, divisional board and finally by the executive committee of the main board. Amounts over 100,000 pounds sterling would go to the main board itself (figures relate to 1982 values).

Another more subtle form of control appeared to be via the internal promotion system. Promotion between companies within British Metals was common and managing directors and sub-divisional and divisional directors who wanted to get on were likely to adhere to policies decided at higher levels. These were transmitted down the hierarchy of boards through overlapping memberships. Thus, while the chairman had stressed in the annual report that the move to more product design and development was best left 'under the control of the profit centres concerned', whether an MD started to move in this direction would be likely to be used in judging his performance. Policies were also transmitted by advice and encouragement, as the CNC case described below illustrates.

There was also some evidence of more direct control over operating companies as revealed by the way in which, while interviewing for the research was taking place, a divisional director entered one of the factories and went straight to the shopfloor to talk to one of the unions without first informing the MD and then, without notice and without knocking, walked in on the MD during our interview with him.

Nevertheless neither this overbearing central control nor the operation of the internal labour market for senior management was capable of overcoming resistance from below if those in lower positions held little expectation of promotion between operating companies. One had the impression that there was a middle stratum of local management for whom such promotion was not a real possibility and for whom it therefore had no incentive or control potential.

There was some feeling, by one of the MDs in particular, that decisions, such as whether to buy CNC machines, were sometimes imposed from above.This manager also felt that the company was weak at the centre and that it created problems for itself by having conflicting policies - for example by setting up Design Co Ltd., which was then not used fully because it did not have enough CNC machine tools. A contrasting view was put by the manager of the Design Co Ltd. facility who argued that the provision of more centralised toolrooms (which Design Co Ltd. could have become) would make the group more vulnerable to industrial action, and less easily managed.

Reasons for innovating

The original drive to introduce NC machines in British Metals stemmed from a belief of the then Technical Director as early as 1971 that as tooling became worn it used and wasted more of the metal being pressed or stamped. If tooling could be replaced more often and more cheaply he estimated that British Metals could save approximately 8.5 million pounds sterling per year on metal costs. He and the Group Training Manager, with the support of the MD of the appropriate division, decided that British Metal companies needed educating on the uses and benefits of NC, so an NC machine was purchased and installed in the Training Department.

Around the same time the divisional MD asked the MD of one of the companies in his division to carry out the first of three surveys assessing the potential use of NC machines with British Metals companies. In each case he was advised 'no' as systems at that time were too expensive and difficult to program.

In 1974 a new entrant to the corporate training department was given responsibility for NC as one of his three areas of responsibility. About the same time someone who had been a key person in the development of new technology within British Metals returned to the company after two years at Cambridge, where he had been writing a CAD package.

These two and a programmer/operator began doing work for British Metals companies to demonstrate NC techniques, and around 1975/76 another survey was done for the divisional director which concluded that CNC had become feasible. The software was better and easier to program, and therefore less expensive. It could do 3D twisted shapes with relatively easy programming (useful for the complex dies needing to be machined). In 1977 a 3D contour milling machine was purchased, Design Co Ltd. was set up, and the subsidiary company MD responsible for the survey bought a CNC machine for his own company, which would be programmed by Design Co Ltd. and the program sent to the company down a telephone link.

The decision to innovate within the operating companies

Within one of the two British Metals companies studied (which we will call British Metals A) there had been enthusiasm for CNC from the start. This was the subsidiary headed by the MD responsible for the various surveys on CNC feasibility, and the first one to buy CNC in the group.

According to the MD, the original impetus for innovating was the shortage of highly skilled toolmakers. He regarded toolmakers as 'technician artists' but they were underpaid and hard to find. The company was still having trouble getting good toolmakers despite the recession, with the most capable youths going into technician apprenticeships rather than craft apprenticeships. With CNC taking over the more complicated machining it was seen as a way of reducing the demand for this scarce labour resource.

However, once the MD saw CNC machine precision parts within a production rather than toolroom facility he decided there was greater potential in that direction rather than in toolmaking. About the same time British Metals made a corporate strategic decision to move towards precision engineering as a product-market and this strengthened his own policy to move in that direction.

A further factor was CNC's contribution in reducing lead times. Subsequent to the recession beginning, customers had been insisting on shorter lead times.

Two final factors pushing British Metals A towards CNC were the great keenness of the group to introduce CNC into some of its companies (both the company chairman and the group technical director had high profiles in the engineering industry - the latter sitting on a government committee examining ways of speeding up microelectronics process innovations) and the availability of a substantial government grant to meet 20 per cent of the capital cost of the CNC machine.

The story within British Metals B seemed to be quite different. Two CNC machines had been bought a lathe and a miller - largely, it seems, as the result of pressure from outside the operating company itself. The MD responsible for the decision had moved on by the time of the study so it was difficult to establish what had happened. Reasons given to us for the purchases included anticipated skill shortages; the usefulness of CNC for repeated batches for when a die needed replacement or repair; greater accuracy; faster tooling changeover; and for carrying out split die work.

Not all of these reasons were wholly convincing. The company knew that it had (or would have) too many toolmakers and the CNC lathe was not used for split die work anyway. Others, within British Metals B and in Design Co Ltd., suggested the decision was thrust upon the company, which had been selected as a guinea pig. The previous MD was said to have been very keen on CNC, and is now chairman of another British Metals division where he is pushing for more CNC usage. The group technical director had visited the company several times to encourage them. In any event the division and not the operating company had provided the money for the machines.

Management of the change and industrial relations aspects

British Metals A, the smaller company which was first in the field with CNC, was a 'family' company in the sense that both the MD and the Works Director had started as apprentices in the company. The MD's secretary was married to the CNC programmer. Everyone called the MD by his first name and there was a casual, friendly atmosphere. There were no recognised unions within the company, though some people were union members. There was no formal collective bargaining and employees were on individual rates of pay set by the MD and the Works Director. The MD said that he paid over the rate and gave extra benefits to keep the unions out. There was a works committee which represented the shopfloor and which the MD 'consulted'.

This works committee was informed when the decision had been made to buy the first CNC machine. This was accepted, partly because the men had had experience of earlier innovations. They had, apparently, feared the introduction of spark erosion machines earlier but had adjusted to these.

Programming the CNC machines was done primarily by someone who was described as having previously been a mediocre designer. He was deemed to have good mathematical skills but little machining experience. Against the advice of the CNC machine manufacturer, who advised that the programming office should be attached to the drawing office, the programmer's office was put next to the CNC machines. The operator of the first CNC machine to be installed was described as a good toolmaker and, although very keen, was not thought sufficiently good at mathematics to be a programmer. Nevertheless he did do a minor programming course and was expected to do the programming of simpler movements and prove tapes. The programmer said that he had to leave scope to the machinist, especially on feeds and speeds and which cutter to use, and he expected the operator to override him.

After some years experience with CNC some workers were still worried about the loss of skills. Some operators felt that they had more control, through programming, but others felt they had less. Some felt stress from the speed of the machine. If it went wrong it did so quickly and was hard to catch and stop before a very large workpiece might be ruined. One operator said he worried at night about mistakes.

Attitudes varied about whether people would want to work on CNC. The older men appeared less keen. Some felt it was not useful for toolmaking, but most interviewed said they thought it was going to come, so they ought to accept it and get experience with it. Though some preferred the hand and bench work and the variety of conventional toolmaking one older man had wanted to try CNC but had not been allowed to because he was too valuable where he was.

At British Metals B the situation was quite different. There was a high level of union membership and the strategy adopted by management was to buy the CNC machines and install them first at the Design Co Ltd. site 'to iron out the bugs'. The programmer and operator were recruited and trained by Design Co Ltd. In the first instance they attempted to recruit these from within British Metals B but no-one from within the company was considered suitable for programming and so an outsider was recruited. It was decided to recruit three operators for the two machines and these were selected from internal candidates.

The programmer was put into the technical services office with the draughtsmen and was given responsibility for programming and tape proving. However, the operators were allowed to override the tape, were given some programming training and were expected to alter programs because of things like tool wear. The programmer could in turn use the computer on the machine, the union did not insist on the operator being there and often the two would work together. This degree of union acceptance had not, however, always existed.

Although the unions agreed to accept the machines in the first instance, this may have been a case of the convenor accepting them only to find the men were not behind him. The convenor had not seen new technology as a bargaining issue and AUEW policy was to put no obstacle in the way of new technology. At meetings of the union members in the toolroom, held in company time, the convenor put the official line and told his members about other companies' experience that he had learned from through the quarterly district meetings.

Nonetheless, the members began to put pressure on him not to accept the machines. First, it was clear that there was lots of apprehension in the toolroom about the machines and fears for job security, should new technology come on a large scale. The MD blamed this attitude on the media. Second, the toolroom began to argue that the introduction of the machines was a chance to increase their income, but this chance had to be seized at the outset as once the machines were in they would lose their bargaining power. The toolroom argued en bloc for an increase in pay for everyone and a guarantee of no job losses as a direct result of new technology. After a year of negotiations, during which time the machines remained at Design Co Ltd. and were used for production there, the conflict was resolved at the time of the annual pay settlement. The agreement was that the union would accept the machines like any other piece of equipment with no special pay increases, and there was no concrete new technology agreement.

Benefits and problems

At British Metals A the CNC machine had been evaluated some time after its introduction. The MD reported that the return on capital from the CNC machine was at least as good as that from the conventional machines, and possibly better because he had left out certain factors such as a reduction in inconsequential work, for example polishing and bench work, in his calculations. Product quality was reckoned to be better; machining time was three to four times faster on repeat jobs, which reduced lead times, and up to twice as fast on one-offs. It was felt that CNC had boosted the image of the company, which was already known as an innovative firm. Other claimed benefits were less heavy copy-milling work and more white-collar, brain work, both of which may have made working at British Metals A more attractive to the type of person who would normally apply to be a technician-apprentice.

A problem was that of getting enough of the right kind of work to keep the machines fully utilised. For this two extended shifts were needed but the work was not available.

No reduction in staff numbers was reported, and it seemed unlikely that there would be any in the future, given this company's chronic shortage of skilled men. With regard to pay, as the toolmakers were paid on an individual basis there were no rates or payment systems to alter. The MD said that CNC operators were paid the same as a good toolmaker, although the two men on CNC turning had been given a little bit more because they were learning to use new skills.

One worry amongst operators with regard to skills was that hand and touch skills might be lost through using CNC and some men were unwilling to work full-time on these machines for this reason. Another worry was that the company move to more repeat work was really a move to precision machining for production rather than for the toolroom, and this in the long term might affect the type and variety of skills needed.

Within British Metals B the CNC machines were only beginning to be fully utilised at the time of the study and no evaluation had been done. Up to that time there had been no change in staff numbers, pay or payment systems caused by the introduction of CNC. Productivity on the CNC machines, targeted to be twice as fast as the conventional machines, was only 30-40 per cent faster, and any attempts to increase this productivity was having deleterious effects on quality. These are likely to have been transitional figures, however, although it did seem that there was a lack of knowledge, skills and perhaps enthusiasm for CNC in British Metals B, which may have contributed to the slow start for this technology. Indeed, the MD made the interesting comment that he felt that the new technology had shown the need for a new kind of person in the organisation - one who understood how to change the company and manipulate people, i.e. 'man management'.

Conclusions

In many ways there is little that is new in the case studies reported here. The variations in form of work organisation associated with CNC machine tool usage found in our four factories replicate quite closely the Sorge *et al.* (1983) study of British and German factories. Our findings also corroborate Wilkinson's (1983) study of the effects of new technology on skill composition and occupational structures which by no means unequivocally supported the de-skilling thesis. There are, however, a number of features of these case studies which are worth emphasising. One of these is the context in which CNC was introduced in the factories as described here. In every case management's main concern, in deciding about CNC purchase, was with improving the quality of the product. The possibility of gaining competitive advantage by shortening lead times in production, and the reduction in work-in-progress and therefore in working capital were the important factors taken into account in evaluating investment in CNC machine tools. In many cases the decision to buy CNC was pushed by technical managers who were very much more interested in the technical possibilities of the equipment than in its effects on work organisation or skill requirements. Furthermore, there is a distinction to be made between decisions based on the relative advantage of new CNC equipment over old, but still functioning production facilities and decisions to add to production capacity. In the latter instance, management are choosing between new conventional versus new CNC equipment and the price of the latter, for a given output rate, is so favourable it is almost inconceivable that conventional machinery would be bought.

It is also worth noting, at least in the British context, the extent to which management were fearful, unnecessarily in most cases, of union reaction to their proposals for new technology. This accords with recent survey evidence in Great Britain (Daniel 1987) showing the widespread acceptance by British workers of technological change.

This fearfulness may itself be a reason for a third striking characteristic of CNC introduction - the lack of consultation with unions, or with groups of workers generally. Despite widespread advice to management in Great Britain from government agencies, management associations and publications, none of the managers in the cases reported here engaged in consultation as a pro-active measure. All consultation was reactive, the result mainly of union pressure.

As one would expect in a British case study, unions played a major role in the introduction of CNC. Except in one case, where management did not behave in a particularly intelligent way, unions did not oppose in principle the introduction of CNC and did not, therefore hold up the process in any specific way. Nevertheless, the complexities of negotiation with unions, and establishing which unions had rights over which new occupational categories, took time and effort. It would appear that the relatively high degree of union strength in these British factories did operate to the workers' advantage, though much union effort was expended in protecting sectional interests of particular worker groups.

Finally, there does appear to be little evidence in these cases of skill diminution. In virtually every case skilled workers continue to operate the machines themselves, and report that substantial skills are still required to run CNC machine tools. Many of them have, in addition, learned programming skills which they are using either in a formal way because they have been 'promoted' to the part-programming office or informally because as operators they are collaborating with the part programmers in proving tapes and setting up their machines.

Nevertheless, it is not our conclusion that CNC usage had no de-skilling effects or will always be unopposed by workers so long as management use appropriate consultation procedures. Our intention, in providing detailed case study material about the introduction of CNC machine tools in four British factories, is to illustrate a connection between the wider institutional, economic and historical context of the firm and the specific location where new technology is introduced. This material should illustrate the theoretical considerations set out in, for example, Burawoy (1985), Francis (1986) and Wood (1982) which argue the importance of the specific context for the analysis of the process and effects of the introduction of new technology in the workplace.

Notes

1. In carrying out the research on which this account is based and writing this paper, I have benefited from the co-operation of Mandy Snell Wright and Graham Winch.

2. See, for example, Wood (1982).

3. See, for example, Turner (1971), for a description of the archetypal case of British Leyland.

References

Beckerman, W. (ed.) (1979) *Slow Growth in Britain: Causes and Consequences*, Oxford, Clarendon Press

Blackaby, F. (ed.) (1978) *De-industrialisation*, London, Heinemann

Braverman, H. (1974) *Labour and Monopoly Capital: The Degradation of Work in the Twentieth Century*, New York, Monthly Review Press

Burawoy, M. (1985) *The Politics of Production*, London, Verso

Carter, C. (ed.) (1981) *Industrial Policy and Innovation*, London, Heinemann

Daniel, W. (1987) *Work-Place Industrial Relations and Technical Change*, London, Frances Pinter

Francis, A. (1986) *New Technology at Work*, Oxford, Clarendon Press

Jenkins, C. and B. Sherman (1979) *The Collapse of Work*, London, Eyre Methuen

Pavitt, K. (ed.) (1980) *Technical Innovation and British Economic Performance*, London, Macmillan

Great Britain

Prais, S.J. (1976) *The Evolution of Giant Firms in Britain*, Cambridge, Cambridge University Press

Sorge, A., G. Hartmann, M. Warner and I. Nicholas (1983) *Microelectronics and Manpower in Manufacturing*, Aldershot, Gower Publishing

Turner, G. (1971) *The Leyland Papers*, London, Eyre and Spottiswoode

Wilkinson, B. (1983) *The Shopfloor Politics of New Technology*, London, Heinemann Educational Books

Wood, S. (ed.) (1982) *The Degradation of Work? Skill, Deskilling and the Labour Process*, London, Hutchinson

261

10
Transforming Industrial Work in Finland

Pertti Koistinen

Introduction[1]

In the tradition of social sciences our research would be regarded as an approach of contingency theory, because it stresses the social conditions within which the application of new technology takes place in industry.

Although we have studied the use and effects of new production technology, such as NC and CNC machines, on industrial work, in this interpretation of the results we want to draw attention to the analysis of both national conditions and those of individual enterprises. We regard among other things as structural conditions the crisis of the Finnish industry followed by the crisis of economic growth and reproduction. Then we estimate those typical means with which enterprises have tried to adjust to new situations.

The empirical data of the study were collected in three modern engineering plants. The choice was based on a preliminary survey of 20 plants. The plants analysed here as examples belong to larger Finnish concerns as independent profit centres and have a significant role inside the concern as far as their technological level and economic status is concerned. The concerns are Finnish-owned multinationals and large-scale enterprises for Finnish standards and each has held a leading position in the development of the Finnish metal industry.

Enterprise A is a hoisting gear factory. It is an independent profit centre in one of the world's leading lift enterprises. Enterprise B manufactures special machining equipment, for example for the car industry, and is also a profit centre of a leading national large-scale concern. Enterprise C is a machine-tool factory, which makes tools both for its own concern producing electrical equipment and for outside customers. Our samples may be exceptional as to their larger than average size, their relations with the concerns or their new and partly self-developed technology. On the basis of the preliminary survey they are considered to represent, however, to a considerable extent how technological innovation is realised in a small country which is facing a period of transition in its production structure. Through their history these enterprises present the phases of birth and expansion in the Finnish metal industry.

The empirical material of this study is based on interviews, field work, statistics, newsletters and histories available in the enterprises and local organisations. At the enterprise level we interviewed several times about 30 managers, clerical staff and supervisors. After a week's workplace inspection, done with three researchers in each enterprise under study, we interviewed about 80 workers at their workplaces. At the local level we visited neighbour enterprises which utilise the same local labour markets. We interviewed also the staff of local employment offices and schools for vocational training and also met the representatives of trade unions. When analysing the background information we focused on the role of our case study enterprises.

National characteristics in the process of economic development and modernisation

Sociological theories have claimed that small countries are dependent on external factors. As to their national success and command over development it is crucial how they succeed in adjusting themselves to specialised markets and how they succeed in adapting their social, economic and cultural traditions. In this respect small countries have developed special strategies to solve problems concerning their development. According to Eisenstadt (1985: 44) it is evident that, whatever the solution is, specialisation makes a country dependent on and sensitive to changes in international markets, because they cannot bring about changes in demand. This state of matters is not restricted only to the economy, but it concerns culture, science, technology and politics. The same analogy is often applied when the development of production technology in small countries is evaluated and particularly in their sporadic enterprises, which are too weak in resources and too small in size to participate in technological development (Walsh 1986: 17, 32).

The width and character of that dependence or independence are naturally connected with the line of specialisation chosen by the country (Eisenstadt 1985: 45). In this respect the discussion about country-specific models is most interesting. These models denote relatively coherent modes of interaction in the relationship between the economy and politics, modes with which each society has renewed its economic, social and political relations (Kosonen 1985: 113). One of the main arguments has been that the co-operation between the Nordic countries has created common characteristics in their economic and social development as for example in social security and in the behaviour of labour markets. Although universal features of the development of small countries are present, the comparison of the Nordic countries has brought into discussion the hypothesis of a Danish, a Finnish, a Norwegian and a Swedish model. The accumulation and renewal model of the social state was developed as early as in the 1930s in these countries, but the heyday was in the 1960s, continuing till the depression of the next decade. Since then each country has tried to solve its economic problems as well as its relations between the economy and the social system in a specific way.

The country-specific models of the Nordic countries could be characterised as follows:

- it has been characteristic of all the Nordic countries to base their economy on one dominating export branch. These carrier branches have been supported by other sociopolitical decisions, for example by means of technology, investments and labour market policy. The Nordic countries illustrate how small countries have to specialise and develop control and subsidy systems for flexibility and adjustment as well as for maintaining economic and technical rationality;
- the basis of economic adaptation in the Nordic countries has been in political mobility. It has meant an apparent class compromise between capital and labour in order to maintain competition under external pressures. The content and form of this compromise have differed from country to country, but for instance in Finland modernisation and national adjustment to external pressures are a basis for national strategy. The urge for adjustment and the interpretation of national benefit can be seen also today, when discussing the challenges of the world

market and new technology (Koistinen and Särkikoski 1986). Although the economic and political basis of national competitiveness is breaking, the ideology of national benefit and competition seems to prevail;

- the Finnish model differs in its reactive adjustment line from that of Sweden, which can be characterised as the most organised one (Kosonen and Pekkarinen 1985: 170-71). The basic programmes behind the Swedish model have been those developed by trade unions after the war. Thus the Swedish programmes backed by the Swedish Social Democrats have also insisted upon economic control. In Finland the trade unions have accepted the requirements of enterprises to regard investments as of primary importance and to accept state subsidies for enterprises. This has given capital almost unrestricted power to operate in technological rationalisations, which for its part explains why employers have been able to realise rationalisation investments without significant political control;

- one aspect of Finnish social history is that the so-called external factors are more significant in the formulation of social tension and the political rights of the working class than in other Nordic countries (Alapuro 1985: 89). This can be interpreted to mean that in Finland industrialisation, technological development and modernisation in other spheres of the society have begun at a somewhat later stage than in other countries and that the ruling class was able to prevent and manipulate the social tensions. This observation seems to fit all the essential stages of social change which are linked to changes in industry, technological development, the economy and social structure;

- the Finnish model is the result of a long dominating project in the spheres of the economy, politics and culture. In Finland the political discussion has always been abstemious and politically attached to the right rather than to the left wing. Thus it has supported the continuity of rationality of production. This means that in Finland there is no tradition of discussion about economic democracy, quality of working life and solitary alternatives of societal development as in Sweden. The effects of such harmonious existence become apparent in the standards of the social and political demands of the Finnish working class being much lower than those in Sweden, and in the ability of the Finnish workers to control the quality of working life being poorer. Thus for instance the Finnish exporters of technology

find planning in Sweden much more pretentious and demanding more co-operation with personnel than in Finland.

All these factors have significance when we consider how rationalisation of production has been interpreted by the different social
groups of Finnish society.

General conditions of rationalisation policy in Finland: the crisis in the mode of production

National models are to be understood as the result of long-term
development. They reflect the way each country has tried to adapt
itself to the state of the world economy and the way they have
tried to meet the requirements from within society. It is realistic to
say that the crucial parts of the Finnish model have been
formulated since the Second World War. The principles are clearly
reflected in the industrialisation of the forest sector and in the
institutional, social and political system underlying it. The
industrialisation carried out by the forest industry has produced a
country-specific enterprise structure and a mode of interaction
between enterprises and society. We assume that it has also guided
the enterprises in choosing their concepts for rationalisation and
how concepts have been accepted sociopolitically.

When considering technological development and the way
enterprises have utilised labour resources it is important to notice
that enterprises are divided into two separate groups according to
their size. In Finland there are large-scale enterprises which produce either export products or counterbalance imports. They are
widely supported through a system of trade policy, technology
policy, financing, as well as other socioeconomic systems of
society. On the other hand, there are also small enterprises which
operate by filling the gaps of large-scale industry or are tied in a
system of subcontracting.

Industrialisation created a specific interaction between different branches. The increase and continuous growth of the metal and
especially engineering industry till the 1980s can be seen motivated by the demand for technology in the wood processing industry. This industrialisation created the structural conditions for
the consensus of economic policy. When the wood processing industry and other branches motivated by it became the basis of
international exchange it was obvious that political mobilisation

tended to support it. Society has supported the key branches as to their technological development, the enterprises have been given unlimited authority to rationalise and through the position of competitive branches the nation has learnt that competition is the saviour of a small country.

In the course of industrialisation a specific type of enterprise-community relation developed, with industrial communities around enterprises. This type of enterprise-community relation has played an important role in the socioeconomic development of communities and industrial culture as well as in allowing enterprises to realise their own modes of rationalisation. It can be said that the communities dominated by one large enterprise illustrate how rationality of production and modernisation of society have been tied to each other. This structural quality of society has influenced industrial labour and how the working class experienced and interpreted the blessings and curses of industrialisation in its own social history. During the last years social scientists have put forward the thesis that the Finnish working class has taken a place in 'the sunny side of factory' (Haapala 1986). If this were the case, it could be explained by the fact that in the one-enterprise communities the enterprises had quite broad concepts of rationalisation. Enterprises have been compelled to participate in developing communities in order to safeguard production and its renewal. On the other hand, the positive interpretation of workers could be interpreted by the fact that industrial growth has so far been constant and has offered at least some future to the surplus population coming from agriculture (Haapala 1986, Koskinen 1987). When still considering the fact that so far the working class has been saved from the negative effects of overindustrialisation and greater declines of industry, it is understandable that the Finnish working class has till now supported the rationalisation of industry (Koistinen and Lilja 1987).

In our opinion these are the special national characteristics which have to be taken into consideration when evaluating the present technological standard of Finnish industry and its structural competence to compete, as well as the social consequences caused by the strategies of rationalisation in production. In fact the industrial development has been exceptional in Finland because the increase in employment based on manufacturing industry continued even in the 1970s and at the beginning of the 1980s, whereas it stopped in other OECD countries as early as at the turn of the 1960s.

The wood processing industry seemed at least up until the 1970s to be playing the part of carrier branch, and the metal industry was its motivated branch, which since the late 1960s took the leading role in manufacturing industry as a deployer of a new labour force. As a result of this growth it has risen from the 1950s to the 1980s as a central area of production in our national economy. The present standing of the economy is reflected by the metal industry, producing in 1984 26 per cent of industrial gross production; it employed 35 per cent of industrial workers, and its export share was 36 per cent of industrial exports.[2] In terms of industry's internal structure, its growth broke down the traditional model of growth based on one sector, and the metal and engineering industry became a significant exporter. The growth of the metal industry was faster in Finland between 1970 and 1984 than in other OECD countries, and faster, for example, than in West Germany (Brotherus 1984) and also faster than in the other Nordic countries.[3] As a result of this development the metal industry became also a large-scale employer. Its demand for labour continued steadily up to 1975.

Now a crisis seems to affect this growth development, because according to the estimates of the industry's own experts 'the development of our industry and infrastructure has reached a saturation point'.[4] This saturation may be ascribed to the changes having taken place in the factors speeding up growth. The motors behind growth in the Finnish metal industry were, among others, an expansive domestic construction programme, investments by domestic industry, an exchange relationship in commerce between socialist and capitalist countries profitable to Finland, and the relatively cheap, motivated and skilled labour force. Now the effect of these growth factors has either decreased or part of them have undergone structural and qualitative changes. Experts on the metal industry estimate that the same growth trend as in 1970-83 can only be brought about with the help of exports. The problematic state of this saturation stage is again emphasised, since the benefit derived from foreign trade and exports is hard to realise; according to reports on foreign trade, Finnish industry is not heading for strong growth areas in exports, but rather towards slow growth in traditional production areas (Leskelä and Ylä-Anttila 1984). In other words, Finnish enterprises are struggling in 'mature' markets of industrialised countries. An exception to this is, among others, the electronics industry, which has undergone a strong period of growth, although the same has taken place in other countries, too (Lovio 1986).

The metal industry's attempts at renewed growth can be seen in its interest in developing global, national and enterprise-related strategies. Industrial research units in the Nordic countries have, for example, studied whether co-operation between the Nordic countries could create bases for new growth.[5] The Nordic Council has set up a commission under Volvo's managing director, Per Gyllenhammar, to investigate the development possibilities of economic co-operation. Finland's and Sweden's metal industry's central organisations have negotiated on the future possibilities for the industry (Brotherus 1984: 3) and the Finnish Metal Industry's Central Federation reported in 1984 on the development alternatives open to the Finnish metal industry. In all these reports the central idea is to form a new strategy for the metal industry. According to our observations the need for strategic planning and choice has been noted also in the planning of individual enterprises. For example, studies in strategic planning have spread into the enterprises' managerial training, and international enterprises especially have founded strategic planning departments. The task of these departments is to evaluate the enterprises' possibilities of choice in changing circumstances. In our opinion these matters emphasise that the choices related to production and rationalisation of the production process are a part of that strategy planning, to which individual enterprises and the metal industry's employer organisations are driven as a consequence of the economic crisis of the 1970s.

The adaptation crisis in the metal industry is seen also in its use of the labour force. There was a continuous growth in the demand for labour from 1960 to 1975, more than in the manufacturing industry in general. In 1975, however, a downward turn began, and the demand for labour dipped, despite a continued growth in production volume.

The stagnation in the demand for labour and the pressure to rationalise the existing labour force is seen also in the enterprises' own estimates. According to the average estimate there was too large a labour force in the enterprises between 1973 and 1978 and only later, between 1979 and 1981, did the enterprises see a need for additional labour. After 1981 the enterprises considered they had too many workers in the lower wage brackets, not especially workers possessing professional skills.[6]

Today the situation in the metal industry is characterised by enterprises trying to introduce flexible production and a flexible use of the labour force, as a result of the adaptation crisis in production and, related to this, the stagnation in labour demand. The attempt to use the labour force flexibly has meant pressure on the state and on the trade union movement. The enterprises have attempted to break away from legislation governing their operation, and from the accord of the labour market organisations, so that they could more easily use the labour force in a flexible way.

The national line in the behaviour of Finnish enterprises - general aspects

We have already discussed national models and the crisis of reproduction in the Finnish economy. Now we try to estimate how the national line emerges from the behaviour of private enterprises. We start with a theoretical discussion and then characterise some strategies of the Finnish enterprises.

According to Bechtle (1980: 47-55), within the general strategic conditions in the branch we can still distinguish the strategies of individual capital and of individual enterprises. Individual enterprises can shape the conditions of their value process, production status and the continuity of production, in accordance with society's general conditions of production. The competitive mechanism is, however, only one factor which directs enterprises' strategy choices, besides such measures influencing the value process as the employment of the labour force or other social conditions. These can have particular effects on the enterprise's competitive standing depending on its status and the nature of its production process. In this sense, individual capital has a certain autonomy and leeway. The enterprises employ their autonomy strategically to deflate external pressures on them, as well as such pressures as those determining the state of competition and market and price mechanisms. But Bechtle's interpretation does not provide any clues how the enterprise strategy is determined and what significance the strategy has in shaping the production and work process. For example the autonomy strategy may have different impacts if an enterprise is trying to control the global development of markets and technology (Ernst 1983, Räsänen 1985), or if the enterprise is adapting to the developments of markets and technology. Bechtle's concept of enterprise autonomy strategy does not allow us to evaluate the national contextual factors either. We consider, therefore, that Bechtle presents a general, sociologically oriented interpretation of autonomy strategy in individual capital, but he does not go into the content of the autonomy strategy or the environment where it could be realised.

Each of these factors, however, essentially influences from where the autonomy derives, and how it can be realised. If we consider, for example, the content of the autonomy strategy, then the interests related to autonomy probably vary according to the organic composition of capital and the conditions of competition.

The changes in the conditions of capital accumulation and of competition between individual capitals are perhaps the main reasons why industrial enterprises are seen to move away from traditional models of business management and competition towards new modes of competition. It has been shown in historical analyses and through case studies of modern enterprises that the strategies have gone beyond rationalisation of the production process to include control of markets and of technology, and generally a wider direction of social life (consumption, cultural traditions etc.). In this sense the individual enterprise should not be considered only as an individual production unit with specific internal processes, but rather as an institution related to society as a whole. In enterprise strategy this is reflected in the fact that 'strategic activities involve concentration and centralisation of capital by major take-overs and mergers, but they may also include expenditures on R & D to control technological development, large marketing campaigns to open up new markets or restructure old ones, and forming of more or less formal coalitions with other firms and agents' (Räsänen 1985: 90). This picture of a wider competition emphasises investments and the enterprises' strategic planning choices. It mainly suits diversified large enterprises, which can shape economic, technological, political and social conditions of competition, and which can modify external conditions as part of the enterprise's internal decision-making area, while the corresponding strategy for smaller enterprises emphasises their adaptation to given conditions. Later we will argue that the enterprises of a small country may follow a more adaptive strategy.

In these circumstances of wider competition business management influences labour deployment mainly by other choices than those directly related to labour processes. In the enterprise operations rationalisation of labour lay-offs, dismissals and closures of departments and individual production units are based on aspects related to business operations, and labour processes are subordinate to them (Tainio *et al.* 1985). And we can say that management treats labour tactically.

As we have referred to earlier, the adaptation crisis which industrial enterprises faced in the 1970s in several industrially developed countries took on quite special features in Finland, in its economy, politics, labour markets and social policy. We should emphasise further that factories and industrial work do not undergo modernisation in a vacuum, but in interrelationship with the surrounding society. The modernisation of industrial work and of factories can take place only if society also becomes modernised and begins to operate along the lines required by modern capitalism. For this reason the interrelationship between the enterprises and the community should be evaluated as a whole.

The adaptive enterprise strategy

Studying various Finnish enterprises of various sizes and from different production areas, Honko *et al.* (1982: 33-39, 40-44) observed that these enterprises in the 1970s followed a relatively clear operating strategy. The content and accent of the operating strategy varied according to the size of the enterprises and to the relation between the organisation structure and the production area; but the strategy was relatively constant for each production area, for different products and different technological set-ups. It was considered as a common feature that these enterprises followed the line of small enterprises in their operations. Such features as an attempt to adapt to markets, an attempt so specialise in products, and to have flexibility of operation were evident.

What has been stated above can be considered the dominant features, but since the enterprise strategy is tied to changes in enterprise structure, when the enterprises become multi-branch, multinational, more concentrated, or when complex and new types of functional enterprises are formed, the traditional, adaptive strategy of small enterprises gives way, at least in part. This means that the operation models of the aggressive enterprise are introduced. Then enterprises differentiate their labour deployment and try to exploit national differences, using *divide et impera* tactics in business management.

The adaptive strategy cannot be demonstrated by figures or by empirical examples, but its main idea should be seen as a principle labelling the operation of individual enterprises. How the adaptive line is realised in practice, differs according to the enterprises' organisational and production characteristics. When focusing on the argument made above, we paid special attention to the general development and organisational structure of the enterprises under study. We analysed their planning pressure points, their staffing policy within enterprise operations, and their community relations.

The enterprises have an adaptive orientation to product markets and behave like small units. But as soon as they internationalise their operations their relation to the community of origin starts cooling. The enterprises exploit the infrastructure of the area of origin but they do not want to be bound to the fate of the local community any more. In this orientation the enterprises already follow the strategy of large, dominating companies. But the enterprises differ from each other, for example, in the position of the personnel management, the qualification policy and the way of profiting from community relations.

Enterprise A had a clear, active aim to draw profit from the professional skills of its personnel and acted as a pioneer. Enterprise C was also active in its choice and training, whereas the strategy of enterprise B was to profit from the qualifications on the external labour market and train in this. In community relations enterprise A was reserved, enterprise B broke away dramatically from traditions and enterprise C showed a cool withdrawal.

Internationalisation of behaviour of the enterprises
Internationalisation of production will create special pressures in the behaviour of enterprises. Although Finland's domestic market is the third smallest in gross national product compared to OECD countries (Luostarinen 1982: 134) the internationalisation of production of Finnish enterprises is still in its early stages.

The expansion of exporting goods and the break away from the traditional mode of international co-operation took place in Finland after the mid-1970s. Among the units under study, enterprise A belongs to the mature stage of internationalisation of a large enterprise. Enterprise B is also in this mature stage as the internal manufacturing unit of a large corporation, mainly aiming at exports; and enterprise C is at the initial stage, as a unit operating within an enterprise.

From the point of view of labour employment and work we can say that pressure towards rationalisation and assimilation brought about by the internationalisation process of production is only beginning in Finland. Since internationalisation has so far affected only the enterprises' top sector, and since it has mainly been export of goods, Finnish enterprises have succeeded in international markets rather because of competitive prices, and especially due to relatively cheap labour in relation to the skills and motivation of workers. Now when the enterprises are more and more tied to international markets they are obliged to change their managerial behaviour. We can presume that in future employers will aim at the same type of managerial strategies in Finland as in competitive countries. This means that enterprises will deploy their labour reserves tactically and will try to break from the national traditions in staffing policy if they form a restrictive factor in price competitiveness. On the other hand, the enterprises will try to exploit national differences and take advantage of social benefits linked to labour renewal and exploitation possibilities. It is probably not an exaggeration to suppose that this internationalisation of enterprise operations will bring conflicts to enterprise staffing policy, labour market contracts, union possibilities of control, the individual work conditions of employees and the development of their demands.

Technological innovations as a way of adaptation

Finnish machine shops, in aiming at production adaptation have made choices typical of small enterprises also in technical and organisational questions. In analysing the technological development in machine shops from the early 1950s until today, we have observed that in technical colleges and in enterprises there has been an active international scientific dialogue and an interest and ability to incorporate technological innovations from abroad. It is typical of this dialogue that in Finland there has always been the problem what kind of technology would be more appropriate for our typical small series production organisation, and whether the choice of technology would reduce our technological dependence. This dialogue is invoked in connection with all the essential technological innovations. As examples we can mention the discussions about alternatives in developing machine tools and the control system of automatic machine tools. It is typical of Finland that in machine shops functional production organisation, for example, has never been realised in its pure form but that a certain intermediate form between functional and group organisation has been adopted. Another interesting discussion occurred with the choice of programming language of machine tools. There was a long discussion about which language is appropriate in small series production.

Technological renewals have been experienced in Finland from a spectator standpoint. The delay in technological modernisation has usually meant a freedom of choice in modes of adaptation or creation of a specific mode of adaptation. The creation of modes of adaptation is evident, among other places, in the development of specialised types of machine tools, and in the development of CNC systems. It is also demonstrable in choices related to modes of work organisation, such as the small group organisation experiments in machine shops, which were systematically tried out in 150 machine shops in the early 1980s.

In the Finnish case it is important to note that enterprises have drawn their technological examples at different times from different countries: after the war and especially in the 1950s and 1960s technological innovations in the metal industry came from Sweden by subcontracting relations with Swedish machine shops. Co-operation with Sweden and the other Nordic countries has been strong both in production and in research. For example, in 1968 the central organisations of the metal industry in the Nordic countries set up a common committee to promote the research possibilities of the machine-shop industry, to develop co-operation between countries and to supervise the common advantages of the Nordic countries. On the another hand, the trade relations between Finland and the Soviet Union have had their own special influence on the technological development of Finnish enterprises. A review of the discussion in the scientific journal of the engineering industry between 1950 and 1970 shows that Finnish enterprises, in their product development, have tried to predict the need of the Soviet market. Co-operation with socialist countries is also evident in Finnish enterprises having bought machine tools there, and, for example, from a co-operation project with the Soviet Union to develop new technology.

At the enterprise level the choices related to production techniques and organisation fluctuate, but in all our examples the technological rationalisations of production have played an active role in the enterprises' adaptation strategies.

- In enterprise A expansions and the installation of new machinery took place in different stages in 1977, 1979, 1981 and 1982. Enterprise A, and especially our gear workshop under study, is an experimental unit within the whole lifting division.

It was set up in 1982 and set in operation in 1983, so its machines are new, and its labour organisation and operations system are in an experimental stage. The objectives of the new workshop were to cut production costs by 30-40 per cent, to reduce the time for accomplishing an order to four weeks, to raise stock turnover to between 20 and 30 per year, to implement a flexible manufacturing system and production with little manpower (an unmanned night shift), to automate the assembly and transport system, and to implement computer-aided production management and material flows. Employees, whose average age was 23 in 1983, were trained for cell production as independent operatives of FMS groups. So the distinctive features of the work are not only CNC machines, but an overall system of CNC machines, computer-directed machine tool centres, automatic transport systems, and manually operated machine-tool groups and robots working as additional machinery. All in all this organisation enabled a two-shift system to run on 25 workers.

- In evaluating the technological level of the specialised machine-tool production department of enterprise B, a distinction should be drawn between parts manufacturing and the actual machinery construction. In parts manufacture the machine base was gradually renewed throughout the 1970s, so that 30 per cent of the machine base are CNC and NC machines and the remainder are manually controlled. Labour organisation in this part of the manufacturing process is functional and there are 35 employees in the department. The actual machine construction, which consists of construction work, parts assembly, machine fitting and testing, is carried out in small groups. The small groups are formed under the lead of the older machine constructor, and they consist of workers of different qualifications. In this small group organisation there are 44 workers. Project engineers are responsible for the projects and supervisors are responsible for social co-ordination. The technological level of this department is mainly determined by the organisational structure of machine construction, such as the project form of co-operation in production and planning, the small group organisation of manufacturing, and the high know-how. From 1979 the enterprise has developed quality circles and from 1982 computer-aided stock control. Thus the unit is organised on a workshop basis.

- In enterprise C the more profound changes are linked to the implementation of group organisation. From 1973 onwards they have gradually aimed at functional production organisation. In 1976 they switched to the so-called workshop organisation, and in 1982 to small group organisation, which is characterised by a certain combination of all production and quality checking. The change in organisation meant that the production schedule could be shortened by 30-40 per cent. At the time of our study the unit had eight CNC machines and eight NC machines. Their total share of the machine base was 17 per cent. The technological level of the production unit is not high if compared to automated machines, but from an efficiency viewpoint, the crucial feature is probably its organisational structure. This also indicates that special attention has been paid to labour rationalisation in the factories of concern C. For this reason the enterprise has a labour research department at its disposal.

As a conclusion we can say that Finnish enterprises have been open to various adaptations and experiments in technical and organisational systems. An analysis of technological development in the machine industry after the Second World War shows that Finnish machine shops have actively imitated technological advances; but the principles of functional production have never been implemented according to the pure ideas of large-series production. Neither have Finnish machine shops been bound, for example in computer adaptation, to any single type of solution; they have rather tried to choose adaptations which suit the small-series production of their own machine shops. Together with these characteristics, special features have been observed also in labour deployment.

Flexibility as a concept for rationalisation of labour

The ideas and normative concepts of how the production process should be organised in order to maximise both economic and socio-political profits have varied in the course of time. Automation, for example, has been discussed throughout the history of industrialisation, but its objectives have been interpreted according to the understanding of the problem at each particular point and the possible solution in the light of available knowledge.

Thus, for instance, at the stage of establishing industrial organisation, automatic systems were planned on Taylorist ideas of a strict division of labour and the simplification of tasks. Later automation has been used to improve the quality of work and to improve productivity.

At present industrial systems are expected to be flexible. Fluctuation in demand, customer-oriented planning, and the need to answer all demand available imply flexible production systems. The significance of these factors has grown essentially since the crisis of the 1970s, but there are also other reasons that have made the objective of flexibility a current idea of planning. One of those reasons is the effort of enterprises to free themselves from the norms of labour legislation and from the bonds caused by occupational safeguarding of organised labour, which have limited the management's prerogatives. While labour markets have become strained, different groups of workers have agreed to the redesigning of tasks, and re-division of labour has contributed to the realisation of the objectives of flexibility. Workers have consented for the sake of employment.

Concepts of production emphasising flexibility seem to be a modern principle of planning in industrial countries of both capitalism (Maurice 1986, Mannari 1986) and socialism (Sachse 1986).

The main differences in the development of different countries are seen in how this demand for flexibility is realised in the utilisation and renewal of the labour force, i.e. how work is developed/adjusted/submitted under the demands of flexibility in production. In Finland employers have aimed at quantitative and qualitative flexibility as well as that of saving expenses on labour. These different objectives of flexibility can be achieved by changes in working hours, or by adopting new technology and new management methods by which to influence the content of work. There are numerous examples of these means both in Finland and in other countries, but given the different aspects of flexibility we would like to emphasise that the means of rationalisation realised by enterprises should be considered as entities. The analysis of purely technological solutions is not enough for estimating the qualitative changes in work, because the quality of working life depends also on sociopolitical decisions.

In our cases flexibility was aimed at by several methods. In the use of labour we identified the following tendencies:

- the quantitative demand for labour stagnates and enterprises use the internal labour markets more effectively;
- selection, career planning and training are used as means of flexibility and disciplining of workers;
- flexibility of the labour force is achieved through versatility and employment policy;
- intensity and flexibility of the production process are achieved through organisational modes and opportunities offered by new technology.

Towards a more effective shaping of the internal labour markets

As late as in the 1960s, during the period of so-called extensive growth, the enterprises in the metal industry based their entire growth on the exploitation of surplus labour freed by structural changes in society. Thus, enterprises recruited labour from the country and from vocational groups outside their own domain. The utilisation of unskilled labour was possible because the enterprises based their production processes on strict division of labour and used management methods which made the guidance and control of work depend on numerous foremen (Kavonius 1979; Hirszo-wicz 1981). When the enterprises of the metal industry at the end of the 1970s were forced to emphasise flexibility and quality in production, they were also obliged to develop new technology and new models of organisation. This also meant that enterprises had to develop more intensive forms for the utilisation of labour.

The breakthrough of the intensive forms of utilising labour was the transition from traditional control methods of the foremen to semi-autonomous working teams. Shops and small-group organisations became functional organisations. Where production organisations were renewed, technological improvements were also made. In the utilisation of labour this meant that enterprises used internal labour markets more effectively instead of quantitative fluctuation. Consequently, the training of personnel and the planning of personnel policy in general became more crucial when considering productivity. Later the utilisation of internal labour markets was revised so that enterprises abolished personnel policy norms, restricting them to refer only to decreasing core personnel. This has meant that enterprises seek to meet variations in the work

279

volume by using external labour reserves, for instance by sub-contracting and renting manpower as well as buying services, besides the core personnel. Our samples present these aspects.

In the enterprises under study the quantitative demand for labour examined at corporate level generally stagnated in the mid-1970s. If the number of employees is related to business turnover, the picture of the stagnated demand for labour also holds for expanding concerns or their individual units. This stagnation, even when the production volume has increased or the quality and flexibility demands on production have risen, has become possible by reorganising the tasks of the decreased core personnel. This has required the examination of the task distribution of vocational groups. It has required the expansion of areas of responsibility concerning the amount and quality of production as well as cost responsibility. The decrease in the size of the core personnel has meant that the enterprise's own internal labour market, that is personnel transfers, allocation of completion time for tasks, employment policy arrangements and various types of substitute arrangements, has become an active part of personnel policy.

-   The number of personnel of enterprise A has risen, but the increase is explainable through corporate acquisitions and particularly through the growth of its units operating abroad. The size of the staffs of individual units has varied. The desire to maintain mobility between units situated in different areas appears in personnel policy. Mobility of personnel is also maintained between Finnish units. This is emphasised in the enterprise's labour policy, particularly in the 1970s. The internal mobility of personnel is visible both in the expert help received from central units under Finnish regional administration and as short-term transfers of individual workers. Workers are borrowed for a few months or weeks from a unit situated about 60 km away. Otherwise, enterprise A has balanced its varying volumes of work through subcontracting, accounting for approximately 20 per cent of the production value, and by using overtime and unmanned shifts. In addition, the internal transfers between different work posts come into the picture, occurring through substitute personnel arrangements and the versatility of the workers. As a result of various regulatory means, such as the concern's internal mobility, the division of labour between enterprise A and its subcontractors and the mobility occurring inside unit A,

280

employment is stable and labour turnover has been minimal in recent years.

- In enterprise B the number of employees of its mother concern began to decline in 1974. The number of employees in enterprise B itself began to decline in 1980, though the number of workers in the unit manufacturing machine tools has risen. But when considered in terms of production volume development, the number of workers in the unit manufacturing machine tools has also dropped. The stagnation in the demand for labour has meant in concern B, too, that the transfer of workers inside the concern between production units located in different areas and between different departments of enterprise B has become the guiding principle in personnel policy. This is evident in the form of the three main lines of personnel policy. First, personnel planning is considered a part of the company's overall plan for its plants. In this way fluctuations in the need for labour are to be balanced and harmful personnel turnover is to be prevented. Among the methods used are training, transfers and temporary arrangements, temporary overtime and subcontracting. Second, each time when hiring workers, it must first be verified whether qualified persons and people capable of development exist within the company. Third, further training and retraining are to prevent the under-use of personnel.

- The situation in enterprise C is basically the same as in enterprise B. Personnel development in the concern began to decline in 1974. The labour force in the concern's local plants has also decreased evenly since 1974, though business turnover has increased. The number of employees in unit C, which manufactures tools, started dropping in 1978. The decrease in the size of staff and its fluctuations in different units show that work volume regulation is chiefly influenced by the mobility of the labour force between the concern's plants in the same area. While the number of workers at the local plants of concern C was stable in 1983-84, clerical staff increased by 5.7 per cent. In the same period in enterprise C the number of workers dropped by 2 per cent, while the clerical staff rose by 3 per cent.

Enterprise examples confirm that the use of internal labour markets has formed an important means of allocating work volume. Internal labour markets have been effective because the means provided by them in Finland are not limited by any regulations or sanctions. Operations are in practice simply part of the employer's right of direction.

For the workers, the use of internal labour markets means vocational mobility, variation in tasks and a change in both job location and environment. Tracing in the sample firms the number of employees having changed job titles, we noted this to be quite general. In enterprise A, 53 per cent of the employees had maintained the same job titles while employed, and 43 per cent had changed at least once or twice. Changes in job titles were even more frequent in enterprise B, where only 15 per cent had maintained the same titles and 53 per cent had changed three to five times during their periods of employment. In enterprise C, 45 per cent remained in the same job titles and 36 per cent changed job titles once or twice.

It is, however, important for the workers to ask whether a change in job title also means career advancement. On the basis of pay records of workers changing job titles, the employees were classified by those whose career had regressed, those where the effect was unclear and those whose career had advanced. According to our estimates, a change in job title generally seemed to lead to career advancement and only in exceptional cases to regression. Differences between enterprises show that in enterprise B, where job title changes were most common, changes led to advancement in 80 per cent of the cases and were unclear in 20 per cent. Correspondingly, in enterprise A percentages for career advancement and for unclear effect of change in job title were 38 per cent. In enterprise C, where job title change was also quite common, 36 per cent represented career advancement.

From the examples we can see that enterprises have leeway in organising the work and in personnel management. The management has been able to justly manipulate the professional and social effects on the personnel according to age, experience, training and their adapatability.

Sharpened selection of personnel

An improvement in the selection of the labour force has, on the one hand, been made possible by the continuous surplus of labour and the division of regional labour markets by silent agreements between enterprises and has, on the other hand, been required by the new quality demands of the production process (Koistinen

1985: 86-90). Selection of the labour force occurs no longer only once, nor is it concerned only with the vocational skills of the workers, but has become systematised. This is demonstrated in our sample enterprises since

- in filling new jobs, priority is given to workers presently in the company;
- in hiring new workers, the enterprises use the local employment agency only on rare occasions;
- enterprises have their own hiring organisations and direct contacts with the vocational schools in the local and economic region;
- vocational school graduates go through a first selection in the enterprise's own industrial school or 'internal training', which generally surpasses the level or training provided publicly;
- only after the enterprise's own training and the practice and test period associated with it does the selection and hiring of workers occur;
- career development and further training in the employment situation is connected with success at work, the right behaviour and work motivation.

The system of selection described above has created a new system to discipline the personnel and select only persons who accept the conditions and claims of industrial work. While selection continues during the employment period, it is based on such factors as motivation, social background and type of personality. Modern enterprises seek even more qualified people with corporate spirit, who are motivated and accept corporate economic realities. The career development of present-day workers is tightly bound to this motivational viewpoint. Thus these characteristics stress that in the rationalisation of industrial work the control of social and political realities also plays a remarkable role.

Seen from the workers' point of view, the career development linked to the enterprise's personnel policy can at the same time mean being tied to the fate of the enterprise while gaining possible vocational skills. At the time of the study we noted whether the workers had received vocational skills on the job or had had them when hired. In enterprise B 57 per cent and in enterprise C 81 per cent received the vocational skills associated with their work in the firm. The acquisition of vocational skills tied to the enterprise was further stressed by the fact that 19 per cent of enterprise B's employees had been hired without any special skills. Enterprise A was an exception since employees had almost without exception come from vocational schools and received only additional training from the enterprise.

The sharpened selection of personnel became possible in a situation where the demand for industrial labour stagnated. When the difficulties of finding a job increased, enterprises were able to sharpen their criteria of recruiting. According to our research, another crucial reason for sharpening the selection is the fact that in regional labour markets there has existed a 'silent agreement' among the enterprises not to compete for the same employees and thus not 'to buy' them from within other enterprises. This silent agreement has led regionally to qualitative segmentation of labour markets.

Shaping the content of work

According to our study, part of the strategy of modern enterprises is the creation of labour force flexibility through employee versatility. Present day employees are not hired for any specific job or job title (filer, milling machine operator etc.) nor for a definite production department, but inside the enterprise they can be directed to work concerned with several job titles. Nowadays it is typical for employees to be trained for two or three different occupations. To attain this versatility the sample enterprises had training and practice systems both inside production cells and going beyond them, through which readiness to perform in various jobs was developed by the workers. This expansion of the employees' occupations in production was obviously successful, which means that the work content profile was relatively large and at least broader than that, for instance, of the industrial clerical staff in office work.

In order to depict the content dimensions of work and to compare differences between plants and vocational groups, we have borrowed the 'spideridea' developed by Sachse *et al.* (1980) and made our own application (Koistinen 1984). The content of work is described as having five dimensions:

- level of vocational skill demanded by the work;
- routine/diversity of the work;
- physical/intellectual nature of the work;

- level of freedom of action;
- individuality/co-operative character of the work.

Figure 10.1: Content Profile of General Machine-shop Work

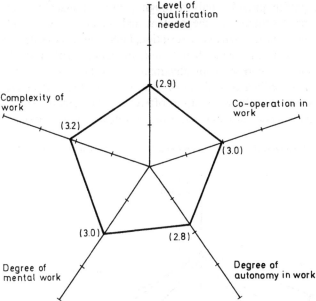

Each dimension was evaluated on a scale of one to five points. When we summarised the values of all the 80 workers studied into one general content profile to describe 'machine-shop work', we arrived at the situation presented in Figure 10.1.

The profile shows with regard to the required vocational skill (point value 2.9) that machine-shop work demands skills attained during comprehensive school and at least two years of vocational school, plus on-the-job training. The dimension routine/diversity of the work shows that the ratio between them is almost 60:40 (point value 3.2), the routine part consisting of tasks which remain the same, using the same tools or operating methods. Machine-shop work is still combined mental and physical labour, because 60-70 per cent of the working time is made up by manual tasks. The dimension concerning the degree of freedom has a point value of 2.8. If the extremes in this dimension are a tied/free possibility to affect such matters as the amount of work, production methods, tools, job site etc., we can characterise machine-shop work as being partially free. The fifth dimension depicts co-operation at work. The extremes on this scale are individual/co-operative work in co-operation with different vocational groups in planning the work as well as in its realisation. The point value of 3 demonstrates that machine-shop work is generally co-operative work, performed jointly in the vocational group.

The profile provides only a rough picture of machine-shop work. The description of the content and nature of their work would need a more extensive description, including work tasks and the characteristics linked to their completion and control. It would also require the workers' own situational interpretation concerning the internal conflicts of their work. But if we are satisfied in this sense to use only the information offered by the content profile, we can summarise our main results in the following observations.

Figure 10.2: Content Profiles of General Machine-shop Work in Enterprises A, B, and C

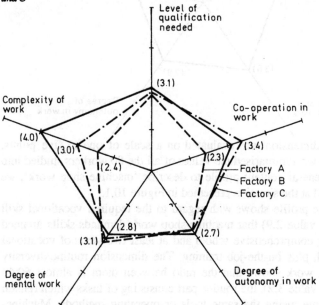

Similar rationalisation pressures have been exerted on the work in modern plants, which affect technical and organisational systems, control of work, and desires to benefit from vocational skill. Despite the general development, differences between enterprises still exist. Figure 10.2 shows that enterprise B differs in the extensiveness of tasks from, for instance, enterprise A, which has the most advanced technological system among our cases (machine tool centres, CNC system and cells, transfer robots etc.).

286

Differences between enterprises also remain in a detailed examination when we compare, for example, the vocational profiles of CNC-machine and CNC-cell operators (Figure 10.3). The differences in the content profiles of work must therefore be explained in terms other than of production technology factors, such as through the differences in production organisation and its tradition.

A third claim affects the idea that in the characteristics of the content of work the differences between occupations are still maintained.

Figure 10.3: Content Profiles of Work among CNC-machine and Cell Operators in Enterprises A, B, and C

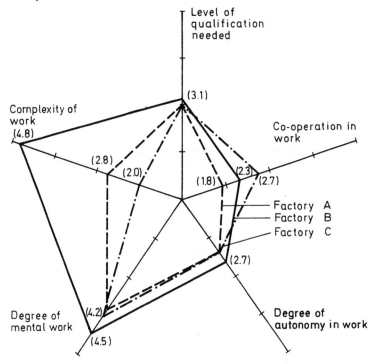

Figure 10.4: Content Profiles of Mechanical-manual Work, CNC-machine Operation and Assembly Installation in Enterprise A

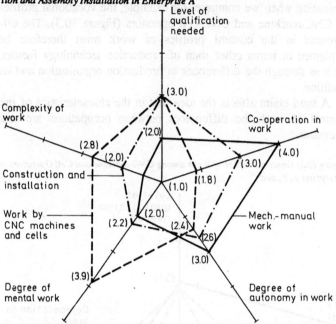

Figure 10.5: Content Profiles of Mechanical-manual Work, CNC-machine Operation and Assembly Installation in Enterprise B

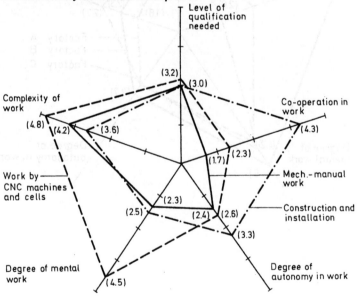

Figure 10.6: Content Profiles of Mechanical-manual Work, CNC-machine Operation and Assembly Installation in Enterprise C

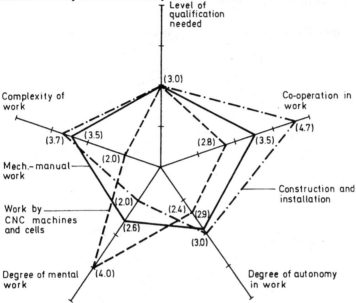

Figures 10.4 to 10.6 point to two factors. First, they show that the work on CNC cells represents a broader and more harmonious vocational profile than traditional work performed on mechanical-manual machines. Second, they show that assembly and installation work maintain competitiveness with regard to the characteristics of content of work. The diversity of this work must be compared to the work of CNC-machine and cell operators.

The model for flexible use of labour

If we pay attention only to the processes at the enterprise level we realise that the case studies concerning the Finnish engineering plants support Atkinsons's (1984) idea of flexible employment relationships. He points out that the revolutionary aspect of the new model of employment relationships is that it signifies a new type of distribution of tasks as well as professional and social standing within the enterprise. This work distribution does not derive from the so-called Taylorist work distribution according to work achievement, but is based on the functional specialisation of the tasks in their entirety. This means a functional division of work both among the enterprises, on the one hand, and inside the plants on the other hand (Figure 10.7).

Figure 10.7: Labour Force Resource Structure of a Flexible Enterprise

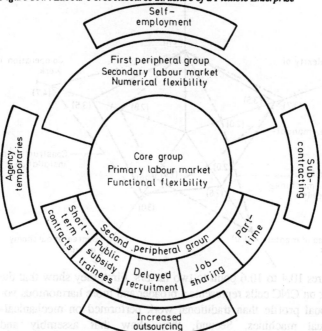

The first functional division of work takes place when the enterprises' labour markets are divided into their own internal labour markets and into external labour markets exploited by them. Such exploitation is evident, for example, in the increase of temporary contract jobs and use of the special services of independent enterprises, as well as in using subcontractors and other external services. This distribution of tasks enables the enterprises to regulate their work volume quantitatively and to control their labour reserves functionally (Atkinson 1984: 28). Our studies of machine shops show that the enterprises concentrate internally only on those established and restricted jobs which are essential to their product and competitive status.

The second level on which the distribution of tasks is evident is the division of internal labour markets into primary and periphery labour markets. If the above-mentioned division of jobs has significance in terms of the enterprise's strategy, then the division of labour inside the enterprise has significance in various jobs, in controlling the enterprise's internal production process. The modern enterprises would seem, according to Atkinson (1984: 28), to be attempting to divide their internal labour markets into primary and periphery labour markets.

Although the Finnish material seems to support Atkinson's models, one can question whether or not the flexibility model is a normative model which describes the aims of the management rather than its practice. If we take into consideration how the state of local and regional labour markets, the social ties of enterprises as well as the trade union surveillance affect the behaviour of enterprises, it appears that Atkinson's model is a simplification.

Our empirical material indicates clearly that management has profited from its better standing and has realised rationalisations almost unrestrictedly, and consequently atypical employment relationships have increased (Bruun 1985). But if these efforts are compared to those of, for example, the working life humanisation boom of the 1960s and 1970s, the influence of the new employment relationships model could be considered as not fully developed. Our examples indicate that there is no such large-scale attempt at developing a uniform personnel policy as there was with legislation at the beginning of the 1970s or in the golden age of the so-called Fordist industrial relations model. At the end of the 1960s and beginning of the 1970s industrial relations were characterised by consensus-ideology. According to this ideology, the co-operation of the labour market organisations and agreement procedures were renewed, and a corresponding renewal of labour legislation was put into effect, related, among other things, to participation in organisations and working life democracy, health care at work, work safety, the quality of the work environment and labour policy legislation. This 'desire for compromise' that appeared in the 1970s throughout society and a temporary cut in the labour reserves went a long way to explain the labour market organisations' desire for an active personnel policy. This activation of personnel policy took the shape of an attempt to create some kind of administrative organisation in personnel policy in all larger-sized enterprises, and an attempt to create some kind of internal minimum coherence in personnel policy (Koistinen 1984: 320-333). For the time being we cannot show a corresponding general line covering various policy levels, such as the enterprises' personnel policy, bargaining procedure as well as the relations between legislation and the labour market organisations. But anyway, some new tendencies in personnel policy and deployment can be observed, which can be explained mainly by the changing economic conditions of enterprise operations and by the enhanced position of employer groups.

Conclusions

At the beginning we asked what the role of small countries in the implementation of new technology would be. Following contingency theory, we looked at features which describe the national experience in Finland, the crisis in production structure and the exceptional position of the metal industry. We also evaluated the strategies used by enterprises and how the labour force has been used as a means of adjustment.

This view does not underrate the significance of technological change, but emphasises the need of a more holistic picture. The technological change is a question of fate for Finland, too, as it has to solve problems connected with the economic and political system's ability to function. That is why the question of technology and the future of work should be politicised and understood as a crucial question for the future of society.

There has been a certain consensus in Finland on how the country adjusts to external conditions. Till now Finland has not experienced any problems caused by overindustrialisation and the decline of entire branches of production, and this is why the working class has also given support to the rationalisations (Koistinen and Lilja 1987). However, during the last years rationalisations, amalgamations and industrial restructuring have meant such a profound crisis in the socioeconomic and vocational position of the economically active population that they threaten to break down the traditional model of the renewal of labour based on a social state.

Concerning sociological theory we suggest that in the future we should, by using comparative studies, develop such a theory of technological change that would hermeneutically and historically relate separate phenomena to the entities of the whole system. The historical view is especially important when we evaluate the success of technological innovations. At present industrial sociologists are too much preoccupied with the current production rationality. This engagement has meant that the social effects of the new technology are estimated according to the benefits it has for the operation of the system. A trait of this techno-economic rationality can also be seen in our analysis, but by referring to the crisis of the model of economic renewal we have suggested that the question is not only what happens to jobs but that the difficulties of adaptation also concern the very industrial system. In these days there is a strong dispute between those who support the current rationality and industrial system and those who would like to revise the trend of industrial and social development. This general argumentation can be more crucial for the future of industrial labour than disputes on rationalisation agreements. There are signs that those wider issues have lately become topics of discussion in Finland, too, whereas formerly only automation and the design of work were discussed.

Notes

1. In writing this chapter I received important and useful contributions from my colleagues Tuomo Särkikoski and Timo Tikka.

2. See *Metal Industry's Year Book* (1984).

3. See *Economic Growth in a Nordic Perspective* (1984), p. 106.

4. See *Selvitys Suomen metalliteollisuuden kehitysvaihtoehdoista* (1984), p. 7.

5. See *Economic Growth in a Nordic Perspective* (1984).

6. See *Metal Industry's Year Book* (1984).

References

Alapuro, R. (1985) 'Interstate Relationships and Political Mobilization in the Nordic Countries', in *Small States in Comparative Perspective. Essays for Erik Allardt*, Oslo, Norwegian University Press, pp. 93-108

Atkinson, J. (1984) 'Manpower Strategies for Flexible Organisations', *Personnel Management*, August 1984, pp. 28-31

Bechtle, G. (1980) *Betrieb als Strategie: Theoretische Vorarbeiten zu einem industriesoziologischen Konzept* (Enterprise as Strategy: Theoretical Approaches to a Concept of Industrial Sociology), Frankfurt/M., Campus Verlag

Brotherus, J. (1984) *Metalliteollisuuden tulevaisuuden kuva. Tekniikan päivät 1984* (The Future of Metal Industry), Helsinki, Suomen Teknillinen Seura

Bruun, N. (1985) 'New Forms and Aspects of Atypical Employment Relationships in Finland', in K.-P. Tiitinen (ed.) *Työoikeudellisen yhdistyksen vuosikirja*, Helsinki, pp. 63-75

Economic Growth in a Nordic Perspective (1984) Det Okonomiske Råd Sekretariatet, Copenhagen, ETLA, Helsinki, IUI, Stockholm, IOI, Bergen

Eisenstadt, S.N. (1985) 'Reflections on Centre-periphery Relations and Small

European States', in *Small States in Comparative Perspective. Essays for Erik Allardt*, Oslo, Norwegian University Press, pp. 41-50

Ernst, D. (1983) *The Global Race in Microelectronics: Innovation and Corporate Strategies in a Period of Crisis*, Frankfurt/M., Campus Verlag

Haapala, P. (1986) *Tehtaan valossa: Teollistuminen ja työväestön muotoutuminen Tampereella 1820-1920* (In the Light of the Factory: Industrialisation and the Formation of the Working Class in Tampere, 1820-1920), Tampere, Osuuskunta Vastapaino

Hirszowicz, M. (1981) *Industrial Sociology: An Introduction*, Oxford, Martin Robertson & Company Ltd.

Honko, J., A. Prihti and K. Virtanen (1982) 'Critical Areas in the Capital Investment Process of the Enterprises: A Study of the Success and Failure of Strategy and Capital Investment in the 30 Largest Finnish Industrial Enterprises', *Helsingin kauppakorkeakoulun julk.* B:57, Helsinki

Kavonius, M. (1979) 'Teknologisen kehityksen vaikutukset ja mahdollisuudet sen hallitsemiseen' (The Consequences of Technological Development and the Possibilities to Control It), in *Työ ja teknologia* (Work and Technology), Helsinki, Metallityöväen Liitto, pp. 6-16

Koistinen, P. (1984) 'Teknologiset uudistukset ja työvoiman käyttö. Tutkimus Suomen paperi- ja kartonkiteollisuudesta' (Technological Innovations and the Use of Labour: A study in the Finnish Paper and Cardboard Industry) *Työvoimapoliittisia tutkimuksia*, no. 47, Helsinki, Työvoima-ministeriö

Koistinen, P. (1985) 'The Use of Labour in Modern Plants of Engineering Industry: Some Conclusions of the Finnish Case Studies', University of Joensuu, Karelian Institute, working papers, no. 5/1985, Joensuu

Koistinen, P. and K. Lilja (1987) 'Consent Type of Occupational Adaptation to New Technology: Observations from the Finnish Case', manuscript

Koistinen, P. and T. Särkikoski (1986) 'Teknologinen yhteiskuntakuva hegemonian välineenä ja perusteluna: Kysymys yhteiskunnan tulevaisuudesta ja sen johtajuudesta' (Technological View of the Society as a Form of Ideological and Political Hegemony: The Question of the Future of Society and to Whom Belongs the Leadership), manuscript

Koskinen, T. (1987) 'Sociological Analysis of Paper Mill Community as an Anatomy of Finnish Society', manuscript

Kosonen, P. (1985) 'Public Expenditures in the Nordic Nation States - the Source of Prosperity or Crisis', in *Small States in Comparative Perspective. Essays for Erik Allardt*, Oslo, Norwegian University Press, pp. 108-124

Kosonen, P. and J. Pekkarinen (1985) 'Norden dagen efter' - pohjoismaisten mallien murros' (The Country-specifics of Nordic Countries in Transition), *Tiede ja Edistys*, no. 2/1985, Helsinki, pp. 167-178

Leskelä, I. and P. Ylä-Anttila (1984) 'Pohjoismaat junnaavat hitaan kasvun markkinoille', *Talouselämä*, no. 18/1984, pp. 40-42

Lovio, R. (1986) 'Emerging Industries: Interactions between Production, Technology and Markets in a Small Open Economy', Technical Research Centre of Finland, Research Notes, no. 554/1986, Helsinki

Luostarinen, R. (1982) 'Suomalaisten yritysten kansainvälistyminen: Motiivit, strategiat, ongelmat ja vaateet' (The Internationalisation of Finnish Enterprises: Motives, Problems and Demands), *Kansantaloudellinen aikakauskirja*, no. 2/1982, Helsinki, pp. 132-146

Mannari, H. (1986) 'Employment Structure in French and Japanese Firms', paper presented at ISA Symposium, Session III: Science and Technology in Social Change, Delhi, 18-22 August 1986

Maurice, M. (1986) 'Flexible Technologies and Variability of the Forms of the Division of Labour in France and Japan', paper presented at ISA Symposium, Session III: Science and Technology in Social Change, Delhi, 18-22 August 1986

Metal Industry's Year Book 1984. Federation of Finnish Metal and Engineering Industries, Helsinki

Perez, C. (1983) 'Structural Change and Assimilation on New Technologies in the Economic and Social Systems', *Futures*, October, pp. 357-375

Rautiainen, H. (1985) 'Sopimusvapautta pakotteiden sijaan' (More Freedom than Sanctions into the Contracts), *Teollisuusviikko*, 3 October 1985

'Report of Finnish Technology Committee', *Valtioneuvoston kanslian julkaisuja*, no. 1/1982, Helsinki

Räsänen, K. (1985) 'Industrial Enterprise and Extended Competition', in *Problems in the Re-description of Business Enterprises*, Helsinki School of Economics, Studies B-73, Helsinki, pp. 85-95

Sachse, E. (1986) 'Theory and Practice in the Field of Social Policy with Respect to the Scientific Technological Progress in GDR', paper presented at the University of Joensuu, 8-15 September 1986

Sachse, E., B. Stieler and G. Sperber (1980) 'Erfahrungen bei der quantifizierten Bewertung von Arbeitsinhalten in der materiellen Produktion' (Experiences with the Quantified Evaluation of Work Contents in Material Production), *Sozialistische Arbeitswissenschaft*, no. 1/1980, Berlin, Verlag Die Wirtschaft

Schumann, M., E. Einemann, C. Siebel-Rebell, P. Wittemann (1982) *Rationalisierung, Krise und Arbeiter. Eine empirische Untersuchung der Industrialisierung auf der Werft* (Rationalisation, Crisis and Workers. An Empirical Investigation of Industrialisation in the Shipyard), Bremen, Kooperation Universität/Arbeiterkammer Bremen

Selvitys Suomen metalliteollisuuden kehitysvaihtoehdoista (1984) (Alternatives of the Finnish Metal Industry), Helsinki, Suomen Metalliteollisuuden Keskusliitto

Tainio, R., K. Räsänen and T. Santalainen (1985) *Suuryritykset ja niiden johtaminen Suomessa* (Managing Large Corporations in Finland). Tampere, Weilin and Göös

Teulings, A.W.M. (1985) 'The Power of Corporate Management: Powerlessness of the Manager', paper presented at Helsinki School of Economics, *Studies*, no. 3-73, Helsinki

Walsh, V. (1986) 'Technology, Competitiveness and the Special Problems of Small Countries', background paper submitted to the OECD-Finnish Government Seminar in Helsinki, 29-30 January 1986

Watanuki, J. (1986) 'Welfare Policy, Welfare Society and Welfare State - Japan's Case', paper presented at ISA Symposium, Session I, Delhi, 18-22 August 1986

11

Technological Changes in Two Dutch Factories: Control, Flexibility and Learning

Jan Berting and Hans van de Braak

Introduction

Social choice or industrial convergence?

Although the thesis of work organisation's relative autonomy with regard to technology seems to be accepted among East as well as West European social scientists (Grootings 1986: 279), at least in principle, this does not answer how science, technology and characteristics of work organisation are *de facto* related.

Accepting the idea of social choice in relation to the introduction of new technologies in work organisation (Child 1986: 40), we want to know which choices are available and to whom, under which carefully specified social, political, economic and cultural conditions, and what are the outcomes of this decision-making.

The central idea of social choice with regard to technology runs counter to the industrial convergence thesis claiming that there is no real choice because each industrial nation has to mobilise its best resources of production. So each nation has, as Kerr (1983: 45) remarks, to utilise the best modern technology. Moreover, this urgent need to mobilise the best resources of production implies that there is also the best organisation of work in relation to a specific technology. The present stress on social choice may be considered as a new stage in industrial development, connected with the introduction of new types of information technology. It

296

must be remembered that a lot of systematic evidence on industrial development supports the industrial convergence thesis, the technological variable being cross-culturally quite strong in explaining social behaviour on the job, in the factory, and in job-related systems (Marsh 1984: 86).

The present state of this debate requires a careful analysis of the specific relationship between technology and the organisation of work both within different branches of industry and within different production processes. It may be that at least part of the empirically observed industrial convergence is a consequence of the acceptance of the logic of industrialism by those who decide on the introduction of new technologies in work organisation. As Hirschhorn (1984: 3) says: 'The managers, union leaders, designers, engineers, and educators who together shape our new technologies operate under traditional industrial assumptions. Many still believe in dividing up the work, creating semiskilled jobs, and planning the work flow entirely from the back office'.

It is easy to see that industrialisation, conceived as the interrelated development of the division of labour, of specialisation and mechanisation - a process implying on the level of production organisation, standardisation of parts, continuity of work flow, rigid integration of parts within the factory as a whole, and reduction of work to simple tasks - must have consequences as implied by the convergence thesis. New types of research, starting from the assumption of social choice in relation to technology, have to lay bare the (new) foundations of choice and the consequences for the organisation of work.

Two Dutch case studies: aircraft industry and lift-truck attachment manufacturing

We have studied two firms in the Netherlands, both of which have introduced NC and CNC machine tools, but differ widely in some major respects such as market conditions, complexity of production and work process, plant history and nature of international cooperation with subcontractors:

1. A long-established aircraft factory (production of turbo prop and prop-fan jets). This factory is engaged in both civil and military production and is, moreover, contributing to the

development of space technology.

2. A company that is engaged in the manufacturing of lift-truck attachments (e.g. fork clamps, pulp bale clamps) and related products such as hose reels and masts for handling materials in all kinds of industries. This factory is part of a North American Corporation.

Both factories may be considered as leaders within their branches of industry and are operating in highly competitive international markets. Nevertheless, the differences between the two cases are considerable in many respects.

The lift-truck attachment factory has recently been built in one of the eastern provinces of the country in which no prior establishments of the firm existed. This firm designed and built a factory in which very advanced production techniques were introduced (computer-aided design and manufacturing system, robotics connected with welding, automatic handling of transport and storage). At the time of our research (spring 1986) the process of introduction of new technologies had not yet been completed. Although the firm has two other factories in the western provinces, most of the workers in this new plant were recruited from the area. The company decision to build this new factory in the Netherlands was strongly influenced by the fact that important subventions were made available by the Dutch government (Ministry of Economic Affairs). The policy of the government is connected with two goals: 1. the development of new types of economic activities in areas which have undergone major economic transitions (in this case the collapse of the textile industry); 2. the acceleration of the introduction of new technologies in industry in order to maintain or corroborate the international economic position of Dutch industry.

The aircraft factory is, by contrast, a long established one, characterised by an organisational structure and culture which seem to be rather resistant to changes emanating from technology.

Prior to new developments during the last years - the launching of two new types of airplanes leading to the acquisition of important orders in the international market - the firm was obliged to fire about 2,000 workers. At the end of 1984 the firm started the recruitment of some 800 new workers, most of them highly qualified. The firm is very dependent on state participations and state research orders (for example military aircraft and other types of defence orders, the Airbus programme, aerospace products).

298

Goals and organisation of the study

We have primarily paid attention to the analysis of

- the nature of the introduction of new technologies in the work organisation. What are the main assumptions of the decision-makers who have adopted new technologies (NC/CNC machine tools in these cases)? Is there an awareness of social choices with respect to the organisation of work? If so, in what ways are these choices related to the main characteristics of the existing work organisation? Has a specific model of introduction of new technologies been developed? In what ways are new technologies actually introduced and what are, in this respect, the roles of the workers within the factory and of the labour unions?
- the effects of the introduction of new technologies on work organisation in order to get some pertinent data which may enable us to specify the relationships between technological changes and work organisation. In connection with these propositions we will try to describe in what ways technological changes within the two factories are related to changes in the qualification levels of the workers, to changing learning processes, to changes in the hierarchy (both with regard to its structure and the nature of interactions between different levels), to new types of integration and accompanying changes in the organisation's flexibility to both clients' demands and problems arising within the organisation itself.

We organised with the help of the personnel managers several series of interviews within the two factories. We interviewed employees and workers on different levels within the hierarchy, in order to get a description as complete as possible of the problems connected with the introduction of new technology, taking into account the different perspectives on this issue that may prevail among different interest groups within the organisation. These interviews were held during the last months of 1984 and lasted one hour/one hour and a half each. During the first months of 1986 we returned to both factories for another series of interviews. In some cases these interviews were held with the same persons, but also several 'new' people were questioned. The second series of interviews was organised in order to complete our data in those cases where we had discovered some gaps in our information about

299

changes that had occurred within the factories since the end of 1984. We hoped to get some information concerning effects of technological changes as assumed by some of our respondents in 1984. Approximately 30 persons were interviewed (20 persons in 1984 and 10 in 1986). We used a checklist during our open interviews, containing topics related to the main hypotheses. We also studied company documents containing information on: (changes in) the labour force (number of workers, required skill level, lay-offs etc.), technical descriptions of production processes, lay-out of the machinery on the shopfloor, social policy, the effects of the introduction of new technologies on the work organisation, the economic position of the branch of industry, especially in relation to the international market etc.

The promises of new technologies

An important question facing management in capitalist societies is that of which contribution new technologies offer to the organisation of production, considering a competitive environment. Though the introduction of automation in the manufacturing process is far from new, it is often stated that microelectronics promises to provide substantial advantages in the area of flexibility, reduction of manufacturing costs, and the like. According to a popular observation, the development of automated manufacturing seems to point to a direction where factories with small-batch production tend to resemble continuous-process industries. An important effect of the new technologies is that the latter are losing the comparative advantages springing from the economy of scale. The activities performed on the product are done automatically by machines, and the function of the production worker is merely to watch and take corrective action. Whether this is a valid observation has to be discussed afterwards. Anyway, traditional arguments favouring the deployment of automated manufacturing refer to reduction of unit costs, improvement of product quality, and shortening of production time. Although these arguments are still valid, market opportunities to realise mass production and small-batch production have changed substantially in recent years. So, reduction of the batch size is a common management objective. This situation has, first, been triggered by the conception that sales can be increased by providing customers with a wide range of product variants. Second, there is an increased awareness, caused by the extremely high interest rates in the preceding period, that large stocks of half and final products are costly. Thus, the reduction of stocks and storage costs means smaller production runs. A third factor which tends to reduce the production runs is technology itself: new materials and components shorten the economic life-cycle of commodities. Moreover, microelectronic technology tends to provide opportunities to enhance the flexibility of production systems. In sum, reduction of the batch size has increased the need for flexible manufacturing systems. Flexibility means here that automated machine tools can be utilised both in single-item production and in small-batch production, with minor adjustment times.

Apart from the desire to improve productivity, the arguments favouring automated small-batch production refer mainly to close tolerances, following from three demands on contemporary commodities. First, fabrication of parts out of one piece of raw material saves weight. This kind of fabrication allows less dimensional tolerances since inaccuracies can no longer be corrected at final assembly. Second, reduction of indirect costs since parts with closer tolerances show less wear and tear and thus need less maintenance. Third, it contributes to the easy replacement of defective components all over the world (especially important in the aircraft industry). The basis for close tolerances, precise machining and automated small-batch production is the numerically controlled machine.

Basic conceptual framework

Before entering upon our case studies, it is necessary to outline our basic framework, starting from the so-called labour process debate. In his well-known book, Braverman (1974) takes the view that work study engineers are merely acting as the eyes and ears of management to steal knowledge from the workers of how jobs are done. The advantages to management of splitting programming from operating machine tools are claimed to be that wage costs are reduced and management can exercise tighter control over the shopfloor. Noble (1980, 1984) takes the argument a stage further by arguing that not just the use but also the design of NC machine tools has been influenced by management control considerations. However, against the Braverman de-skilling thesis major objections can be formulated. For example, tight control of labour and the need to maximise output from individual workers may not be management's most dominant concern in every case, if existent at all. The central problems faced by management are not so much control but rather such matters as obtaining orders, handling their relations with the capital market, with customers' demands, and the like. Furthermore, technological and market opportunities vary across firms and industries. If then correcting the framework of Braverman and Noble, we should realise that there is no universal capitalist labour process, nor is it feasible to make any valid and tenable conclusions about the impact of new technologies of such a general nature as those of Braverman. Any conceptual framework should seriously take into account the peculiarities of the various firms and industries to be studied. It may thus be expected that the introduction of NC machine tools in the aircraft industry might be relatively indifferent to criteria such as cost-effectiveness or optimum utilisation of equipment, in as far as aircraft firms combine the manufacture of civil and state-subsidised military aircraft. The remaining metal working industry, such as the automated manufacture of lift-truck attachments, may in contrast be more eager to reduce stocks and storage costs as well as increase sales through product variety.

The manufacture of aircraft: the Prodair case

We will start with the aircraft factory. Our leading expectations may be summarised as follows:

1. The firm's primary interest in automated machine tools for the manufacture of aircraft fuselages is expected to derive mainly from its co-production in aerospace and military aircraft programmes.
2. The actual introduction of automated milling and related machines is expected to be triggered by the very nature of aircraft manufacture where high quality, certified safety, and customers' demands concerning performance, aerodynamics, noise volume, fuel economy and service count heavily in a highly competitive buyers' market.
3. Since the manufacture of aircraft is by tradition a matter of craftsmanship, related to the need to maintain a high level of flexibility in an extremely complex assembly process, the in-

troduction of automated machine tools is expected to have only minor effects on the organisation's structure and management style.

4. In as much as the manufacture of aircraft shows a tendency towards high quality, machine workers in the metal working department as a rule are expected to meet high qualifications and skills, including tasks in the area of on-line programming.

5. Since aircraft manufacturers are highly dependent upon the periodical need of airlines to renew, partly at least, their air fleet, employee recruitment as well as lay-offs are expected to alternate, more or less apart from the introduction of labour-saving machinery.

The Netherlands is keen on making its presence felt on the smaller airline market. Its aircraft industry has built an enviable reputation in this field with short-haul airliners. Unable to internalise the production of engines and parts, the firm under study has relied on suppliers elsewhere in Europe. Its most successful airliner, for example, is about 60 per cent British-supplied (engines and wing sections). Final assembly also requires delivery of fuselage sections, engine nacelles, and empennage from West Germany and France. With over 60 years of experience the firm has established itself in the world aircraft industry.

Aircraft manufacturing consists in principle of two processes. First, the development of different types of aircraft, and second the design and production of these types according to customers' wishes. We will confine ourselves to the second, so-called customer version process. The manufacture of aircraft is highly dependent upon the customers' wishes. These may refer to aircraft performance and/or to the transportation function, such as range of action, aspects of design (VIP, cargo etc.), electronic equipment, cabin lay-out, passenger and luggage capacity and so on. Adaptation of the aircraft to customers' wishes is enabled by the fact that the complete aircraft consists of two main parts, i.e. a basic part which is not variable (air frame), and a variable part which allows deviations. Thus, several customer versions of aircraft may be discerned, the so-called short-haul family.

The customer version process of an aircraft passes through three stages. The first stage refers to the production of drawings specifying the customer version of a type of aircraft. The second stage concerns production preparation, i.e. production data (test instructions, quality prescriptions etc.), materials, production means (tools, buildings) and needed manpower (planning, recruitment, training etc.). The third stage has to do with the manufacturing process, resulting in the final assembly of fuselage frames, engines, wings, electronic systems etc. As an aircraft consists of thousands of parts (50,000-100,000!) the production scheme contains detailed information about the quality of needed products, their mutual connection, the responsibility for manufacturing and so on. Thus, the production scheme forms the basis for production preparation and production planning. In more detail the production scheme contains different kinds of summaries. For example, a summary of segments which are collections of defined activities for each type of aircraft, a summary of passing times and delivering frequencies between work stations of production lines.

The introduction of new technology

Four types of technical changes may be discerned in the manufacture of aircraft. First of all, the development of advanced aero-engines, such as turboprop and prop-fan. As the aircraft firm happens to obtain engines from a supplier, we will leave this type of aircraft technology aside. The same applies to the technology of aviation electronics. What remains are glue techniques for connecting parts, and (C)NC machine tools for metal-cutting. As far as gluing parts of the airframe (for example flaps) is concerned, this new manufacturing technique proves to be not only more reliable than conventional riveting or welding, but it also meets more precise and close tolerances. The application of glue technology originates from the production of space vehicles and military aircraft as well as from ship-building. Glue technology is furthermore important since it adds to the interchangeability of parts, which enhances service opportunities (spare parts). Likewise, the interest in automated machine tools for metal-cutting seems to be triggered by the space and military programme in which the aircraft firm under study serves as a co-producer (for example infra-red satellites and airfighters). In so far as military aircraft are concerned, in 1975 the new fighter of the NATO airforce was adopted as a replacement by Belgium, Denmark, the Netherlands and Norway. Regardless of a unit-cost penalty, the airfighter being of US design and built as a collaborative effort on both continents, the European aircraft industry opted to establish production facilities for co-producing the new airfighter. One American engineer surmised that the higher unit costs entailed by such a move would be compensated by technology transfer. He stated that the European aircraft manufacturers 'are interested in procedures, quality control, configuration management, all practical things such as precise machining and close tolerances' (Todd and Simpson 1986: 165). In other words, they wanted to gain from access to process innovations as well as to product innovation. As a result, the aircraft manufacturer under study obtained new milling machines, whereas other co-producers established new plants for building wings or were enabled to use military aircraft technology in developing new lines of shipboard navigation systems. Indeed, the introduction of the first NC milling machines in the case study plant took place in the early 1970s. We may thus provisionally conclude that our manufacturer of commercial aircraft might benefit from the military-induced introduction of numerically controlled machine tools. This kind of equipment offers well-known advantages in the area of precise machining and close tolerances, which comes in very useful in meeting airliners' specifications regarding part of the airframe. In addition we may provisionally conclude that technical criteria, i.e. quality, dominated at the expense of cost-competitive criteria, i.e. price.

Now we will turn to the technology of shaping metals in the manufacture of aircraft, i.e. the fabrication of fuselage parts. Although a multitude of metal-shaping processes are used in the metal-working industry, we shall look briefly at three of them as they are (were) used in the aircraft industry. The traditional shaping process in fuselage manufacture used to be forging. Forging is the process by which the shape of a piece of metal is changed by hammering or squeezing. Another way of shaping is joining metals. Joining techniques include mechanical ones, such as riveting and screwing, or non-mechanical ones, such as welding or gluing. Traditional forging as a way of metal-shaping in the manufacture of fuselage parts has been replaced by cutting by means of machine tools. A wide range of such machines have been encountered in engineering workshops. The most relevant type of shaping machine in the metal-cutting department of airframe building is the milling machine. Alongside conventional equipment to be used for small pieces of work, particularly two general types of numerically controlled machine tools have been found in the airframe workshop since the early 1970s: point-to-point positioning machines and continuous path contouring machines. Since about 1975 the aircraft firm under study has also had at its disposal four computerised NC milling machines with manual data input.

Those four milling machines, meanwhile incorporated into a DNC system, which means that programming takes place in connection with the computer-aided design system, are exclusively utilised for the manufacture of military fuselage parts. The main reason for programmable automation, whether on-line or off-line, lies not so much in the reduction of manufacturing costs or shortening of delivery times, but particularly in the improvement of product quality as desired and specified by the customers. Since numerically controlled machine tools for metal-cutting are highly expensive, the company under study tends to develop these machines in co-operation with the manufacturer, for example in as far as milling machines for sun panels are concerned (space programme). As a rule, the programming of automated machine tools is done by the operator himself. However, programming, machining, tooling and the like are not combined as far as the DNC machine tools are concerned. As already mentioned, the DNC equipment exclusively utilised for the manufacture of military parts, is connected with an off-line design department.

Effects of technological change

The effects to be expected on the quality of work are such that the CNC milling machines - programmed by the design department - demand less skill as well as afford lower wage and less work autonomy in comparison with on-line programmed machine tools. In addition, to optimise the utilisation rate of CNC machines three shifts are needed instead of two. In as much as work qualifications are concerned, formal education is by no means sufficient to match operational requirements. As a rule, millers, turners and kindred metalworkers, leaving lower technical school, have to pass through the two-year in-company school and need additional on-the-job training as well as job rotation to meet shopfloor requirements. Apart from a tendency towards upgrading, as far as on-line programming/machining jobs are concerned, there is a persistent need for high-qualified manpower (i.e. higher technical school certificate).

Dealing with the effects of technical change in the manufacture of aircraft, we may discern first and second-order effects. Primary effects pertain to, for example, skills, wages and qualifications of the workers concerned, whereas secondary effects refer to the company's organisational structure and its internal/external labour market. Although the introduction of automated machine tools shows a tendency to be accompanied by upgrading of the workers' skills and qualifications, this may only be an intermediate stage. The use of DNC equipment in connection with off-line design equipment for the manufacture of military airframe parts shows an opposite, i.e. downgrading, tendency. Anyway, it is hard to anticipate what the net effect of advanced automation in the manufacture of aircraft will be in the near future. Turning to the secondary effects, the supply of workers shows no problems since the industry has traditionally a wide, magic appeal to youngsters, which enables the aircraft firm to maintain strong selection criteria. From the company's own training school the core of group leaders, designers, and other members of the middle management layer are selected. The internal labour market offers ample opportunities, for example for machine-tool operators, to move into higher jobs in the area of work preparation and production planning. There is only a shortage of DNC machine-tool operators, leading to 10 per cent (total at the metal-cutting department: 130) being recruited from outside the firm.

With regard to manpower volume, the plant employs about 10,000 people, other domestic plants included (1985). In 1983 this figure was about 8,300. Since the manufacture of aircraft is highly dependent upon demand fluctuations, i.e. the periodical need of airlines to replace their fleets, this feeds back to the manpower flows. In 1982 it was decided, in consultation with the trade unions, to reduce the volume of jobs by 1,400. This reduction was, among other things, prompted by a decrease in demand for civil and military aircraft, as well as by the unsuccessful joint venture with an US airframe manufacturer. Since 1985 until now, however, about 600 new jobs have been added to the payroll as a result of the production of two new short-haul air liners. Today, total manpower employed counts about 10,600, all plants included (1986). In sum, we may presume that there is no specific or systematic relationship to be found between the introduction of automated machine tools and the outflow of personnel. It is rather the buyers' market for aircraft which determines manpower flows.

Turning to the company's organisational structure, the same presumption may be stated. Since small-batch aircraft manufacturing involves much craftsmanship and specialist knowledge, work preparation and production planning are highly decentralised.

Group operation and collective responsibility at the various production lines add to this picture of an organisation where the hierarchy tends to be long. The hierarchy's essential purpose is to solve problems while maintaining a high level of flexibility rather than to lead people as in mass-production industries. Thus, technological and subsequent changes as induced by automated machine tools are confined to the metal-cutting department and leave the organisation as such relatively untouched. 'Social' rather than information technology appears to be highly relevant in as far as the production of the new airliners has prompted a reorganisation of the whole company.

The preceding discussion shows that the introduction of new technologies is, in this case, neither connected with long-term planning nor with a policy to install in the near future a completely integrated system. In comparison to the automobile industry the aircraft industry resembles more the traditional, non-integrated workshop with custom-made car production than the rigid system of assembly-line production. In the aircraft industry the awareness is very acute that in an extremely complex production process such as the construction of airplanes, together with the strict norms with respect to reliability and interchangeability of all elements, it is important to maintain the organisation's high flexibility vis-à-vis changing conditions.

We have seen that this industry is highly dependent on military production orders and on state subventions as well as on market conditions which make the launching of new types a necessity. Under those circumstances the changing conditions in the buyers' market are more important for the company's survival than the introduction of labour-saving technology as such. This may explain the fact that the working climate seems rather relaxed, giving ample room to numerous types of consultation and idling on the shopfloor.

In this factory there are no specified procedures to handle the actual introduction of new technology. Owing to the specific way in which Dutch labour relations are organised, the labour unions have no grip on the technological changes as such. Moreover, within the specific culture of aircraft production most workers seem not to be motivated to resist new technological developments. Although in several cases workers on the shopfloor were asked to give their opinion on new types of machines before final decisions were made, this depended rather heavily on informal networks within the organisation.

The manufacture of paper roll clamps: the Attatruck case

Our leading expectations with regard to the introduction and effects of technological changes in this plant may be summarised as follows:

1. The company's interest in automated machine tools and related equipment for the manufacture of lift-truck attachments, such as paper roll clamps, is expected to derive mainly from its small-batch production.
2. The actual introduction of numerically controlled machine tools and related equipment is expected to be triggered by the need to supply cost-competitive and high-quality products.
3. Since the manufacture of lift-truck attachments, such as paper roll clamps, happens to be a brand new industry, the introduction of flexible automation is expected to have far-reaching effects on the quality and organisation of work.
4. In as far as the manufacture of lift-truck attachments shows a tendency towards flexibility, overall cost reduction and quality improvement, machine workers are expected to be flexible in employment, meet high qualifications and be able to do related jobs, including tasks in the co-ordination of computer-aided design, manufacture, logistics and the like.
5. Since the plant under study is engaged in a highly competitive market for high-quality and custom-made products, automated machine tools and related equipment are expected to save labour and reduce the hierarchy.

In contrast to the aircraft case, little systematic knowledge is available about the industry of lift-truck attachments such as paper roll clamps. This is indeed a brand new industry, more or less apart from the manufacture of industrial lift trucks. We can observe a market for efficient material-handling tools, and vehicles as internal transport means such as business cars and lift trucks are no longer viewed as dead capital. Instead, there is an increased tendency to either buy or lease such transport means. As far as the industrial lift truck is concerned, technical changes refer to locomotion (engine, electronics), economy, reliability and performance (for example lifting height, side positioning). In sum, lift trucks are increasingly used to optimise the movement and storage of goods and material in all kinds of industries.

309

The world industry of lift-truck attachments is controlled by a handful of Japanese and American companies. In as far as paper roll clamps are concerned, the case-study plant has four European competitors. It is part of a worldwide corporation with headquarters in the USA; European headquarters are located in the Netherlands with three plants.

The plant under study is engaged in manufacturing material-handling tools. These tools are lift-truck attachments (fork clamps, pulp bale clamps, for example), and related products (such as hose reels and masts) for handling materials in all kinds of industries. During the past 30 years, the field of material handling has developed into a highly sophisticated and important branch of industry. As a leading worldwide manufacturer of industrial lift-truck attachments, the US corporation under study has played an important part in this development. Much of the impetus behind this growth stems from the realisation that the impact of material-handling extends far beyond the simple movement and storage of goods and materials. Efficient material-handling systems can substantially shorten manufacturing cycle times, lower inventory levels, reduce product damage and provide better space utilisation. Attachments that enable the conventional lift truck to become a more versatile and efficient material-handling tool help industries improve material-handling productivity and cost efficiency.

Founded in 1943, the corporation serves the growing worldwide material-handling needs through fully owned plants located in nearly a dozen countries, as well as through exclusive distributors located in other important markets. The growth of the corporation has been founded on two basic lines, i.e. material-handling equipment/hydraulic cylinders, on the one hand, and its capacities to solve various problems in the area of material handling, on the other. Although basic handling functions are essentially the same the world over, specific requirements differ between market areas. The company's international organisation aims to respond quickly and efficiently to the special needs of the individual markets it serves and to provide the local engineering, manufacturing, sales and service capabilities to meet those needs. The corporation invests in new machinery and equipment to support quality improvement and cost-reduction programmes. Several new robotic welding units have been installed in plants and presently the corporation is in the process of equipping the newest manufacturing plant (i.e. the plant under study) where the latest technologies and

310

state-of-the-art manufacturing techniques are to be represented. The corporation has purchased and is installing in this plant computer-aided design and computer-aided manufacturing systems. These facilities enable design and manufacturing engineers to analyse data and generate detailed drawings utilising advanced computer technology. A common engineering data base is stored in the computer memory and can be recalled as needed for new designs, design changes or modifications, and for numerous other engineering and manufacturing requirements. Initial CAD/CAM applications will be new product design and testing, tools and tool design, computer-design nesting of flame-cut parts, numerical control programming and the preparation of various technical publications. The primary benefits of CAD/CAM will be increased productivity, shorter design cycles, improved design quality, reduced lead times for special products and lower costs.

The introduction of new technologies

The plant under study was newly built in 1982 and was planned to have a fully operational production line in 1986. In contrast to the manufacture of aircraft, the manufacture of paper roll clamps is relatively simple. Parts of the clamp are cut from pieces of raw material, i.e. plates, and then pass through processes such as bending, welding, drilling, cutting, painting and final assembly. The production line concerned consists of five flexible manufacturing units, i.e. a flame-cutting unit, a robot welding unit, a CNC work centre for metal-cutting, a CNC-controlled storage unit and a robot painting unit. Between these manufacturing units two automatically controlled vehicles are planned for internal transport. From the very beginning the corporate management had a fully-automated system in mind. Negotiations with the Ministry of Economic Affairs resulted in a considerable state grant, without which this technological innovation would not have taken place at such speed and at this point of time. Thus, the paper roll clamp plant under study acquired the status of a demonstration project for flexible production automation. Meanwhile a computer-aided design system has been purchased for the nesting of parts by the CNC flame-cutting machine. Since product development is done at the US headquarters, all drawings on tape have to be adapted to the European market (metrical system), and the CAD system is expected to facilitate this translation process. Likewise, the welding and painting robot as well as a CNC work centre for metal-cutting have been installed, while a small pick-and-place robot supplies the various tools. What remains to be deployed is the CNC-controlled storage unit and the automatically-controlled vehicle transport system.

Work organisation

Our case study plant is characterised by small-batch production which may be ascribed to the so-called just-in-time conception. This conception holds that long delivery times and large stocks of final products are too costly in a competitive environment. The subsequent need to adjust machinery quickly and deliver the final products with no delay is basic for the introduction of flexible technology. In addition, the deployment of automated machine tools, for example, allows a continuous process of product improvement and lowering of manufacturing costs. As far as the product quality is concerned, the newest models of paper roll clamps require less welding, save more weight and afford a better positioning of the lift-truck to move and store, even in narrow corridors (for example side-shift carriers).

Automated machine tools also offer the opportunity to meet customers' specifications, since customers vary from seaport to newspaper industries. As a rule, there is one standard paper roll clamp, with the exception of its opening range, which depends upon the material to be handled. For the rest, automated machine tools are utilised in single-item production. The special clamps constitute about 30 per cent of all final products.

The actual process of introducing new technologies, i.e. CNC-controlled flame-cutting, storage, as well as robot welding and painting units, is guided by an internal project group with an external consultant. Furthermore, a dozen working groups are active in specific task areas and report to the project group. Working groups invite various sales representatives from machine-tool manufacturers to quote and finally order, for example, a painting robot or automatically controlled vehicle. Various problems have arisen with the introduction of automated machinery since the machine tools happen to be prototypes, its software needs to be adapted to the European market, and higher qualifications are required from the workforce.

We may conclude that the introduction of new technologies in the manufacture of paper roll clamps hinges on the plant's need to reduce manufacturing costs as well as to supply high-quality commodities in single, custom-made and small-batch production. The substantial state grant, which promoted the plant to the status of demonstration project for flexible production automation, has only accelerated the pace of technological changes. As already mentioned, the top-management of the lift-truck attachment corporation had a fully-automated system in mind. Indeed, the Dutch plant for the manufacture of paper roll clamps is intended to serve as an example for US plants.

Effects of technological change

Turning to the effects of new technologies at work, we may again discern primary and secondary effects. Running automated plants requires a workforce of higher qualifications, preferably a medium-level technical school certificate. Programming is a minimum requirement since shopfloor programming, connected with a central data base (drawings!), is the rule. That is to say, on-line programming is done by the foremen, while operators adapt and correct the available programs. Additional training courses are needed, for example to operate the new robot welding and CNC-controlled storage unit. Furthermore, capacities are needed to understand and feel responsible for the whole logic of flexible manufacturing.

Job enlargement has been an immediate consequence of the ongoing process of automation. Another consequence refers to reduced career opportunities within the plant, since jobs are substantially enlarged, at least in practice, and workers are supposed to be widely employable. For example, they are expected to replace each other as far as possible and to look for other work to be done when automated machine tools are running. A secondary effect, intimately connected with the foregoing, has to do with the organisational hierarchy. About four years ago (1982), when the plant was newly built, the hierarchy was made up of several layers, from plant manager, department officer and (assistant) foremen to operators and engineers. Today (1986) the hierarchy has been drastically reduced to two layers, i.e. plant manager as the top layer and foremen, operators and engineers making up the bottom layer. In as much as manpower flows are concerned, the volume of employment is generally dependent upon the economic environment. Since the early 1980s the market for industrial lift trucks has practically collapsed, which has not left the workforce untouched. However, the introduction of new technologies in the plant has in due time particularly made redundant the (assistant) foremen.

We may thus conclude that the automated manufacture of paper roll clamps indeed has upgraded the quality of work, but tends to reduce career opportunities and to result in a net loss of employment.

Comparison and discussion of the two cases

Main differences between Prodair and Attatruck

Although both factories are confronted with problems connected with the introduction of new technologies, they differ widely in many respects. To summarise the main differences - which are partly interdependent - we can mention the following items:

1. the size of the factories and the nature of the relationship between them and the firms of which they are part;
2. the important role of suppliers in providing essential parts of the final product (Prodair);
3. the size and shape of the organisation and their concomitant complexity with regard to
   - the organisation's hierarchy (number of strata and nature of interaction between them);
   - the nature of technological changes and the interdependency between different technological strategies in the area of production (compare Attatruck's production process, consisting mainly of such activities as welding, milling, grinding and cutting, with Prodair's intricate production process connected with developments in gluing technology, the development of information technology as part of the final product, the use of new products derived from space technology, the development of engine technology) and
   - the ensuing complexity of the division of labour, the nature and types of specialisation, opportunities to organise continuous production lines within an integrated production process;
4. the nature and complexity of the final product itself, connected with 3. and with

5. the changing role of craftsmanship;
6. the personnel policies and manpower flows;
7. the international market position, especially with respect to customers' demands;
8. the nature of the relationship with the state as partner and/or source of subventions.

The introduction of new technology and learning processes

Considering the wide differences between the two cases with respect to the variables summarised above, we expect to observe differences between them in both the introduction of NC/CNC machine tools in the production processes and the effects of the actual introduction of those new technologies on the organisation of work.

Considering the debate on the industrial convergence thesis, we have to look whether there are any similarities in these processes, in spite of the dissimilarities existing between our two cases. The description of our two cases does not provide a solid base for testing macro-social hypotheses about industrial development. Nevertheless, it may indicate in which respects the findings run counter to such hypotheses concerning social choice versus convergency. International co-operative and comparative research may contribute to a further clarification in a next stage, using the results of a wider range of case studies. It must be kept in mind, while discussing the two cases, that the similarities between them are far greater when we concentrate on the introduction of NC/CNC tool technology as such, i.e. when we compare Attatruck as a whole primarily with those departments of Prodair in which technological changes take place in comparable production processes.

The analysis of the two cases seems to confirm our hypotheses. In Attatruck the introduction of new technology is connected with an encompassing view of the management on the role of technology and its development in the organisation of production. The case exemplifies the realisation of the engineer's utopia of a completely integrated system in which all parts have their meaning as components of a whole. Ideally, the system is able to react in a flexible way to all the problems which may pop up in the organisation's environment because all of them are anticipated in

315

the system's design. The introduction of technology has been accompanied by the promises or expectations of full integration and control on the one hand, and complete flexibility concerning the responses to environmental changes, on the other.

Revisiting the factory a year after the first interviews, we noticed some changes in this perspective of technological development. In the first place it was realised by management that this type of flow production is accompanied by an increasing vulnerability of the production process, because in an integrated system the breakdown of a single machine may block the total process. This implies that the maintenance of the technological system has become an object of utmost care.

Moreover, the dependency on external advisors increased considerably during the introduction stage. External advisors related to firms which offer software to handle the introduction of integrated production systems promised much more than they could actually accomplish. These advisors, as a rule, sell the engineer's utopia without paying attention to the basic flaws in the particular organisation's model, especially to the basic tenet that complete knowledge of future problems is impossible. Thus a lot of basic errors came to light, both in the hardware and software, which were difficult to solve (for instance the interconnection of subsystems).

In the third place, and related to the problems mentioned earlier, the system became more dependent on the workers on the shopfloor and their ways of handling problems in the production process, especially their new ways of learning. By now it is evident that complete control and flexibility are goals which cannot be achieved. Labour continues to play a pivotal, though changing role in the production process. The dependency of the organisation on the workers' learning processes seems to increase under these circumstances. At the same time, it is not primarily the workers' specialised knowledge that plays this role, but their general potential to solve problems arising from the interaction between man and machine, a solving of problems that is based on a thorough theoretical know-how enabling them to formulate the problem-solving in such a way that it can be integrated in the system's software programs. This emphasis on learning abilities is related to changes in the organisation of work, as the role of supervisors changes in the direction of being a facilitator and co-ordinator. The workers rotate in a broad range of tasks while learning themselves and instructing less experienced workers in ways of solving problems. Thus the workers' general skill level rises and the organisation's need for workers with specialised skills to handle problems in a more or less fixed way is decreasing.

This observation seems to be in line with Hirschhorn's (1984: 163) conclusion:

> 'Postindustrial settings integrate work and learning. The new technology does not de-skill workers: they must learn to manage technical transitions from one machine state to another, from expected to un-expected machine events, and from one product design to another. The workers' knowledge will have a double character: in solving unstructured and unanticipated problems they will learn how to learn.'

In the Prodair case the introduction of the NC/CNC machine tools is not part and parcel of the organisation's appearance as an integrated system. Partly the introduction of new technology is a consequence of outside demands connected with military orders, partly the introduction of new technology is a response to changing requirements connected with customers' demands and with reliability and safety standards of the product. The interrelations between several technological developments which are connected with the production process, the complexity of this process itself, together with the concomitant awareness, based on a long experience, that system-integration may decrease considerably the flexibility of the production process, are factors which are not amenable to a strong belief in promises of an integrated approach to solving the major problems of production. In fact, this is the case within Prodair. However, comparably to Attatruck, it has been observed that the learning processes of the workers play an important role in connection with CNC machine tools and will continue to do so in the next years.

Choice and convergence

The preceding observations may lead to the conclusion that recent developments ensuing from the introduction of new technology give rise, at least partly, to a new type of convergence with respect to the role of learning processes and a changing development of the division of labour. These conclusions do not shed much light on the development of industrial life as such, although an

317

accumulation of knowledge concerning those processes may do so.

The description of the two cases also discloses many differences in development which may be partially dependent on social choices.

Looking at our data, we first of all are struck by the fact that in both Attatruck and Prodair a rising importance of theoretical knowledge in the organisation can be discerned very clearly. In Attatruck both management and workers remarked several times that the original craftsmanship of, for example, welders and fitters had largely become obsolete. This observation is in line with what has been said about 'learning to learn'. In Prodair we witnessed the recent dismissal of 2,000 workers and the beginning of a campaign to select some 800 new workers with a higher educational (and theoretical) background. In the latter case, however, industrial craftsmanship, based on both qualifications acquired in the educational system and on in-plant training, still remains an important part of the production system.

Our second observation concerns the organisation of work. In Attatruck a new division of labour has been developing, based on the primacy of theoretical knowledge. In the new division of labour only those workers who are able to catch up with the requirements of the new system - i.e. by learning the basics of information technology - can be retained. Those who are not able to follow this trend - or who are not motivated to do so - are definitively out. Those workers on the shopfloor who have managed to catch up with the new developments experience more autonomy than in their former jobs. They have been able to initiate interactions to those responsible - as white-collar employees - for designing and programming tasks. Those initiatives have been facilitated by the fact that the intermediate supervisory level has disappeared and the role of the first-line supervisors has changed (facilitator/co-ordinator). It is difficult to say which will be the long-term consequences of those changes. Will 'learning to learn' be a stable element of the organisations' future? It may be so. However, we have to add two remarks in this connection. In the first place we visited this factory in a transitional stage. Only a few workers, apparently selected from a large supply of labour, managed to catch up with the new developments. Second, in this transitional stage their original background as highly skilled workers was still useful as the workers concerned could observe on the shopfloor any inadequacies of programming and they could also take measures to prevent damage. But what will be their future when the CAD/CAM system operates fully and when the feedback from the shopfloor may be of less importance? Perhaps some of the highly motivated and capable workers will, in this transitional period, manage to become part of the control system itself. The next generation will most likely not have those opportunities - already now very scarce - for upward mobility into the lower ranks of the control system. Attatruck has to be very flexible in its reactions to changing customers' demands. The production process is sophisticated, but the product they offer is relatively simple, although offered in a great variety. The important issue is that the firm must be able to respond quickly to the changing needs and demands of individual customers. Under these circumstances the need for learning to learn may be rather modest, once the introduction problems have been overcome.

The market conditions for Prodair are quite different. Their product is very sophisticated and the demands of the customers are binding. But in contrast to the customers of Attatruck, the customers of Prodair want a product that is not only highly reliable but that also has a considerable longevity and is adapted to the demands of their market. The cost of each unit product on this market is less important than on Attatruck's market. In the long run, the workers' capacity of learning to learn may be a commodity of even greater value within this type of production process than it is at present.

We observe in Prodair that technological developments are subordinated to the social organisation of the firm. In this highly complicated assembly process much is dependent on the professional skills of the workers, including their ability to adapt to changing conditions by actively seeking solutions to the problems they are confronted with. In Prodair the functioning of the organisation is highly dependent on the intricate networks of informal relations which are used to solve problems that were (and often could) not be foreseen by the designing and programming departments. During a long period the organisation's formal hierarchy has been relatively stable.

In this connection we put forward the following hypothesis: The less an organisation has experienced major changes caused by technological innovations in the past, the more the management will be convinced that forthcoming technological changes will not affect the organisation's structure and management style. Although Prodair was to be faced with an important change in its production as the manufacture of two new types of airplanes was drawing near and an enlargement of scale was considered to be inevitable, Prodair's management did not expect far-reaching changes in the formal hierarchy nor in the organisation's informal structure. Up to then highly sophisticated technological innovations had been introduced in Prodair - such as the production of new materials related to the space programme, advanced techniques for gluing metal elements that have to be operative under extremely severe conditions, application of advanced information technology in the production of certain elements of the planes - but these innovations were related to specific departments of the factory and did not disturb the social organisation as such.

In the case of Prodair we observe that in this highly complicated production process management's opportunities to control the workers, by dissociating the labour process from the skill of the workers, is rather limited. In fact, as a consequence of the high standards of reliability that are required in every instant of the production process, it is obligatory for new workers who have finished their technical training in the formal educational system to have a two-year in-plant training before they are allowed to be integrated in the regular production process.

We conclude from the comparison of Attatruck and Prodair that: the more complicated the production process (for instance the production of airplanes as compared with pulp and paper attachments), the more important the social co-ordination of tasks and the higher the relevance of 'social technologies' in comparison to information technology's (potential) contributions.

With Prodair's organisation we could not observe the development of a new division of labour as was the case with Attatruck ('shrinking' of the intermediate supervisory levels, changing interaction between designing and programming departments and other office tasks, on the one hand, and task execution on the other, although in Prodair the autonomy of workers in relation to the back office increased in the case of NC programming).

Moreover, neither in Attatruck, nor in Prodair did the labour unions have a noticeable influence on the technological developments and their social impact on the organisation. The Dutch system of industrial relations is especially effective on a national level but trade unions do not have effective instruments at their disposal to be able to pursue specific goals in relationship with technological change inside the enterprise. Neither have the committees for joint consultation within the firm a grip on the decisions that are connected with technological innovations. The trade unions are just beginning to formulate their general policy towards information technology. They are certainly not opposed to technological changes but are trying to corroborate the future workers' positions (for example by negotiating technology agreements with the employers).

Tentatively, we formulate in this connection the following hypotheses: the stronger labour unions' organisation on the national level and the stronger their orientation to issues connected with the distribution of commodities (wages, salaries, holidays etc.) the stronger the position of management with regard to decisions on the introduction of new technologies within their firms.

Moreover, the more the population at large is convinced that technological innovation is a necessary condition for increased economic growth, the stronger the position of the managerial elites who introduce new technologies in industrial and administrative organisations.

Furthermore, if the trade unions are in a weak position to counteract management's technology policy and the public at large is convinced of the inevitable character of technological change, management's position will be all the stronger and decisions concerning the application of new technologies will be of such a type that existing power balances and leadership styles will remain unaffected (especially in large firms).

Finally, the more rigid an organisation's formal structure (especially hierarchy), the stronger the tendency to consider technical changes as having a relatively low potentiality of changing the organisation's structure and management style.

Conclusions and final remarks

The two cases we have discussed do not allow us to formulate any general statements on organisational consequences of technological changes in production that are really in line with one of the approaches outlined previously. It is evident that a study that is restricted to two cases does not permit us to say sensible things about general developments within production and about the macro-economic and societal consequences of technological changes. It may be that Prodair represents a segment of Dutch industry that will be superseded by a quite different organisation of production. Why is this organisation relatively stable when

321

confronted with new technological developments? Do we observe in this case an opposition between traditionalism and modernisation? Will the 'traditional' structures crumble away under technology's impact? We do not think so, looking at the market relationships that are prevailing in this area and at the nature of the product that is delivered. Nevertheless, it may be that Prodair represents an industrial segment of the Dutch economy that is as such of decreasing importance in comparison to the type of production represented by Attatruck. If Attatruck is indeed representative of the production relationships in the years to come, then the societal consequences of this development will be tremendous. Although many long-established dividing lines within organisations will disappear - as is evident in the Attatruck case - we do not think that these changes imply an 'end of the division of labour' in economic life as such. Restricting ourselves to the capitalist countries, we do not see a logical link between technological and organisational changes as described in our cases, and a transition to new types of ownership and control of the organisations concerned.

Both cases corroborate Bell's thesis that the post-industrial society is organised around knowledge for the purpose of social control and the direction of innovation and change.[1] Both cases highlight the growing importance of theoretical knowledge, conceived as the primacy of empiricism and codification of knowledge into abstract systems of symbols. But does this development imply the coming of a real meritocratic or credential society, as Bell states? Here we make some reservations. In the first place, we are not convinced that the growing importance of knowledge implies *ipso facto* that ownership and control will be in the hands of those persons who have excelled in the educational system. Moreover, if this were the case, it would still be a rather poor type of meritocratic society in which only a minority of the adult population occupies positions in economic life without the large masses being integrated. Such a credential society must be full of antagonisms between employed and unemployed people.

Finally, the credential society is connected with individual achievement, primarily in the educational system. As several authors, among whom Bell himself, point out knowledge is a collective good and the new production relationships imply increasingly collectivistic orientations and types of organisation. Thus there must be a growing tension between 'merit', as an individual characteristic, on the one hand, and the collectivistic types of co-operation in which it is difficult to assess the contributions of each of the participating individuals separately.

Both cases indeed give us indications that opportunities for individual advancement during working life will decrease in the (near) future as the promotion ladders within organisations become shorter. It may be that increasing inter-generational social mobility will be accompanied by decreasing intra-generational mobility (working life mobility).

There are no indications of a systematic downgrading of the quality of work when we leave apart the shrinking opportunities for advancement within the organisations concerned. This observation does not imply that the older types of craftsmanship will continue to exist. In fact they are being replaced by new jobs and new requirements, as we have observed. The new jobs are by no means of a degraded type. They require both autonomy and the ability to see one's job as part of an integrated system of networks.

However, it follows from our description that the subordination of the jobs to the system's rationality is much more outspoken in Attatruck than in Prodair, where the social system regulates the type of application of technology. The Attatruck case is much more in line with Noble's analysis of the role of management in the selection process of new technologies and their application. The Prodair case is quite different from the Attatruck case in this respect. The difference may be connected with the fact that Attatruck is part of an American multinational organisation while Prodair is not. The differences may reflect different styles of management, in combination with the fact that in Prodair it would be illogical for the management to extend control over labour under present circumstances because its dependency on craftsmanship within the organisation cannot be neglected.

It follows from our two cases that the same technological development may have different consequences. The nature of the consequences is dependent on the specific configuration of variables, such as prevailing market relationships, strategic decisions taken in earlier stages of the organisation's development, images of societal development both within the class of managers, the working classes and the population at large, and the type of organisation of labour. Neither the structural side of social life nor the decisions of the actors as such determine the outcomes of technological changes. The outcomes depend on the specific combination of structural conditions - seen as the result of earlier decision-making in society - and the goals the participants try to achieve. This is neither a case of hard economic or social determinism, nor of voluntarism.

Note

1. Bell in *The Coming of Post-Industrial Society* (1978) emphasises the increasing importance of theoretical knowledge. This development explains, according to Bell, present and forthcoming changes in advanced societies, '...the primacy of empiricism and codification of knowledge in abstract systems of symbols that, as in any axiomatic system, can be used to illuminate many different and varied areas of experience' (p. 20). 'In postindustrial society the labour theory of value is being replaced by a "knowledge theory of value" because it is clear that the "value added" components in a set of national income accounts are due, increasingly, to the contribution of knowledge workers, and the kind of knowledge that these men can draw upon' (Bell 1980, p. 237). Moreover, he points out that this codified knowledge is a collective good because 'no single person, no single set of work groups, no co-operation can monopolize or patent theoretical knowledge, or draw unique product advantage of it' (ibid, p. 237).

References

Bell, D. (1978) *The Coming of Post-Industrial Society. A Venture in Social Forecasting*, New York, Basic Books

Bell, D. (1980) *The Winding Passage*, Cambridge, Abt Books

Braverman, H. (1974) *Labor and Monopoly Capital. Degradation of Work in the Twentieth Century*, New York, London, Monthly Review Press

Child, J. (1986) 'Technology and Work: An Outline of Theory and Research in the Western Social Sciences', in P. Grootings (ed.) *Technology and Work. East-West Comparison*, London, Croom Helm, pp. 7-65

Grootings, P. (1986) 'Technology and Work: A Topic for East-West Comparison?', in P. Grootings (ed.) *Technology and Work. East-West Comparison*, London, Croom Helm, pp. 275-302

Grootings (ed.) (1986) *Technology and Work. East-West Comparison*, London, Croom Helm

Hirschhorn, L. (1984) *Beyond Mechanization. Work and Technology in a Postindustrial Age*, Cambridge, Mass./London, The MIT Press

Kerr, C. (1983) *The Future of Industrial Societies. Convergence or Continuing Diversity?* Cambridge, Mass./London, Harvard University Press

Marsh, R.M. (1984) 'Whither the Comparative Study of Modernisation and Development?', in M.B. Brinkerhoff (ed.) *Work, Organisation and Society. Comparative Convergences, Contributions to Sociology*, no. 53, Westport and London, Greenwood Press

Noble, D. (1979) 'Social Choice in Machine Design: The Case of Automatically Controlled Machine Tools', in A. Zimbalist (ed.) *Case Studies on the Labor Process*, New York, Monthly Review Press

Noble, D. (1980) *America by Design. Technology and the Rise of Corporate Capitalism*, Oxford, University Press

Noble, D. (1984) *Forces of Production. A Social History of Industrial Automation*, New York, Alfred Knopf

Todd D. and J. Simpson (1986) *The World Aircraft Industry*, London, Croom Helm

Zimbalist, A. (ed.) (1979) *Case Studies on the Labor Process*, New York, Monthly Review Press

Appendix
Typology of Machine-tool Technologies

Roger Kesteloot

The research results which are discussed in this volume are related to the study of production processes which make significant use of machine tools. More particularly, a common feature of all the national studies compared in this volume is the use of machine tools under 'computer numerical control' (CNC). However, the term CNC sometimes has different meanings according to individual or local interpretations. In order to exclude any misunderstandings about the variable which was to be held constant if maximum comparability between cases was to be guaranteed, i.e. the 'technology' itself, an overview will be presented in this appendix of different types of machine tools.

Such a typology can be based on several criteria. First, machine tools can be classified according to the type of activities for which they may be used. Thus, a distinction can be made - in the industrial sector we have been studying - between metal-*forming* and metal-*cutting* machine tools. According to a widely accepted definition, metal-forming machine tools are used for transformation of materials by pressing, cutting off, bending, drawing, thumping, punching and analogous operations. Metal-cutting machine tools, on the other hand, are machines which cut metal by turning, boring, drilling, grinding, threading, milling or the like.

Other classifications can be based on, for example, the material of which the tools are made, or their degree of accuracy of operation. Also, distinctions can be made between the types of energy by which they are driven.

More relevant to our kind of research, however, is a typology which is constructed around the characteristics of machine control. In this context, we define control as the determination of the space- and time-related aspects of the contact between tool and workpiece: the speed of operation and the positioning of workpiece and tool, the duration of the operation, the sequence of operations, etc.

The 'basic' type of machine, around which, historically, machine construction industry has developed, is most frequently called the 'conventional' machine tool. Its major characteristic is the fact that its operator (for example, the turner or driller) adjusts tools and workpieces guided by the specifications for the machining of the piece set out on a traditional blueprint. Also, he adjusts tools and workpieces by directly manipulating handles, wheels, and other controls.

Numerical control (NC), as applied to NC machine tools, works in quite a different way. This is a form of programmable automation in which a program of instructions, designed for a particular workpart, controls the sequence of operations to machine the workpart. New workpart designs are accommodated by means of new part programs (Herroelen 1982). Of course, recurrent use of the same program is possible. The numerical codes which control the operations represent both geometrical and technological data. The geometrical information is related to the consecutive positions of workpieces and tools (measures, tolerances, characteristics of the surface to be machined), whereas technological data refer to machine specifications, characteristics of the tools to be used, etc.

With the typical NC machine tool, the instructions are put on punched tape. Each group of perforations on the tape corresponds to one single movement as, on a conventional machine, executed by the operator. In order to execute the program, the machine contains a control unit, by which the program is read, interpreted and translated into mechanical operations. According to the degree of sophistication of the machine, it may also contain a feedback system, by which information on program execution is sent back to the control unit.

Production by means of NC equipment constitutes a rather rigid form of automation, the main economic advantages of which are consistency in performing repetitive jobs and increased labour productivity. Its most efficient use is to be found in the production of large series of very restricted numbers of relatively simple product types.

With CNC, microelectronics has been introduced on the metal-working shopfloor. The basic technical system largely remains the same as with NC, but now a substantial part of the control unit of each separate machine is formed by a (mini-) or micro-computer. This provides the possibility of storing control data in the memory of each individual machine, which enhances overall operational program memory compared to NC systems of the same size. Furthermore, the individual microcomputer creates the possibility of relatively easy direct intervention in the control program on the machine and the workplace itself.

Still another difference from standard NC machine tools is the possibility to avoid punched tape data transmission. With CNC machine tools, programs are mostly (also) stored on electronic media such as floppy disks.

All in all, this means that, at least in theory, the advantage of flexibility is added to the NC characteristics of speed (productivity) and accuracy of repetition. Moreover, microelectronic control also gives higher reliability and sharper margins of fault measurement.

Until now, we have only discussed types of single-purpose machine tools. A major characteristic of technological evolution in metal-working, however, has been the search for integration of different types of cutting, forming and supporting operations into more complex technological units. A first step has been the construction of *machining centres*, which physically are still formed by a single 'machine', but on which combinations of operations of at least two different types of tools can be performed (for example turning and boring).

With Flexible Manufacturing Systems (FMS), the single-physical-machine stage is left behind. An FMS can be defined as a group of processing stations - numerically controlled machine tools with automatic tool interchange capabilities - linked together with an automatic material (workpart) handling system that operates an integrated system under computer control (Herroelen 1982). In such a system, not only tool/workpart contacts but also the choice, supply and positioning of tool and workpart are determined - in theory - by computer control, for several processing stations simultaneously. In theory, these flexible manufacturing systems could bring about (in terms of management interests) an optimal combination of, on the one hand, efficiency of automated large-batch and mass production and, on the other hand, flexibility of piece-by-piece oriented production. In this way, the previously existing efficiency and productivity gap in small-batch production is filled:

- efficiency can be reached by total integration of production units, which is realised by means of a central computer, starting from which the whole process of production can be changed and controlled (also called Direct Numerical Control);
- flexibility can be realised by making use of CNC machines and robots, which allow for on-the-spot changeability and adaptability of programs (Raeymaekers *et al.* 1985).

Field of Application of Flexible Automation of Production

Batch Size / Product Structure	Piece Work	Small Batch	Medium Batch	Large Batch	Mass Product
Simple Products & Product Parts				Rigid Automation	
Simple Final Products & Composite Products					
Complex Final Products & Composite Combinations	Handwork				

Source: Herroelen & Lambrecht 1985, p.16.

One problem with a definition of flexible manufacturing systems (FMS) is that it leaves open the question of what is to be considered as a 'group' of machines. In recent pertinent literature, authors often make a distinction between flexible manufacturing cells (FMC) and flexible manufacturing systems. Quite arbitrarily, one can define an FMC as a group in which four or fewer machine tools are integrated, and an FMS as a group of more than four.

There is also a discussion on the distinction between what is sometimes called a flexible transfer line and a flexible manufacturing system. Such criteria as the size of batches and the number of different products to be machined on them - which can be quite decisive for the market choice in making specific hardware/software combinations - are mostly used to distinguish the first type of automation (less flexible) from the latter (more flexible).

References

Herroelen, W.S. (1982) 'Automation of Small Batch Production - from Numerical Control to Flexible Manufacturing Systems', *Bedrijfseconomische Verhandeling*, no. 8204, Leuven

Herroelen, W.S. and M. Lambrecht (1985) 'Innovatie op het gebied van produktie- en voorraadbeleid' (Innovation in Production and Storing Policy), in *Innoveren en Ondernemen*, Antwerp, Vereniging voor Economie

Raeymaekers, A.M., E. Henderickx and R. Kesteloot (1985) 'Flexibele productie-automatisering in de metaalverkende nijverheid - onderzoeksmodel m.b.t. productie- en arbeidsorganisatorische aspecten' (Flexible Automation of Production in Metal Firms - Research Model for Production and Work Organisation), RUCA working paper

Index

AccuRay process control system
101-8

adaptive enterprise strategy
272-3

aircraft industry 297-8, 302-8,
314-24 *passim*

aluminium foil industry 25,
63-72

APEX (Administrative, Professional and Executive
Association) (Great Britain)
230

ASTMS (Association of
Scientific, Technical and
Managerial Staffs) (Great
Britain) 230, 231

Atkinson, J. 289, 291

Attatruck (Netherlands) 298,
309-14, 314-24 *passim*

attitudes of workers to new technology 3; in Czechoslovakia 45, 51, 55; in
Federal Republic of Germany
219-25; in German
Democratic Republic 66; in
Great Britain 240-1, 242,
257; in Hungary 98, 106-7,
114-15; in Poland 163; in
Soviet Union 124, 129-30

AUEW (Amalgamated Union of
Engineering Workers) (Great
Britain) 230, 239, 240,
242, 244; and new tech-
nology 231, 243, 245, 256

autonomy of workers: in Federal
Republic of Germany 209-

10, 220; in Finland 285-6;
in Great Britain 244-5; in
the Netherlands 306, 318; in
Poland 158-62; *see also*
responsibilities; supervision

Baden-Württenburg metal
industry strike of 1978 196

Bechtle, G. 270-1

Belgium 165-86

Bell, D. 322

Betriebskollektivvertrag
(German Democratic
Republic) 62

Braverman, H. 227, 228, 301-2

Britain *see* Great Britain

building machinery industry
144-64

CAD (computer-aided design): in
Great Britain 232, 236-8; in
the Netherlands 298, 306,
311

CAM (computer-aided manu-
facturing): in Belgium 169;
in the Netherlands 311

car industry 37-8

case study method of research
17-20

Che-Peh-Ou machine tools
(Soviet Union) 120-39

CIM (computer-integrated
manufacturing) *see* CAM

CMEA (Council for Mutual
Economic Aid) (COMECON)
5, 96, 145

331